JESUS *Above* SCHOOL

A Worldview Framework for
Navigating the Collision Between
the Gospel and Christian Schools

NOAH SAMUEL BRINK

WESTBOW PRESS®
A DIVISION OF THOMAS NELSON
& ZONDERVAN

WestBow Press books may be ordered through booksellers or by contacting:

WestBow Press
A Division of Thomas Nelson & Zondervan
1663 Liberty Drive
Bloomington, IN 47403
www.westbowpress.com
844-714-3454

ISBN: 978-1-6642-8682-5 (sc)
ISBN: 978-1-6642-8683-2 (hc)
ISBN: 978-1-6642-8681-8 (e)

Library of Congress Control Number: 2022923753

Print information available on the last page.

WestBow Press rev. date: 1/17/2023

To my Dad.
For nearly five decades, your faithfulness to the gospel of Jesus has shaped the hearts and minds of your students – myself included. I've never met a person who has lived a more consistent commitment to a truly Christian educational philosophy. *May it Never Be* that the thousands of students you have taught lose sight of the Jesus you put before them. Though you did not write this book, they are as much your words as they are my own.

Soli Deo Gloria

CONTENTS

INTRODUCTION

In Courtship with the Gospel, Christian Education, and Biblical Worldview

Fifteen years ago, one of my mentors died, leaving a huge void at Evangelical Christian School in Memphis, where I was teaching and coaching. As a result, the Head of School asked me to teach the biblical worldview course ECS required for new faculty induction. My mentor had co-created the course, but it was primarily all in his head. By God's grace, he had asked me to team-teach the course with him the summer before he died unexpectedly. Realistically, he did most of the teaching; my contribution was a lot of notetakings and organization of the content.

Being asked to replace an irreplaceable man, I was honored, a bit scared, and certainly didn't really know what I was getting into. I was curious and naïve enough to jump in and was quickly inspired by all I read to get up to speed. By God's grace, I stumbled into a framework which helped me make sense of the essential categories while enabling me to explain it to our teachers.

I certainly didn't have all of this figured out when I started developing a worldview curriculum, and I still don't. Maybe my inadequacy might encourage you to walk through these pages with me. Quite a few years into getting my head around teaching about the Christian worldview, I'm still trying to make it accessible to people like myself: every day Christian educators longing to make sense of the world in light of their need for and gratitude to Jesus.

As I became more comfortable with the content, I whittled down the course's skeletal framework and used it as the foundation for two other worldview classes: an adult Sunday School class and a tenth-grade Bible class. Both helped me see how the framework could be applicable to people in all areas of life and simple enough for adolescent understanding. Due to the murkiness and overuse of the concept, the lessons I've learned in teaching about worldview have convinced me how important simpler articulation is.

Gene Frost, former Head of School at Wheaton Academy, unexpectedly drove the worldview course's evolution when he wrote *Learning from the Best.*[1] His book mentions a handful of schools which demonstrate certain best practices among Christian schools, and one of his chapters addresses Christian worldview development programs – specifically our program at ECS. The bulk of his chapter on ECS focuses on our faculty worldview course as the foundation of the other things we were doing.

While I wasn't teaching the course when Gene started researching ECS' program, I had stepped into the role soon after it was published and began fielding calls from educators who read his book and were interested in what we were doing. They wanted to hear more about the required twenty-five-hour course, the other pieces that had grown out of it, and the effect our initiatives were having throughout the school. Over the next three or four years, a growing number of educators came to Memphis to see the worldview course first-hand and how it began changing the school culture. Yet, it was a substantial commitment for schools to send staff to Memphis for a full week during the summer.

With Gene's prompting, we condensed the course content so it could be digested in two days and created small workshops which welcomed Christian school leaders to Memphis during the school year to provide personal glimpses into what we were doing. After a couple years of hosting our Worldview Symposiums, I began getting requests to add more flesh to the course notes so what we were doing could be more easily accessible in a book form. That's much of what you have here.

Whenever people heard about my worldview course, they concluded that I must be teaching about worldviews: comparing belief systems, pinpointing where they show up in our culture, and offering a response. Certainly, talking about Christian worldview requires an understanding of the different "isms" out there. So, that will pop up in these pages, but only in passing, because I could recommend many books[2] which are far better at unpacking different views. I'm much more interested in speaking toward a framework for a distinctly Christian perspective as it applies to education. While we can learn a lot by seeing things pitted against their opposites, true, good, and beautiful things are best defined by themselves. Once we form a deeper understanding of the Christian worldview, we can better make sense of the other worldviews, rather than the other way around.

While having its place, comparative worldview study isn't what Christian schools most need right now. I've noticed how many Christian schools are more likely to have these comparative courses than providing the tools for understanding the Christian worldview. I find this concerning, especially considering the anemic theology oozing from many churches. We need to more simply define the Christian worldview because we're confusing outsiders by our internal confusion. Not only do we need to provide clarity, but we must also go beyond merely informing the way students think about the world by shaping their hearts, so their desires conform to the spirit of Christ.

Similarly, this book isn't intended to be a manual for critiquing non-Christian ways of thinking. Some people hear "worldview" and automatically gravitate toward cultural engagement, which is certainly another way the Christian worldview has been adapted. Unfortunately, for many of Christians, cultural engagement means looking at different forms of media or politics and pointing out how wrong they are or where they aren't "Christian." In this perspective, the Christian worldview is more of a fence than a lens.

This would be a very narrow understanding of what it looks like to live as Christians in the world. It's similar to Israel's years in exile, as mentioned in the book of Jeremiah. The exiled Jews stayed on the outside of Babylon and opposed it. Yet, Jeremiah trumpeted God's desire for his people to go into their pagan culture and help it flourish. (Ch. 29) This is a large part of what it means to have a biblical outlook on the world, and I hope to raise questions to enable Christians to live in a way which brings about flourishing engagement with the world, not religious opposition to it.

While I've taught about a biblical worldview in multiple contexts using a framework which is broadly applicable, this book is not intended to provide a just-add-water "worldview in a box" curriculum for Christian schools. Christian schools are notorious for finding and quickly trying to implement the latest, trendiest program which another school has found successful. Rarely does this work, because a program which has succeeded elsewhere was developed over years within the culture which cultivated it. While I'd love to succeed like other schools have in their areas of strength, I also realize that what seems to flourish in another community will need to be adjusted so it can flourish in my own context. As much as I've worked to hone my thinking in these areas, I'm not foolish enough to think there's no additional work to tailor it to each school's context.

Along the way of building our program, I visited schools to see what they were doing and took away some things which sharpened our approach. Our worldview course was strengthened by what we saw in other schools. My hope is to provide a framework which is a culmination of the many years of this process so I can empower our abilities to rush toward unpacking how Jesus's gospel drives what we do. That's what I've most enjoyed in my job; that's what I most hope for you.

For Christ and His Kingdom!
NSB

1

YES, THEY STILL NEED JESUS

Confessions of a Recovering Christian School Alumnus

I love Christian education without qualification. It's my starting point because it's central to the heart of this book. It's all I've ever known. I'm all in. I've drunk the Kool-Aid.

I also love the gospel. But even though I've believed the truths of Christianity for as long as I can remember, I wish my love for the gospel was as consistently strong as my love for Christian education. My inability to be *all in* to the same depth is one of the numerous reasons why I still need Jesus as much as I did at the moment of my conversion. Though, I do love the gospel, find myself in a deepening courtship with it, and fully confess that I need it more than I need Christian education.

I start with these foundational loves because they are the critical context for my concerns about how "Christian" our Christian schools really are. I hate that I have this concern, but it's the natural result of the collision I see between the gospel and Christian schooling. For me, the process has been *messy* and idol smashing, and this book is the fallout.

It often seems like the unstated goal of modern, traditional, evangelical schooling is to create a bunch of students who no longer need Jesus – or so they think. Of course, there isn't anyone who doesn't need Jesus. All the more reason to be concerned. Let's make sure we're all on the same page: the goal of Christian education *is not* to graduate students who no longer need Jesus.

While our students have significant exposure to biblical principles, they're likely confused about what it means for Jesus to be at the center of their education (even for those who have legitimate faith). They fail to see the personal presence of Jesus in their school programs because, frankly, our schools present curricula improperly or inconsistently infused with a commitment to Christ's supremacy.

Even more discouraging, we've put enormous emphasis on Christian worldview, such as books (like this one), seminars, workshops, and conferences. Seemingly, these haven't brought us any closer to articulating and implementing the gospel throughout our school cultures. Nearly every summary I've ever read from Christian school accreditation committees has highlighted a particular school's need for growth in biblical integration and faith formation. In fact, I've never seen a review that said a school was where it needed to be, and that's almost entirely based upon the school's evaluation of *itself*.

I hate sounding negative, because I dearly love Christian schooling and have great hope for the movement. But I also can't tiptoe around my nagging concern any longer. Our schools are at a critical juncture with declining enrollments and mounting external pressures. Yet aligning our practice with our philosophy and theology is far more pressing and might be at the root of some of these observable symptoms.

I say this from firsthand experience. I'm the son of a high school Bible teacher. I've been around Christian schools since birth. I'm an alumnus: kindergarten through college. I've taught multiple subjects in seven different grades. I've coached middle school and varsity sports at the very highest level of competition. Major sports and minor sports. I've created and overseen numerous types of co-curricular programs. I've been both mid-level and senior-level administrators, and a head of school. 3K-12 schools, 3K-6 schools, and 7-12 schools. Large, mid-level, and tiny schools. Traditional curriculum and classical. Independent and church owned. Urban and suburban. I've served on accreditation teams and review committees. I've consulted and led workshops for schools around the US and overseas. My own children attend a wonderful Christian school where my wife is a board member. I've seen a lot, and my profound love for Christian schooling has not diminished.

Nor have my fears.

I graduated from a Christian K-12 school thinking one of the goals of the whole process was to bring me to the point where I needed Jesus less than I did when I entered the school – to become more acceptable as a result of my time in that school. Or to *arrive.* Of course, neither I nor anyone else would actually *say* this, but I certainly thought it. If we're honest, it's often easy to think that those of us in Christian school communities are on the right "team." We're the good guys, right? Aren't we the insiders?

Yet Jesus didn't come for the insiders; He came for the outsiders, and if we believe the gospel, we realize that we "good guys" are no less in need of God's pursuing grace than anyone else. Oh, I know we *know* this is true. But we need to live as though we believe it, and the profound truths of the gospel have to be unmistakable in our schools.

Despite my concerns, I'm still deeply committed because I know Christian schools can be places where students can know themselves and the world more deeply through radical dependence upon God's gospel. That's the goal of disciplined growth in the area of Christian worldview, and the Christian school truly can function with Jesus at its center.

Because you're reading this book, I assume you're familiar with the studies and their staggering numbers which project that most Christian school students will graduate without well-formed biblical worldviews or will abandon these views altogether. Not only do these studies reveal that students are "leaving the faith,"[3] I've witnessed significant disgust toward Christian education from many alumni. The majority of my own high school peers won't consider enrolling their children in Christian schools, and other studies suggest this isn't limited to my own experience. You don't have to look very far to notice Christian schools' declining enrollment across the US. Many believe this stems from waning appreciation for the distinctives of Christian education. In *Back to the Blackboard,* Jay Adams adds to this mounting concern by saying that our schools haven't proven themselves to be significantly superior to the public schools as was predicted and hoped for in the 1970s.

Being so tired of blame cast elsewhere, I'm inclined to target our schools' ongoing inability to be truly distinctive when it comes to fostering the Christian worldview's implications throughout the entire school program effectively. In increasing numbers, many schools are imparting a *Christless* Christian education. If we're honest with ourselves, I think we know it.

Progress is slow to address the data about our students' worldviews[4] because schools still try to "do school" the way we've always done it while layering the trendiest "worldview" initiatives onto unchanging, vanilla models. While we want the Christian worldview to be central to what the school does, functionally our schools treat the "Christian" components like add-ons. This is not new; Adams says,

> "Even the most casual survey of the modern history of Christian education shows that Christian schools, on all levels, are little more than adaptations of pagan schools … With very little change, most of the presuppositions, goals, curricula, subject areas, materials, and methods have been brought over into Christian education and 'Christianized.'"[5]

Ouch.

Distinctively Confused

I'm often exasperated by the term "Christian worldview" as it has become an overused and misunderstood concept within Christian education. The onlooking world sees "Christian worldview" plastered on billboards and throughout school communications but cannot pinpoint what makes our schools distinctive (in a way we prefer). Generally, Christian schools are known for:

- what we're *against*, rather than what we're *for*. Onlookers arrive at this conclusion because Christian schools often offer weak or confusing articulations of what they're really about. But they're quite clear about what they're *against,* because their most pronounced "Christian" component is their critique of non-Christian culture; this aligns with Richard Niebuhr's "Christ against culture" label of Christian engagement.[6] As a result, interested families come to the Christian school primarily for retreat and safety. Sadly, I'm not surprised by the Barna Group's 2017 study finding that the greatest reason people put their children in Christian schools is safety.[7]
- swanky programs, facilities, academic prestige, or college-acceptance rates which take a front seat to our missions to such an extent, the non-believer finds it way too easy to accept what is "Christian" about these schools. Parents can stomach it rather comfortably, only because the *product* we offer (success, college acceptance, etc.) is more conspicuous than the Jesus we offer. As a result, many schools are merely influenced by the Judeo-Christian ethic, which makes signing-off on the "religious" components quite easy for the non-believer.
- school structures identical to what's seen in secular schools with the only difference being some "Jesus Dust" sprinkled everywhere. You know what I mean: Bible verses, Christian

lingo, Chapel, and Bible classes – those things which sanctify what's otherwise a secular school.

- "religious" instruction at every turn to the detriment of best practices of sound schooling. Christian curriculum (only), poor emphasis on academic rigor, overly simplistic and absolute "biblical" answers to every question because the spiritual is more important than the physical. These schools don't feel the need to hire or develop excellent teachers or have excellent curriculum, programs, processes, practices, or facilities because they know they are God's people. None of these are as important as faith.

Sadly, this is what the Christian worldview has become for most of the people I've encountered: rules, critiques, tidiness, safety, and spiritual language.

While each of these could have value, none of them are necessarily or automatically Christian, because they could be miles apart from the gospel in the way they're lived-out in our schools. While Christian schools might be jam-packed with biblical references in the halls, at the top of quizzes, and on soccer team warmup jackets, they could be void of the gospel in the philosophy which drives what's produced.

I'm reminded of a reference to famous preacher D.G. Barnhouse given by Michael Horton in *Christless Christianity*. Barnhouse was once asked what Philadelphia would look like if Satan took total control of the city. He remarked that we'd see,

> "All the bars would be closed, pornography outlawed. Streets would be pristine and filled with tidy pedestrians who always smile at each other. Swearing would be a crime. Children would say, 'yes Sir' and no 'Ma'am,' and churches would be full every Sunday where Christ would not be preached."[8]

Tragically, I know far too many schools which would read all the above (except for not preaching Jesus) and think, "That's exactly what we want." They don't want messiness. They don't want dissonance. They want *tidy*, almost as a core value. Yet we often see the biblical Jesus being most critical of the tidiest people in His day because they failed to realize how deeply they needed the One talking to them.

Stanley Hauerwas once said, "I have tried to live a life I hope is unintelligible if the God we Christians worship does not exist."[9] This way of living seems radical to me because I hesitate being *this* different. Yet Hauerwas understands that believing in God and His gospel must speak into all areas of our lives. I don't believe we're intentionally leaving the gospel out. We've just become complacent, which results in lazy (and potentially ruinous) attempts at teaching "Christianly."

It must be more than merely highlighting Christian analogies in class content. Once I asked a teacher how the gospel influences her science classroom; she welled with pride to describe how she showed her class a sampling of a simple organism under the microscope, revealing a heart shape with a cross shape inside it. Another teacher showed me how he had students graph two functions, and the result was an *ichthus.*

Insert face in palm.

These sorts of effort typically flow out of good intentions. I blame teachers less than the schools which have poorly prepared them to know what biblical integration looks like.

We could expect students to draw similarities between Harry Potter, Aslan, and Jesus or make connections between the battle of Waterloo and the fall of Jericho. We could use biblical language at every turn, but we have to get to a place where we recognize that our practices, while justified with Scripture, aren't necessarily Christian if they aren't rooted in the gospel of Jesus. It starts by recognizing that Christianity hinges on what Jesus has done more than what He said.

It hinges on the idea that the gospel fundamentally acknowledges God's mysterious rescue project. Yet, rescue and mystery are both messy. And we struggle with messiness when trying to produce students who are *adequate.*

When the Method is as Christian as the Message

There are two other concerns which have prompted this book (The first being my fear that we're drifting further away from the gospel):

First, it seems like most of our work to develop Christian worldview in schools has been limited to the content of the classroom curricula. Schools which have best developed their ability to teach from a Christian perspective have asked questions about the information and ideas which should show up in their classrooms. If they've journeyed very far into this process, they've even thought in discipline-specific ways, considering what it looks like to teach Mathematics, World Languages, and History from a biblical perspective.

In Christian school circles, it's common to hear people talk about the "integration of faith and learning," and this typically speaks toward the curricula which the school teaches. Typically, Christian educators use this phrase to define what it looks like to teach certain disciplines from a position of faith, which is certainly one of the primary tasks of the Christian school. However, I wish more emphasis would be put on the actual practice of teaching and living among our peers and students as though we have a biblical perspective. This "integration" needs to consider both the "what" and the "how" in our schools. The practices of the school (which could either be Christian or not) are what the school teaches just as much as the information taught in class.

The lasting legacy of the Christian school far transcends the content taught in the classroom, for our graduates will likely forget much of what we taught. They remember the way teachers teach and how they treat their students. Christian schools need to develop philosophies of teaching and learning, assessment, lesson design, and all sorts of educational best practices which are married to their same Christian commitments. While they need to continually consider how to grow curricula rich in biblical truth, schools need to invest just as much time in conversations about what it looks like to teach in ways that reveal their commitments to the essential truths of Christianity.

There is a great difference between what can and should be taught in a Christian classroom and a secular one. However, we often see little variation in how it's taught. Christian schools need to ask questions like "what about Christianity affects the way I assess my students?" or "does the gospel have anything to say about how I define learning success?" "Is my belief that students are prized image-bearers of God central to my educational philosophy and practice?"

We're in far greater need of Jesus than we understand and are far more incapable of fixing ourselves than we'd like to admit. Believing this should cause us to willingly accept some harsh realities, starting with the reality that secular scholars have often done the deepest and most informative work in educational theory. Even more embarrassingly, many Christian schools notoriously look the other way, dismissing the science of data-driven best practices. When I've attended secular school conferences, presentations and workshops are research and data based, almost entirely. Yet the Christian versions quote Scripture and tell loving stories, while I walk away wondering if the presenters are even aware of the research which could better inform their presentations. Not only have many Christian schools not thought deeply enough about how Christianity influences their pedagogy, but they have also fallen way behind secular schools in their attention to pedagogical excellence. Both are unacceptable.

For too long, many Christian schools have functioned as though the actual process of education is essentially neutral. Too often, we teach and assess material without questioning the process. Many Christian schools and their teachers have thought it's sufficient to focus on the content while minimizing the art of teaching, and this simply can't be. It's especially scary, considering that we know that students retain the method far more often than the message. So, we should question how the Christian perspectives of grace, restoration, and brokenness (to name a few) drive the best practices of Christian pedagogy.

Consider asking yourself, "where do themes of hope, repair, brokenness, restoration, or repentance show up in my testing practice?" Did something come to mind immediately?

If we believe words like these are distinctives of a Christian worldview, shouldn't they influence the way we go about teaching or testing?

In his book, *Desiring the Kingdom,* James K.A. Smith says that most of our attention on Christian worldview has focused primarily on the mind – on ideas and thoughts. In doing so, we've neglected the heart and the body. He argues that humans are primarily desiring beings more than we are thinking beings. Similarly in *The Abolition of Man*, C.S. Lewis criticizes modern education because it has removed the wonder from the process. By focusing primarily on the content of Christian education, we tend to focus on students' minds alone. As Smith says, we treat them as bobble-heads. Or, as Lewis says: "men without chests."[10] If schools want to speak more to the desires of the students and treat them as whole persons, we must do a much better job of considering the method used to shape students both inside and outside the classroom.

In *The Pattern of God's Truth,* Frank Gaebelein says our schools should be no less "Christian," if we took away chapel, Bible classes, and lessons about Jesus. He's not suggesting we should ditch our Bible departments or chapel services. But our commitment to the implications of the gospel must be everywhere.

To get there, our schools need a guiding framework which will properly inform whether we're furthering the gospel in the way we "do" education. Most Christian teachers yearn for ways to improve their practice, especially from a Christian perspective; they just don't know which questions to ask. Schools need to develop structures which provide commonality among the staff. This certainly will nurture accountability. But of far greater importance, it will generate a culture of growth as teachers challenge each other to go deeper. As a result, the structure of much of this book seeks to provide a basis for aligning both our content and practice with the truths of the gospel.

Needing Something in Place

This leads to the third problem which prompted this book – the recurringly-voiced theme of schools' inability to both articulate and apply a biblical worldview. Very few schools have frameworks put in place to strengthen their teachers' foundation for and understanding of Christian education and ensure ongoing conversation in the life of the school.

There will always be this need. A teacher could be an alumna of a strong, Christian college and still have never considered how her faith affects her approach to education. Similarly, we can't assume that a seasoned teacher who's also a Christian automatically knows how to teach from a Christian perspective. It takes work; and, schools ought to more proactively equip their teachers to be on the same page and support this aspect of the school's mission.

I've seen many schools tackle this, and there are a few resources for building programs which provide the foundation teachers and administrators need. I'm thankful to have been around schools which have dedicated significant personnel and time to providing support for these programs. There are very practical ways to make progress if the school is willing to make the investments and be patient with the process.

Lord willing, I can frame essential questions to direct a unifying focus on the gospel in our schools. Not only do I hope to provide a structure which has seemed to work, I also want to offer actionable steps to build a program which can make that structure part of the ethos of the school. More than anything else, I've learned that schools need a "common vocabulary" – a vernacular as a starting point to get everyone on the same page. If the members of the school community all use the same "worldview language," the school can do a better job of being distinctive in its mission.

I've often frustrated faculty who have attended my workshops, because I don't provide what many of them hoped for. Much of the available worldview integration material intends to generate classroom lessons or curricula which can be replicated or purchased. Having taught for many years, I understand the request: "Noah, what does it look like to teach my discipline from a Christian worldview?" I've been asked to do countless "worldview demonstrations," with the goal of teaching literature, history, or philosophy lessons to show what "integration" looks like.

I get it. Sometimes, teachers need to actually *see* it, and I jive with the desire to glean something I can actually use. Modeling is a powerful teacher, after all.

However, very little of this book will resemble ready-made, teachable lessons, because learning a handful of "integration nuggets" or analogies might never actually change the way we think about education. It might merely add a new expectation for lesson preparation. That's the last thing we need. Most teachers are running on fumes and wilt at the idea of trying to cram even more into what they already do. Rather than offering several examples to imitate, I'll present a framework of questions which can move an entire school culture toward deeper need for and gratitude to Jesus. It starts by asking a primary, umbrella question which unites the other questions:

What difference does the gospel make?

Asking this question above all others prevents our schools from being little more than environments which assume a handful of truths associated with Christianity. It's the question which moves students to see the uniqueness and beauty of both their faith and education when they leave our schools. Students should graduate knowing they still need Jesus and see this need and the beauty of the gospel as the driving force behind everything the school has offered them.

Most worldview-books outline a handful of essential questions every system answers. As I worked to build my faculty worldview course,[11] I tried to find the overlapping questions in these books and used them to form the core of the structure for my curriculum. The resulting questions can provide a comprehensive application of "what difference the gospel makes" throughout the ecosystem of the school. These questions are expansive and flexible enough to infiltrate every nook and cranny of what's going on in our schools. The challenge, though, will be stepping beyond merely asking the questions once in an in-service, but asking them repeatedly and carving out time where ongoing questioning happens. These questions have given me a scaffolding which supports deeper attempts to consider whether we're really on point with the gospel's demands.

While there's nothing groundbreaking about the questions I'll address, unfortunately we're quick to ask many other questions first: How do we keep enrollment up? How do we improve test scores? Which programs will enhance student experience? How do we get our parents on the same page as us philosophically? Certainly, each of these is important, and they should be both asked and answered. However, these questions are more likely to drive school decisions. And if we're honest, we tend to give the same answers we were given as students rather than having a gospel-framework which guides our reasoning.

When we don't ask the right questions, we add programs to our curricula because it's simply what a school is supposed to do. Other schools have class trips and yearbook clubs, so the Christian school should add them as well and just figure out how to *Christianize* them. Shouldn't we first ask how these programs nurture greater understanding of and love for God? If we haven't asked, we must. If we can't find an answer, maybe the school should be willing to be unlike everyone else. That's OK, though, because the messy pursuit of asking how the gospel affects what we're doing brings us to realize how distinctive our schools really should be.

For example, we may allow people to think our ultimate goal is collegiate success. If we ask these questions, won't we have to reevaluate what it means to be "college preparatory?" Shouldn't we have a gospel-worldview structure which guides whether we should add new courses or change curricula? Are we driven by college admissions requirements and what will help students do better on standardized tests? Do we add cheerleading because other schools have it, or do we make this decision because adding the program furthers our mission?

Yes, we should be excellent! No one's attracted to Christian schools which willingly accept mediocrity. We should hope and even expect for some of our students to be National Merit Scholars or to see our teams win state championships. This is easily and often supported with a biblical mandate to do everything as unto the Lord. (Colossians 3:23) But if we're not careful, these successes can further distance us from the gospel. While I believe in pursuing excellence, this desire needs to be consistent with a structure which regularly takes us back to the gospel.

When we do, our portrait of a graduate will likely focus more on the student who celebrates Jesus more because of her experiences in her school. Our report cards would be more encompassing than mere reflections of how well a student demonstrates mastery of a subject. Our college-placement office would be just as interested in helping students whose calling doesn't include going straight to college, if at all. Maybe, going down this road forces us to have "calling placement" offices, instead. Suggesting this, I realize we're not in Kansas anymore. We should expect that asking gospel-driven questions will shake up much of what we do and turn it upside down.

In *The Advantage*, Patrick Lencioni says that core values drive the decisions of healthy organizations. Is strong enrollment a core value? What about snazzy facilities to improve student satisfaction? What about protecting children from increased gender confusion? If these are core values of your school, you likely won't appreciate most of the rest of this book. I'm willing to bet that these aren't your core values. But what are they? Shouldn't the gospel be in there somewhere? If so, we ought to work to build structures and boundaries to align us with those values.

Is the goal of Christian schooling to produce good people? Is it for students to know Christian truths and how those truths separate them from the rest of the world? Is the goal for students to know and love Jesus and engage the world because they love what He loves? Heading in this direction requires every aspect of the program to be considered in terms of questions which enable schools to determine where they are consistent with the gospel's reordering of everything. We must embrace and run toward this reordering, because that's what the gospel does, and it also generates a mission-consistency which students and the onlooking world desperately need to see in us.

This will require a different culture, a different vernacular, a different set of operating principles – all of which are designed to help the Christian school transcend merely assuming the gospel but proclaiming it. While each school has to establish its own distinctives, I hope the following structure can bring actionable steps toward schools clinging to the Jesus we fundamentally need.

2

NOTHING NEW ABOUT IT

Getting on the Same Page about Christian Worldview

Before getting to the questions, I want to provide a perspective which properly defines a worldview and explain why the gospel ignites a worldview unto itself.

But first, I'd like you to consider asking the teachers in your school for their definition of "Christian worldview." Would they all give you the same definition?[12] If your school uses the phrase to describe its culture and philosophy, shouldn't all primary articulators of that philosophy have the same definition?

I'm fairly certain that your survey would yield myriad answers. Considering that every Christian school I've ever observed talks about a Christian worldview, it's quite important that schools have very clear ideas about it. If the teachers aren't on the same page about what it means, we shouldn't be surprised that our students are also confused about what it means to have a Christian worldview.

"Worldview" is an old concept, but a relatively new term describing how people apply a perspective of everything based on their beliefs. The term has been defined in many ways, but each attempt includes some sort of reference to a universal idea(s) which informs the way a person unifies or defines the particulars of life.

- In *The Universe Next Door* James Sire defines it as "a set of presuppositions about the makeup of our world."[13]
- Similarly, in *How Now Should We Live,* Chuck Colson describes it as, "the sum total of our beliefs about the world, the 'big picture' that directs our daily decisions and actions."[14]
- In *Creation Regained,* Albert Wolters offers that a worldview is "the comprehensive framework of one's basic beliefs about things."[15]

Each of these definitions suggests that a worldview is the way a group of beliefs or ideas affects the way we see everything else. It's a foundational perspective; it's at the core of our deepest convictions. Others, like Francis Schaeffer, have defined it as "the basic way an individual looks at life – the grid through which he sees the world."[16] More expansively, Dr. Armand Nicholi explains after teaching at Harvard University for more than three decades:

> "Whether we realize it or not, all of us possess a worldview. A few years after birth, we all gradually formulate our philosophy of life ... Our worldview informs our personal, social, and political lives. It influences how we perceive ourselves, how we relate to others, how we adjust to adversity, and what we understand to be our purpose. Our worldview helps us determine our values, our ethics, and our capacity for happiness. It helps us understand where we come from, our heritage; who we are, our identity; why we exist on this planet, our purpose; what drives us, our motivation; and where we are going, our destiny."[17]

Nicholi beautifully explains two ideas about worldviews: everybody has one, and a worldview informs and influences a filter for understanding the totality of our most significant life events, hopes, and beliefs. Similarly, Sproul says in *Lifeviews,* "we are not all philosophers, but we all have a philosophy. Perhaps we haven't thought much about that philosophy, but one thing is certain – we live it out. How we live reveals our deepest convictions about life."[18]

I offer a heavy dose of quotes from respected thinkers to make sure we all understand what a worldview is. Many people flippantly use the term as though it's a nifty way of speaking about a person's core, doctrinal beliefs. They may even use "worldview" as a synonym for "dogma." When some of my secular friends learned my job title was "Worldview Director," they naturally assumed I was the school's chief indoctrinator. As far as they understood, a worldview is simply what someone believes. But it's far more than a particular belief-set.

As the above statements suggest, a worldview is a perspective of everything else *in light of that belief set.* Taking this into account, holding to a consistent worldview takes work, because it requires application of beliefs. Yes, everyone has a worldview as Sproul and Nicholi suggest, but a worldview is likely a combination of many competing beliefs and presuppositions, rather than a well-developed, singular worldview.

Since a worldview is an application of beliefs which directs how we engage the world, it's immensely important to make sure we understand those core beliefs which compose a worldview. Any lack of clarity in these beliefs will lead to quite inconsistent or confusing worldviews. As a result, when it comes to Christianity, many believers are prone to some sort of syncretism of Christianity with other non-Christian beliefs because their foundational understanding of the tenets of Christianity is weak.

I imagine this is also a significant reason why so many young people walk away from the Church: they don't really understand what a Christian worldview is because they also have a lot of gaps in their understanding of orthodox Christianity. Likely, their biggest hole is grasping what the gospel is all about. As a result, emphasizing stronger worldview-understanding in our schools requires both orthodox theological training for foundational purposes and a framework for considering how these theological truths drive Christian worldview in our schools.

Presuppositions and Worldview

The foundation of any worldview is a combination of beliefs, assumptions, convictions, values, creeds, or ideals. All of these tend to focus primarily on "brainy" dimensions, yet we should also include what's outside the intellect – like our desires and loves. They are just as important to the foundation of a worldview. Not only do we view the world through a grid made up of our logical convictions, it's also made up of our hopes and longings, which often affect our worldviews far more than our ideas. For our purposes, I'll lump them together under the umbrella of **presuppositions**.

A presupposition is a fundamental idea about the reality we live in, allowing us to form a system of values from which to live. They're different from hypotheses or opinions because they tend to be subconscious assumptions we make about the world and our relationship to it. We typically believe our presuppositions to be true, regardless of or prior to in-depth study. That's where the prefix comes from. For instance, a person may think there is something magical about the world and will approach an unexplainable event with a notion of supernatural activity at work. Contrarily, someone who doesn't believe in any sort of supernatural involvement will go to extreme lengths to understand the same event via natural explanations.

We have many assumptions, and they often connect to our hopes, idols, and deeply-held images of "the good life." As James K.A. Smith says, they tend to proceed more from our "guts" than from our minds. They reside in the core of our beings; they are the loves and desires which shape our thoughts – our philosophies. These loves, desires, and ideas shape the way we receive and interpret our experiences, as C.S. Lewis says in *Miracles,* "What we learn from experiences depends on the kind of philosophy we bring to experience."[19]

Whether consciously or subconsciously, the structure which girds our view of the world informs and determines how we engage and function in it. Ultimately the beliefs which form a worldview answer essential questions like, "I believe people are inherently good," rather than everyday questions like, "I believe Tom Brady is the greatest quarterback of all time." Still, they become the basis for everyday questions: "Should I always trust my child to be honest?"

Presuppositions are primarily concerned with answering foundational questions like: *What is ultimate reality? How does one know what he knows? What is a human? What's the difference between right and wrong?* The four branches of philosophy which correspond to these presuppositions are called metaphysics, epistemology, anthropology, and ethics respectively. There are three related biblical categories which further clarify the nature of these philosophical categories, namely: Creation, Fall, and Redemption.

In one way or another, these seven categories address the "worldview questions" which I found in the books I read to build our faculty worldview course. As a result, these seven categories make up the Worldview Grid which is the structure I'll use throughout this book. It's essential to understand our assumptions in these areas because they form the foundation of our worldviews.

Once we recognize and acknowledge our presuppositions, we have firmer ground for consistent answers to less foundational (but still necessary) questions like: *What is the purpose of education? What do we mean by gender? What is success? Were the Nazis wrong? What is love? Do the ends justify the means? What happens at death?* How we answer these sorts of questions are very much determined by our presuppositions and can be traced to the seven categories of the Worldview Grid.

A Bit of Worldview History[20]

"Worldview" itself is a relatively new word within the Church, especially among English speakers. The German philosopher, Immanuel Kant (1724-804), was the first to articulate it. Kant's word, *Weltanschauung,* is a combination of two German words: *Welt*, which refers to the totality of what's in the world; we translate *Anschauung* as perspective, viewpoint, or outlook. Hence, worldview is essentially an outlook on everything the world has to offer.

Worldview-language became popular within the modern English-speaking Christian Church by men like Abraham Kuyper (1837-1920), Herman Dooyeweerd (1894-1977), Gordon H. Clark (1902-1985), Francis Schaeffer (1912-1984), and Carl Henry (1913-2003). Kuyper and Schaeffer had the greatest influence on me (Kuyper, to the point where I couldn't help but name my son after him), but the legacy of the others cannot be undervalued. Since the groundwork these men laid, Christian worldview has become a popular topic of conversations, books, websites, seminars, and video series in numbers beyond what I can fathom. We certainly have an abundance of resources, many of them giving direct homage to these trailblazers.

Seemingly, much of the commonplace use of the term is due to a worldview-emphasis on Christian college campuses during the mid-twentieth century. Books which resonate with Schaeffer and Kuyper, like Niebuhr's *Christ and Culture* (1951), Gaebelein's *The Pattern of God's Truth* (1954), and Blamires' *The Christian Mind* (1963), found their way onto the desks of many educational leaders who shaped the Christian school movement in the second half of the twentieth century. As more colleges and schools put greater emphasis on Christian worldview, it became more commonplace in other Christian circles, which crossed paths with what was happening in our schools.

My own dad first heard Francis Schaeffer speak at Wheaton College[21] in the late 60's and was changed forever by these "radical" ideas. He started teaching his high school seniors about Schaeffer in the early 1980's, and much of this content seemed new to his students.

While it may seem a newer emphasis for the Church, this recent focus on worldview development is more reformational than anything else, having returned the Church back to what it has historically believed. For instance, St. Augustine's fifth century book, *The City of God,* is one of the clearest examples of early Christians' attempt to make sense of all things in light of the truths of Christianity. Many of the creeds themselves also reflect a commitment to a biblical view of all things.

The reason for the magnitude of the Church's historical writing about Jesus's impact on all things is precisely that the Bible paints the same picture. Any study of Paul's letters reveals his commitment to helping believers understand the implications of the gospel. There are many verses I could reference, but I'll mention just two:

> Romans 11:36, "For from him and through him and to him are all things. To him be glory forever. Amen."
>
> Colossians 1:15-20, "[Jesus] is the image of the invisible God, the firstborn of all creation. For by him all things were created, in heaven and on earth, visible and invisible, whether thrones or dominions or rulers or authorities—all things were created through him and for him. And he is before all things, and in him all things hold together. And he is the head of the body, the church. He is the beginning, the firstborn from the dead, that in everything he might be preeminent. For in him all the fullness of God was pleased to dwell, and through him to reconcile to himself all things, whether on earth or in heaven, making peace by the blood of his cross.

Both passages clearly reflect Paul's insistence that *all things* find their place in Jesus. As a result, believers must learn to look at the cosmos in light of who He is and what He did. Because, as Kuyper beautifully articulates, Jesus says every square inch is "His."[22] The Colossians passage explains both the structure and direction of all things by declaring that Jesus has a restorative plan for it all. This also implies a current deviation from the way things are supposed to be. Yet, we have profound hope because the blood of Jesus's cross brings about reconciliation. Not just to souls, but to everything else as well.

Returning to the twenty-first century, I see a growing trend away from a culture of Christian thinkers. I'm not alone. Mark Noll's book, *The Scandal of the Evangelical Mind* (1994), was one of my "light switch" books which piqued my awareness about this lapse. From the outset of the book, Noll says this scandal of the evangelical mind is that there is *no longer a Christian mind* - or that the intellect is not valued among Christians as much as it used to be. This decline has explained much of the thought-gap I see in Christian schooling.

I've learned that "Christian worldview," typically means one of two things to many Christians (even in educational circles), causing them to miss the point altogether. Many say they know what it means to have a Christian worldview and think little more about it because they've got it covered. These people think it's about basic Christian tenants and/or identifying with a specific Christian subculture. I've had difficulty convincing my peers that developing a Christian worldview can't be so easily dismissed. It takes effort; it's worth the time investment in our schools.

Others have a vague idea of what's being discussed and feel inadequately prepared to engage in it. They retreat. This is the most common struggle I've encountered in working with teachers over the years. They think it's highly philosophical and above their heads. A teacher friend recently told me that she didn't feel too bad about her minimal understanding of the Christian worldview because she didn't consider it as an essential of the faith. She's not alone.

Both responses from Christians are very common – and very wrong – because they fail to see what Christianity is. It's a worldview, and we can't set it aside because we don't see its importance or because we think we have it all figured out. Nor can we run away from it because it's too intimidating. Worldview-thinking isn't a subcategory of Christianity. It's what Christianity actually is. I love how Dorothy Sayers proclaims that "it is vitally necessary to insist that [Christianity] is first and foremost a rational explanation of the universe."[23] In other words, Christianity is primarily a perspective of everything. It says something about life, love, hope, physics, elephants, and limelight hydrangeas.

This is what worldview-dismissive Christians need to hear. Those who insist the that the conversation is not vital to their faith keep it at arm's length and shield themselves by saying they'd rather focus on the essentials, especially those most easily understood. However, learning to see Christianity as a worldview ought not be intimidating; the language doesn't have to be heady. In fact, it should be very common-place because of the many connections and implications we must make to the mundane aspects of our lives. It's not other-worldly. It's all about this world because of the Person who came into this world. It's right here in front of us, staring us in the face in real life conversations and experiences while many people talk about worldview and biblical integration as though they're supernatural concepts for the experts.

While I worry about some teachers giving deep reflection the proverbial Heisman, I'm far more worried by those who fail to see it as essential. We all adhere to set principles which ultimately drive how we view things, and those principles make up our philosophies – our worldviews. Everyone has a worldview, and it's vitally important to employ enough care to consider whether our own worldviews actually jive with the biblical worldview. I fear we rarely conduct such self-autopsies, because we automatically assume to hold a biblical worldview because we're part of the Christian subculture. Or, we don't take a deeper look because we're scared of what we might find out about ourselves. Yet, ole' Socrates' words could never be truer: "the unexamined life is not worth living."

The Grid of a Biblical Worldview

For the purposes of having common questions to house the "worldview terms" which come up in the life of the school, I've come to use seven categories. They serve to frame the way we see the world and ourselves in relation to it through a recognition of who Jesus is and what He came to do. Throughout the questions of the framework, we are confronted by the reality of the fact that God is God and we are not. We often want to put ourselves on the throne, and this form of idolatry is typically at the root of why we most need Jesus.

Let's return to Schaeffer's definition for worldview: "A worldview is the grid through which one sees the world." *World* may loosely be defined as all the particulars of reality including, mankind, nature, ideas, emotions, and events. Also, he doesn't mean physical sight, rather, the way someone makes sense of the world around him. The *grid*, then, is the set of convictions, beliefs, or creeds which determines how one interprets what he sees.

After coming across Scheffer's definition, I wondered what should make up the lines and intersections of that grid. This grid needs structures – boundaries, lines, categories, and boxes. So, I set up a sort of grid of several different "strands," and the deciding factor for the strands was driven by what we see throughout the history of philosophical thought meshed alongside the simplest structure for the story of the Bible.

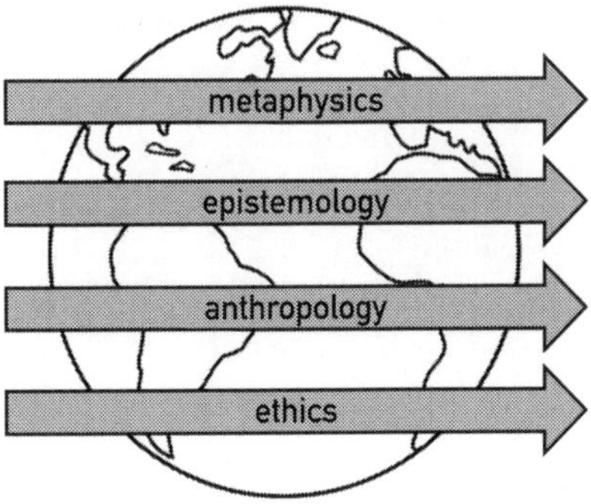

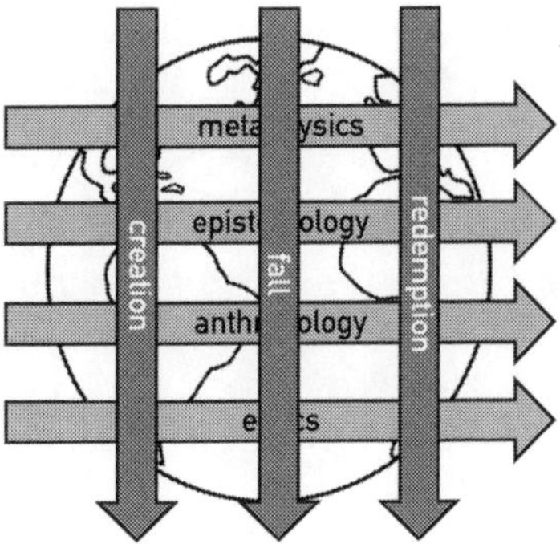

The first four, horizontal lines are more philosophical in nature: Metaphysics, Epistemology, Anthropology and Ethics. Every philosopher and every philosophy has wrestled with these categories.

The vertical lines are more theological in nature, in that they represent the essential framework of the story of Scripture: Creation, Fall, and Redemption. I want to be clear; even though the story of the Bible is one of Creation, Fall, and Redemption, this is the same story which has captured the imagination of every human. So, these categories apply to us all – not only those who read Scripture.

Socrates often said there is little use having answers if we don't first know the correct questions to ask. When a school asks the right questions, it's one of the greatest signs of health. I'd also rather package the ideas of the framework as questions, because they're easier to use in our schools. Using the philosophical terms furthers the notion that worldview requires having a background in philosophy. For the purpose of knowing the history and giving names to them, I'll reference the philosophical terms and will use them occasionally. As far as application goes, I'll stick to the questions far more than the terms. Have no fear.

As we jump into the implications of each category, we'll quickly see how our questions and their answers typically drift beyond the lines of the other categories. They blend together for the same reason the lines between our hearts, minds, and bodies are also murky. Similarly, our beliefs will show up in multiple areas of the Grid, intersecting numerous lines, and we'll find that the vertical, theological categories run right through each of the horizontal, philosophical categories. Therefore, Schaeffer's word "grid" is helpful, because it gives us a mental picture of looking at the world through an intersecting mesh of strands. In our case, it means that we have all sorts of presuppositions, questions, hopes, and desires which collide when we try to do school in light of the gospel.

The Questions of the Grid

When I have taught this worldview framework, I started with the philosophical categories and then explained how every person (not just every philosophy or worldview) has thoughts about the questions associated with these categories. After introducing the questions, we'd unpack the Christian answers to these questions, using these answers as the basis for new questions which shape a more gospel-centric worldview.

For example, were I to focus on the category of anthropology, we'd start by analyzing how every worldview questions what it means to be human. From there, we'd build a case for a gospel-driven view of humanity, focusing on our profound dignity as image bearers of God. Next, we'd formulate image-bearers-concepts to consider what it looks like to engage the world as though we truly believe it. Lastly, we'd consider how that's only possible in light of the gospel, not just biblical truths (rules and stories), but the unique, powerful message of needy image-bearers being saved by the living and active Jesus.

I'll dedicate a chapter to each of these seven questions, but I want to list each of them in one place to help connect the questions to the categories each worldview category addresses:

Metaphysics: "What is the nature of ultimate reality?" or "What's really out there?"

Christians answer this question by insisting that the infinite, personal, triune God of the Bible is ultimate, and all other reality depends upon Him. We'll apply this by asking: *Are we recognizing God as ultimate over everything else?*

Epistemology: "How do we know what we know?" or "What is Truth?"

Christians answer these questions by confessing our dependence upon God and His Revelation. We'll apply this by asking: *"Are we modeling and celebrating dependence upon God's Truth wherever it's seen?"*

Anthropology: "Who is Man?" or "What does it mean to be human?"

In the Bible, Christians see that God created people in His image and tasked us to engage the world through the offices of prophet, priest, and king. We'll apply this by asking: *"Are we celebrating the full nature and calling of the image of God in all members of the school community?"*

Ethics: "What's our standard for right and wrong behavior?" or "How Should we Live?"

Living in the Kingdom of God prompts such a radical ethical view that we must understand our school culture is going to look very different than what we see in other schools, because we recognize that our obedience isn't what makes us good. That's not the source of our hope; it's in God's life-changing grace. We'll apply this by asking: *"Are we cultivating a culture of grace-prompted obedience?"*

Creation: "How ought everything be?"

This is not just a category which asks where everything came from. There are clear, creational norms which must be considered throughout everything that goes on in the life of our schools. We'll apply this by asking: *"Are we pursuing and resting in God's original intent?"*

Fall: "What happened?" or "Where did all of the wrong come from?"

We know that things are not the way they're supposed to be. One of the other dominant themes of Scripture is the resulting effects on the created order because of sin. So, the Fall considers what went wrong and its effects. We'll apply this by asking: *"Are we demonstrating mournfulness and repentance over sin and a broken world?"*

Redemption: "How's it going to be fixed?" or "What does the fix look like?"

Thankfully, God's word also paints a beautiful picture of hope as He has not left the world to its decay. Rather He entered into it to bring about reconciliation. To the extent sin affects the world, God's redemptive plan is about restoring all things back to that original intent. We'll apply this by asking: *"Are we actively proclaiming and seeking repair and restoration according to Jesus's plan?"*

These questions serve as reminders of the gospel because each one of them ultimately confesses God as God and our need for Him. They tell us that God exists; He has revealed Himself; He is the standard for truth, existence, goodness and beauty; our sin is a violation against him; He is the fix. All of these realities chart a course for making sense of our schools in light of the gospel.

As we consider each of these categories, we will consider how the Christian answers to these questions informs our approach to education and where necessary, we'll consider competing perspectives. It's vital for Christian school teachers to understand the ideas which already affect their own assumptions and will certainly combat the students as they engage the world. Knowing both the Christian and non-Christian answers enables us to give a proper target while also diagnosing the cultural trends which surround us and that much more see our need for Jesus.

3

GOSPEL-WORLDVIEW AND MESSY PORTRAITS

How the Gospel Drives a Worldview unto Itself

"Christianity is a world and life view and not simply a series of unrelated doctrines. Christianity includes all of life. Every realm of knowledge, every aspect of life and every fact of the universe find their place and their answer within Christianity. It is a system of truth enveloping the entire world in its grasp."
Frank Gaebelein[24]

In chapter 2, I referenced Dorothy Sayers' statement, "Christianity is supposed to be an interpretation of the universe." I have long loved this *Creeds or Chaos* quote because it surprisingly expands how some might define Christianity. She says nothing about rules, behavior, teachings, or doctrines. Rather, Sayers insists that Christianity has something to say about everything: hope, Saturn, college football, social justice, and very small rocks.

Yes, Christianity ultimately hinges on the life, death, and finished work of Jesus, but this living and active Jesus affects how I see everything else. Even Friedrich Nietzsche (who certainly didn't think fondly of Christianity) remarked in *Twilight of Idols* that "Christianity is a system, a whole view of things thought out together."[25] What he found in Christianity is what caused Nietzsche's greatest distaste. He would have tolerated Christianity were it something like what many skeptics prefer: a hobby like recreational knitting or badminton on the weekends, never getting in anyone's way. Yet, as the son of a Lutheran minister, Nietzsche understood what Christianity was supposed to be: a system which necessitates an intentional approach to all of life.

In *True Spirituality*, Francis Schaeffer says true spirituality (or, that which is good for the life of the believer) is "all of life after that which is contrary to the character of God is removed."[26] More simply, he suggests that everything is good except whatever is in opposition to who God is. Along this line of thinking, there aren't nearly as many "bad" things as we'd often assume; there are also no neutrals. For, if God is the Maker of all things, they must reflect who He is.

This has an important implication for education. Too often, Christians wrongly divide reality into three separate compartments: Good, Bad, and Neutral. If Schaeffer is correct, there is little room to speak of things as neutral. They are either contrary to God's character, or they're good for us. Part of the reason we have such a hard time embracing the implications and concrete reality of our worldviews is our assumption of generally neutral things and ideas. This explains why we've built a separate compartment for the gospel in our lives, relegating it more to evangelism and conversion than to the rest of life.

Our tendencies to build so many compartments in our schools and lives can be traced to our ease of confining the gospel and person of Jesus into narrow categories as well. This is far too small of a view of the gospel; it's bad theology in general. It's anemic, because it lacks what makes Christianity strong. This broken theology is also very much linked to a broken approach to Scripture.

One of my greatest joys has been to read Bible stories to my children in hopes they will see Jesus and His gospel around every corner of Scripture. One of the books we've found most useful is Sally Lloyd-Jones' book, *The Jesus Storybook Bible.* In her introductory pages, she writes about an approach to Scripture which is so radically different than anything I learned growing up. She says,

> "Some people think the Bible is a book of rules telling you what you should and shouldn't do. The Bible certainly does have some rules in it. They show you how life works best. But the Bible isn't mainly about you and what you should be doing. It's about God and what He has done ... No, the Bible isn't a book of rules or a book of heroes. The Bible is most of all a Story about a young Hero who comes from a far country to win back his lost treasure..."[27]

Such a view of Scripture was lost on me as a child. I learned that the Bible was God's Word, revealing what He likes and doesn't like. I focused on the rules and adopted a fear of breaking them. I learned a lot of stories. I matured with a list of the attributes of biblical characters who were loved by God and felt compelled to try to imitate them. Very clearly, I remember the flannel-board Sunday School lessons (where, even the prostitutes looked like wholesome people, with their beautiful, vivid clothes and hair with blonde highlights) with applications at the end of every story about how we were supposed to live.

While I recognize it was never my parents' nor my teachers' intentions, I was taught that the Bible was fundamentally about me. These were the rules that *I* was supposed to keep. These were the people *I* was supposed to emulate. Yet, in saying the Bible is about neither rules nor heroes, Lloyd-Jones insists that children learn that the Bible is about Jesus. Similarly, we're often guilty of making education about the students rather than about Jesus. This is one of the reasons I cringe to see the marquees out front of Christian schools mirroring the public schools' proclamation of the "character trait of the month."

Idols of Success

Though it has since moved in a different direction, my K-12 alma mater had a "Timothy Award" when I attended. Based on I Timothy 4:12, it was presented to the boy and girl in specific grades who most demonstrated Christian character. As the son of the most tenured Bible teacher on campus, I won this faculty-selected award. I remember neither openly speaking about Christianity nor modeling a need for Jesus in repentance of sin. I don't remember embodying joy over the doctrines of grace. Yet I kept my shirt tucked in. I didn't get in trouble. I was respectful to my teachers and involved in my church. I held positions of student leadership. I knew a lot of biblical stories and teachings. I made good grades. In a sense, I did what I had learned from Bible lessons. Sadly, some of the people who won the same Timothy Award profess no faith today. Yet, they *appeared* as Christian as I did.

Many Christian schools have presentations similar to the Timothy Award with criteria likely not very different from what they call their "portrait of a graduate." I'm not exactly sure when this became commonplace, but it's certainly been the rage for the last two decades. I haven't had to dig too far to find numerous Christian schools which have their "portrait of a graduate" clearly detailed on easy-to-find pages of their websites.

I'd rejoice to watch my own students go to college, become faithful spouses, parents, engaged citizens, servants in their community, leaders, and life-long learners, have saving faith and commit to their churches – all things commonly seen in these portraits. My criticism stems from the fact that many of these portraits are absent of gospel, with "Christian" items essentially as add-ons. Performance. A list where students can match the hopes of the portrait while failing to understand or need the gospel. Rarely do these lists allow for deep personal and corporate brokenness or grief over sin. They present everything except an idea of *rescue.*

Many "portraits" don't allow for a student who graduates from school and is hit squarely in the face with the difficulties and realities of life. What about the student who never goes to college? Does the alumna who has a child out of wedlock and nobly raises her son have less value than the alumna who earns a high-powered job and sits on the board of a non-profit? Of course, we'd say "no," but what do our practices tell our current students?

Maybe, our "portrait of a graduate" fascination is a symptom of a crisis in Christian schooling where students don't think they need Jesus anymore. Students graduate, thinking they've arrived. At least that's their goal. They've met the standard, because what's been put before them most clearly is a standard for success they can meet if they work hard enough.

"Arriving" only works when we have a "victorious Christian life" view which has a small view of sin, leading to a small view of Jesus and His gospel. We want God to be our Preventer but struggle to see Him as our Rescuer, because that means that there will be things in our lives from which we need to be rescued. I fear that many of our Christian schools aren't equipped to celebrate rescue, because that gets messy when we want to present success.

I'd rather see students leave our schools realizing that they can't meet the standard and have a context for truly needing Jesus. That's why they need the gospel; it's why they need to be rescued. I hope they become people who cling to the gospel in a way that their desperation and gratitude shapes their views of everything else.

I can only trace the statistics of millennials leaving the church to the distance our schools have moved away from the gospel. The portrait-of-a-graduate phenomena has catered to our students' sinful, intrinsic desires, essentially saying that we want our graduates to know and do the very same things which any secular school could produce – only with a Christian perspective. We want students to perform well on standardized tests, attend elite colleges, earn high wages, yet do it Christianly. Our school literature often reveals that these are the standards by which we tell the world we're doing well. Yet, our graduates see right through it, because we've merely added a qualifier to the sort of successes they already desire. We say they can still gain these things while having a certain perspective toward that success. Eventually, though, students realize they don't need the adverbs and adjectives. The Christian component is a nice addition, but it doesn't detract from or enhance their ability to get what everyone else wants.

If students can get power, wealth, and comfort, great! If they're Christian too, even better! Aren't these the alumni we recognize in our mailings and admission videos? Don't we want onlookers to see how our graduates are as successful or powerful as alumni from every other school, or even more so? In doing this, we allow students to think that the gospel aligns quite well with wealth, power, and comfort.

I've been appalled by statements from Church leaders who have wholeheartedly endorsed politicians who promise to return "power" back to Christians.[28] Of course, this rallies the average church-goers because it appeals to human selfishness. Yet, the gospel has never been about power or merit – well, at least not *my* power or merit. The gospel is about Jesus's work on my behalf. If we truly believe this, we must come to grips with the reality of a gospel-driven school becoming increasingly messy, because the gospel will shake up most of what we've come to believe about success.

This seems to explain why many students leave the faith of their fathers behind; we've done little to enable them to see the goal of Christian education as significantly different than the goal of any other education. We've mistakenly geared our schools toward molding a Christian approach toward their wants, but we haven't considered how we should shape their actual wants. This is critical, because equipping them with a perspective toward these desires still leaves their desires as the ends – as ultimates. That's why we should rethink our approach and structure our programs so they will bend our students' desires further in line with the gospel.

Merely focusing on ideas and perspectives alone is part of the flaw in worldview development, yielding sad results. Yes, a worldview is a perspective shaped by beliefs, but this doesn't go far enough. If we concede that humans are more than brains housed in bodies, but are complex persons made up of head, hand, and heart, we must have an articulation and understanding of Christian worldview which pursues truth and seeks to do it *and love it.*

Desires over Ideas

Last year, I celebrated my twenty-first year in Christian education. During one season in my Christian schooling tenure, I held the title, "Worldview Director," and was tasked to develope our school community's understanding and articulation of the Christian worldview within our school context. I read everything I could get my hands on and thought I had a pretty good grasp of the subject. Then, a mentor recommended the works of James K.A. Smith, a professor at Calvin College. His *Desiring the Kingdom* blew my mind, and I realized how little I understood what it means to have a biblical worldview. Ten years later, I continue to be profoundly moved by Smith's work.

Smith is a philosopher and "academic." He's not against intellectual pursuits. But, he's critical of our disproportionate focus on ideas. For example, there was a war fought between the thirteen colonies and England. As a Christian, how should I think about this war? How should I think about Dante, Harry Potter, thermal dynamics, single digit subtraction, or kickball? What does it mean to have a Christian "perspective?" In a way, this line of thinking turns Christianity into an adverb. When we learn about Shakespeare or Beatrix Potter, how should we do so *Christianly*? Is such a thing possible?

These are the sorts of ideas I considered throughout my first decade in Christian education, and they're still good to address today. We *have* to think about them and do so with precision. Yet, we need to go much deeper.

To summarize one of Smith's points, we must consider the relationship between our loves and ideas. People may hold their perspectives and ideas dearly enough to put up a good fight for their ideas, but rarely would they willingly die for them. I have some pretty strong convictions, but I wouldn't give my life for them. But I'd give my life for my family. Without hesitation. Because I love them.

Smith suggests that we are more driven by our loves than our ideas because we are more desiring beings than thinking beings. We have thoughts and ideas, but what's behind them is our deeply held loves, idols, hopes, and imaginations.

To bring it home to our own school communities: *if what really drives people is their affections rather than their thoughts, the primary task of the Christian school is to shape our students' loves and desires.* Smith says,

> "What if education ... is not primarily about the absorption of ideas and information, but about the formation of hearts and desires? What if we began by appreciating how education not only gets into our head but also (and more fundamentally) grabs us by the gut? What if education was primarily concerned with shaping our hopes and passions – our visions of 'the good life' – and not merely about the dissemination of data and information as inputs to our thinking? What if the primary work of education was the transforming of our imagination rather than the saturation of our intellect?"[29]

Bold implication: *How do we use student literacy to shape loves and desires? What about science? Chapel? Recess?* I get excited to think about our schools grabbing students by the gut! That's truly distinctive. It's infectious and contagious.

We should hope to find new ways to employ our curriculum to love God, what He loves and His gospel, because it's life-giving. Yes, we want students to get excited when they learn about Van Gogh's sunflowers, but we also hope that through their learning, they come to love God and others more. That's a challenging task; it's a lot harder than attaching a verse to a lesson. However, we must dare to accept the endeavor because we don't want to see students merely conform to boundaries set before them. We want to see them *transform*, and we fully believe that this only happens when students come to love God because they see how much they need Him and how good He is. This is where life-long change happens. This is where a foundation built at our schools can stick with them into college and life. This drives our missional hope and confidence because we believe the gospel restores people; it restores families; it restores culture.

Maybe, we should speak of a worldview as engaging the world through an embodiment of beliefs. As Christians, this looks like embodying the core tenants of the faith – embodying need, embodying thanksgiving, embodying hope, embodying rescue and restoration. When we take on these beliefs, our desires change. This is especially true as the Spirit transforms us through our habits being brought into conformity with these beliefs. As a result, much of the conversation about the Christian worldview must consider what it will look like when the gospel starts to seep and ooze out of us.

If we want to see Christianity as a worldview, we must define the Christian worldview in language which is thoroughly saturated by that gospel. Going forward, my working definition for the "Christian worldview" is that it's ultimately *the ability to make sense of the world in light of the gospel.* It's an ordering of our lives (and specifically our school missions and programs) so they might be consistent with a need for and gratitude to Jesus – not merely conforming lives to rules and teachings. I offer this definition, because a common vocabulary is essential to get everyone on the same page. It must be the goal of the Christian schools' entire programs to engender our students' interpretation of all things through the lens of a correct response to Jesus – to the grammar of the gospel.

The Gospel as a Worldview

All worldviews essentially address the same questions, questions of existence, knowledge, humanity, ethics, ideals, brokenness, and fixes. Christ-centered Christianity answers those same questions through the lens of the gospel, because it's the core of what Christianity is all about. When we get into conversations with people about the Christian worldview, we eventually work our way around to asking, "Well, why is *that* Christian?" or "What's Christian about it?"

Sadly enough, most of the answers we get, while consistent with aspects of what Christians hold to be true, provide nothing uniquely Christian. Yes, Christians seek to love others; they put value on human life; they acknowledge the beauty of what God has made; they quote from the Bible. But nearly every other system has the exact same values – just with a few words switched. Many other systems profess some form of a god who made all things. Many non-religious people believe in treating others well, cherishing family, promoting human dignity, and taking care of the world. Foolishly, many Christians think they have a monopoly on such values. Here, I so often see Christian schools fail in their ability to articulate how their practice is Christian. They point to the very same things any other religious school would, just attaching biblical lingo.

While the Gospel connects to many of these ideas, it's bigger than all of them. It's a single idea, a radical idea which turns the world upside down, and it always has been reordering all things. This is precisely what the Jewish leaders in Thessalonica feared about the Christians in Acts 17:6 – their teachings were turning the world upside down in allegiance to King Jesus.

The gospel is not merely what we find in the Bible. It's not just the teachings of Jesus: everything in red letters. It's not what Christians are supposed to do. It's not obedience and moral behavior.

While these statements are certainly in the general vicinity of the gospel, they're not necessarily "good news;" they're not life-giving. In fact, without the gospel, many of Jesus's teachings are terrifying, creating standards none of us can meet. He says, "be perfect as your Father in Heaven is perfect" (Matthew 5:48) or hate our fathers and mothers in order to follow Him. (Luke 14:26) They aren't good news, because none of us do them.

When Jesus was questioned about the Greatest Commandment, He said that the entirety of the Law and prophets can be summed up by the commandment to love God and love others. (Matthew 22:37-40) But we should face the tragedy that none of us love as we should. Far too often, we focus on do's and don'ts as though they are the most extreme of sins. Yet, by Jesus's own words, my failure to love God with *all* of my heart, soul, and strength or my neighbor as myself is far more serious than many of the "cultural evils" which are easy targets. My transgression is against the *greatest* commandment, not an obscure one, and I break it moment by moment. I don't know that I've ever kept this commandment.

In a way, I'm further reminded of this failure each Valentine's Day. As I write a card to my wife saying I love her, I must come to grips with the reality that I don't love her as I ought. I don't love my children as I ought, or my coworkers, or God, or His Church. And, the list of these inadequacies keeps going. It's overwhelming.

Friends, as strange as it might seem, there's good news in this recognition. As C.S. Lewis says in *Mere Christianity*, the gospel doesn't start with comfort; it starts with dismay.[30] Those moments where I become more acutely aware of my sin, I begin to see the weight of my desperation and run to Jesus. My favorite pastor, Richie Sessions, routinely insists, "all you need is *need*." In these lucid moments where I'm moved by my own sin, it's a sufficient and restorative response to say, "and that's why we need Jesus." It's why we need the gospel.

Jesus's teachings are life-giving, but we must understand that the gospel is what makes them good and what gives us freedom to celebrate His teachings. They don't show us how to be good; they show us how very much we need Him because we aren't good. As much as we hear that and (cognitively) know that, it's a struggle for us to live it and feel it.

My church recently organized a conversation to unpack our denomination's new position on human sexuality. This doctrinal statement affirms God's original intent for sexuality within the confines of marriage and addresses orientations outside God's design. But it also speaks to those within the Church who struggle with desires outside God's intent and calls the Church toward a posture of grace toward these brothers and sisters.

Several attendees pushed against this statement. While I respect their desire to fight for doctrinal purity, I also couldn't help wondering whether the real conversation was about believing the gospel or not. It seemed as though people were admitting that Christians are sinners, but they shouldn't struggle with *that* kind of sin.

I deeply appreciate Barbara Duguid's book, *Extravagant Grace*, which deals with this issue in a transparent, convicting, and hopeful way. Duguid says that many people have an unreasonable image of "victorious Christian living" – as though, that's the "good life" that many of us have in our minds. She poignantly reminds the reader that, "if the chief work of the Holy Spirit in sanctification is to make Christians more sin-free, he isn't doing a very good job."[31] Duguid isn't blasphemous; she doesn't have a low view of the work of the Holy Spirit. She's merely helping us understand that God doesn't want us to get to a place where we feel like we need Him less. Maybe, He's even willing to leave sin in our lives so we never forget our weakness and need.

I once took a tour of a Christian school with an admissions officer who told me that *every* teacher teaches *every* lesson from a Christian worldview, and I thought how nice it must be to have a school full of perfect teachers who have it all figured out. Look at your school's website; you might find similar articulations which can't possibly be true. These are the statements of people and institutions who no longer need Jesus because they don't struggle with sin. They're perfectly sanctified.

This lingo has become so integral to our school fabric, we aren't shocked by statements which could only be true were there no need for the gospel: "I just love Jesus with all of my heart," "I give him all of the glory," or "I don't ever have doubts."

Jesus came into the world because we can't love him with our whole hearts, adequately give Him due credit, or do things without wanting to gain glory for ourselves first. That's the reality of sin. That's why we need Him, and this need should be ever-present in the task of education – to prompt need in a way which generates gratitude and drives deep learning in response to what God has done.

Let's be honest, there is a significant gap between these aspiring values (what we want to be), and our actual values (who we are).

I Can't; He Can

My dad taught high school Bible class for forty-nine years, and he succinctly defines the gospel for his twelfth-grade students as **"I can't; He can."** In other words, the gospel says we have a problem which we cannot possibly fix, and that's why Jesus came. He came to live a perfect life, die in our place, and rise again so we can live. That's the gospel: I can't; He can. This is the driving force behind the story of Scripture, and we may not see it more clearly than the structure of the Apostle Paul's letter to the Romans. After building the case that none of us are righteous, he says "But now, a righteousness from God has been made known apart from the law..." (3:21) This is the gospel. What I most desperately need is given to me, not by what I do, but because of the work of the One I have wronged.

As a result, this gospel is radically different from what the rest of the world has to offer. In all our relationships and experiences, a person's merit (what he brings to the table) is what gives him worth. At the end of the day, it's all about transactions. Yet in the gospel, the only thing we bring to the table is the sin from which we've been saved.

This upends the way I view myself and my entitlements. It affects the way I see the world and my place in it, the way I view others, and how I understand my rights, which seem to be central to the American ethos. It affects the way I view Jesus and what He has done. Ultimately, it drives me to have a really big view of God which results in dependence and gratitude. It also forces me to have a small view of myself, yet still see myself as immensely valuable.

The net result is a more tempered view of mankind and a higher view of God. We learn that all people have profound value and conspicuous deficiency. We have value because God made us and was moved to die on our behalf. We're deficient because we needed someone to die on our behalf. It levels the playing field; Christians and non-Christians alike have violated the Greatest Commandment. None of us have moral supremacy – that's why we need Jesus. Christian schools don't exist to produce better people; they're places where Jesus is met and where we learn that He is what's better.

If we believe these things, it radically affects our approach toward education, considering:

A. The gospel is central to Christianity
B. The gospel is radically different than what the rest of society has to offer
C. There is no such thing as a neutral education

If the above statements are true, Christian schools ought to look different from secular education in all their parts. I doubt any believer would challenge the centrality of the gospel, but we must not waver in this declaration. The gospel is what Christianity is fundamentally about – not the rules, teachings, or practices which are often associated with it. It's important to preach the gospel within our schools every day so we don't forget it. Otherwise, just be honest and say our schools are *affiliated* with the heritage and ethic of a religious tradition, but let's not call them Christian. If we can't find the gospel in it, we ought not call anything Christian.

If this unique gospel is central to our mission, Christian (or gospel-centered) schools should look differently, even in how they introduce team sports into their programs. In John 17:14-16, Jesus twice says His disciples are not of this world, just like He is not of this world. And while the Bible says Christians are sojourners in a world that's not our home, shouldn't Christian schools look significantly unlike the world's schools – if we're not of this world?

This presents a unique challenge to Christian Schools, because it forces us to see the deep difference between a Christian environment and a Christian education. Sadly, most of our schools are Christian environments. Donovan Graham speaks poignantly about the difference in *Teaching Redemptively.* Similarly, Gordon Clark says that in those schools which merely focus on their environment,

> "The actual instruction is no more Christian than in a respectable secular school … the program is merely a pagan education with a chocolate covering of Christianity … the students are deceived into thinking that they have received a Christian education when as a matter of fact their training has been neither Christian nor an education."[32]

In *Piety and Philosophy,* Richard Riesen clearly states the necessity and simplicity of an integrated Christian worldview when it comes to our focus within Christian education:

> "The larger point, however, is that both teacher and student come to the process of education with a point of view, a worldview it is sometimes called, which is a synthesis or an amalgamation of convictions about fundamental issues: the nature of man, the existence of God, the meaning of death and so forth ... What I mean can be reduced to the question, does it matter to the way one thinks that one is a Christian? Is Christianity about ideas? Which ideas? Do these influence the way we think about things? It need not be too much more sophisticated or self-conscious than that."[33]

Because Christianity is, in part, about ideas (namely that Jesus came to accomplish what none of us could), we should work diligently against our tendencies to think we're sufficient or that we deserve more than what we have. We fight sin's work which minimizes the wonder of the world around us. We remember that we need Jesus as much today as at the moment of our conversion.

Jesus, the Person

"When faith is conceived of as belief in a person, there is no problem with the connection between faith and life"[34]
- Nicholas Wolterstorff

For much of my life, I've seen Jesus merely as an idea. A rather cool one, but an idea nonetheless. Eight years ago, my niece unexpectedly didn't wake up one morning (she was only three at the time). Like my children, she loved *The Jesus Storybook Bible.* Prior to the night she went to be with Jesus, she wanted to read the story of the resurrection where Mary Magdalene mistook Jesus for a gardener. It excited my niece to think of Jesus calling her name too, and she told her dad that when Jesus did, she was going to get to hug Him. Her parents had no idea how soon she would, in fact, get to hug her Rescuer.

What has happened to me where I don't think of Jesus as being so real that He can be hugged? We so easily lose our fascination. Jesus also tells us that Abraham embraced what God told him, and not only believed it, but *rejoiced* at the thought of seeing Jesus's day. (John 8:56)

Part of living out the gospel means that we must become fascinated with Jesus and allow the gratitude which springs out of it to saturate our communities. In this, essential truths and our loves become rightly ordered. We need these affections put in their right places, because as James K.A. Smith says,

> "Being a disciple of Jesus is not primarily a matter of getting the right ideas or doctrines and beliefs into your head in order to guarantee proper behavior; rather, it's a matter of being the kind of person who loves rightly – who loves God and neighbor and is oriented to the world by the primacy of that love."[35]

As a result, Christian education is not as much about information as it is about formation – a process that forms our loves and affections to love God more and love what He's about. That's a tall task, but a generative one.

A distinctively Christian philosophy of education starts with this very different end in mind. Surprisingly, the goal of Christian education is not a traditional view of excellence (but a biproduct along the way), not if we're committed to the gospel. This traditional pursuit of excellence is man-centered in its faulty assumption about what is good for us. However, the true goal of Christian education is to know and love God more. We should respond by designing the school program around the sort of learning which kindles knowledge and love for God.

Because the gospel is central to Christianity, the school which is committed to a Christian education will repeatedly ask what difference the gospel makes throughout its program. We begin to see the sinfulness of our condition, how much we need Jesus, and eventually have fuller hearts toward Him, demonstrated in gratitude.

Gratitude becomes one of the greatest distinctives of the Christian school; material is taught and learned because of thankfulness for what God has done and thankfulness for our capacity to receive it. As a result, we must design curricula with foundational questions: How will this help nurture a love and need for God, demonstrated through thankfulness? We need to build all lessons, assessments, and programs with this in mind.

Portraits and Older Brothers

As a child, I was taught Jesus's parable of "The Prodigal Son" (Luke 5:11-32) so I might learn to see God as a forgiving God to whom I can always return. I learned to resist becoming like the Younger Brother who squandered away his inheritance. Yet, if I do, God will still forgive me. I also gathered that the Older Brother was more obedient to his dad.

Contextually, Jesus tells the parable to an audience full of Pharisees within a series of similar-themed stories because he wants them to understand how grossly they've missed the purpose of their religion. The Pharisees struggled mightily with Jesus because they felt like they did everything right, yet Jesus didn't give them the recognition they deserved. Rather, he welcomed children, women, the poor, tax collectors, prostitutes, and other forgotten classes.

This context turns the focus toward the relationship between the Older Brother and His Father. At the end of the story, the Older Brother is indignant with his Father, focusing more on his entitlements than on his Father's joy. Yes, the Older Brother is obedient for transactional purposes. In his mind, his obedience merits reward and blessing. He doesn't obey out of love or gratitude but because of what's in it for him. The parable ends with the Father celebrating with the Younger Brother while the Older Brother sulks. The structure of the parable suggests that Jesus is far more critical of the older, obedient brother than he is of the younger, rebellious one.

Clearly, it's easier to teach a classroom full of "older brothers," right? They do what's asked of them; they follow the rules; they fit our "portraits of a graduate." (by the way, YIKES!) I'd wager that our "portraits of a graduate" function like mosquito zappers for Older Brothers who flock to the light and perish. There's no question about what Jesus wanted the Pharisees to understand: they are Older Brothers who will not celebrate with the Father at His feast. Yet these same pharisee-older brothers are the students we often elevate in our schools. Unlike Jesus, we tend to be more critical of the rebellious, non-conforming students than we are of the self-righteous, compliant ones.

I know what you're thinking. Do we really want our graduates to look like the Younger Brother? Will we post updates in our alumni newsletters about graduates who have hit rock bottom? Probably not, and I'm not suggesting we necessarily should. Yet I imagine our championed alumni stories aren't too different from what secular schools produce. We likely highlight those who accomplish great things and have their lives together – *for Jesus, of course.* We do this because we want to attract families, but we do so by offering the very same definition of success the world runs after. All the while, the students in our schools download that the ultimate end of their schooling is to mimic these successful graduates.

Of course, we should celebrate students' hard work and the Lord's giftings even though our fear of sinful pride often prevents us from proper celebration. Also, there's nothing wrong with desiring student obedience, especially when God's laws reveal how life works best. But we must be extremely mindful that the Younger Brother was the one who "got it" in the end while the Older Brother was entirely lost, despite doing everything asked of him.

The Christian school which lives and dies by the gospel must endure and embrace the messiness of allowing Younger Brothers to be Younger Brothers. We're left with the question: would we rather have students "get it" or meet traditional standards of success? They don't have to be mutually exclusive, but what if "getting it" means it's going to get pretty raw and messy along the way?

None of our schools actively try to create Older Brothers, but many of our schools are breeding grounds for students who put their hope in personal merit rather than the gospel. Students naturally revert to this because it gives them control. It's the way the world works. Unless we're counter-cultural, it's what works in our schools, too.

The lesson from the parable of the two brothers draws a very fine line between a relationship marked by conformation rather than by transformation. The Older Brother conformed to what he thought his Father wanted. Just like the Older Brother, the Pharisees thought they could earn the favor of God by meeting a standard (one he set in his mind, rather than one set by the Father). And because they thought they were meeting this standard, they overlooked their deep, personal need.

However, the Younger Brother's relationship with his father is marked by a significant change. Granted, he blew it, and his story reveals the consequences of very poor decisions. Yet he knew he blew it; he knew he didn't deserve his Father's favor. And that's precisely where the gospel lives; it lives in a world where people know they don't deserve God. I want my students to be changed by Jesus, and I long to have programs which are more geared toward that than nurturing conformity. What would it look like if our schools were more likely to produce students who realize how little they deserve than students who feel they met the standard and have their lives together? What would it look like if we drove a stake into the ground outside our schools and declared that we will not allow our schools to become Older Brother Factories?

By the way, not being an Older Brother Factory is a rather rare thing to see among our Christian schools. Our culture almost necessarily forces schools toward becoming hotbeds of conformity, where the desired goal isn't persons deeply shaped by the gospel. Rather, the goal is "the good kid." "The acceptable kid." "The successful kid." "The Older Brother." That's why parents seek our schools out. Without even thinking about it, they come to our schools because many of them subconsciously *want* their children to be Older Brothers. Maybe, so do we.

I fully believe that Christian schools are committed to doing God-honoring things. That being said, the challenge is one of consistency. We need to be more consistent in our efforts to be distinctively Christian, and the following chapters are designed to unpack the questions of the Grid which can help us consistently function like we believe it's good to be rescued by and live in need of Jesus.

PREFACE TO PART 2

I had a seminary professor who started every class by writing the same three words at the top of the white board, reminding us of the true task of deep theological study. In a way, it brought back memories of my mom writing Bible verses on the mirror of the bathroom that I shared with my brothers. By putting these words in such a prominent place, it couldn't be ignored – whether we liked it or not.

"Orthodoxy, Orthopraxy, Doxology" always stared at us from the front of our seminary classroom – normally with arrows connecting the words. Of course, our professor explained what this meant and also why we would continue to see these words without further commentary or reference. He wanted to make sure we never forgot why we had gathered together.

Orthodoxy essentially means straight or right thinking. That's typically what seminary students spend great time and effort to develop. The task of the seminary student is to have sound theology, to know what the Bible says, and to get as near as possible to the straightness and rightness of Scripture.

However, our professor took us to early-Church fathers who insisted that true orthodoxy must lead to orthopraxy (right practice), and that biblical action must lead us to doxology, which we speak of as praise or worship (think of the "Doxology" we sing in our churches). He desired that we'd learn that these three pillars depend upon each other. If our orthodoxy doesn't ultimately lead to worship, it must not be true orthodoxy.

When we worship, it prompts in us a greater hunger to be orthodox in our thinking, which prompts a greater desire to live that hunger out. It's circular. And, that was the goal of putting these words ever-before us – that we never lost sight of worship in our studies, because this would ensure vigor in our studies.

Not that I disagree with my professor, but I prefer a slight change to his reminder. I'd like to replace doxology with *orthopathy*, or "right affections." This balances the equation a bit more. For when our thoughts, actions, and affections work in harmony, this is what worship looks like. That's why Jesus says we must love God with our whole minds, bodies, and hearts. (Luke 10:27) Orthodoxy, orthopraxy, orthopathy. Head, hand, heart. Upward, outward, inward.

The ultimate goal of our schools must be worship. This cannot be negotiated. More than anything else, we should long to produce students who worship the infinite, personal, triune God. To move in this direction, we have to be passionate about our orthodoxy. We probably already seek this in our schools, but it must be within the context of teaching truth in such a way that always moves us to action and affection. And we don't have to do it in such a way that we always start with knowledge. We just need to recognize that true orthodoxy only thrives when married to our hands and hearts.

As a result, this will be the structure of the next seven chapters with each broken down into these three themes. I will spend a great deal of time explaining what Christian orthodoxy looks like in regard to these questions. I'll also try to explain why the Christian answer is what it is, because we always need a bit of an "apologetic" component in our worldview thought process. Not only must our schools be doctrinally sound, it's just as critical that we understand the basis for that soundness. So, these sections will always seek to define how Christians should answer these questions and know why the answers are what they are. We can't apply sound theology (which is what the Christian worldview requires) if we don't first have it. So, I'll pay special attention to this category in each chapter.

From there, I will also address practice (orthopraxy) as well as the cultural implications – the human, relational, emotive, spiritual components of a school that seeks to be distinctively Christian. These two areas are likely where we need to ask ourselves the most prying questions, and I hope to be a catalyst toward that.

My goal is to be a bit more practical[36] in these two sections of each chapter – by providing questions which garner actionable steps toward infusing the Christian worldview through our school communities. I fully realize that one of our needs is to have the theory and understanding in place. Potentially, our greater need is making sure we understand what it looks like to put that theory into practice. So, each chapter will provide tangible examples of things we should consider to better employ the framework.

Living in the Tension

I've never come across a school that isn't looking to get better. In the past few years, I've visited several schools which have caused me to break the tenth commandment – with their beautiful facilities, expansive programs, and gifted faculties. Even *those* schools look to get better. It's only the vastly unhealthy schools that don't see the need to get better.[37]

A few years ago, I had the privilege of being an interim Head of School for a wonderfully diverse Christian semi-urban elementary school. One of the former Heads of School had a mantra that the school would be known for its "relentless pursuit of improvement." Five years later, this was still a part of the culture. This pursuit means we'll also need to hold a little less tightly to some of our agendas, be a little less territorial, and become a lot more willing to ask hard questions and faithfully walk where the pursuit of those answers will take us. But it's going to get messy if you're willing to walk down this path with me and be honest with yourself and your school. Don't navigate around the tension; live in it.

I designed the next seven chapters to create a context of questions to shape our efforts and become more aligned with the grammar of the gospel. While I have some answers and would love to walk through conversations with any of you about greater application of the questions I raise, the greatest gift I can provide is lots of questions. In a way, that will require more work of you and your school as you explore answering these questions. But I firmly believe this is where growth happens – in that process of exploration.

The Grid Questions

1. Are we recognizing God as ultimate over everything else?
2. Are we modeling and encouraging dependence upon God's Truth wherever it's seen?
3. Are we honoring the full image of God in all members of the school community?
4. Are we cultivating a culture of grace-prompted Obedience?
5. Are we pursuing, celebrating, and resting in God's original intent?
6. Are we marked by mournfulness and repentance over sin and a broken world?
7. Are we actively proclaiming and seeking repair and restoration according to Jesus's plan?

4

THE GOD WHO IS THERE ... IN OUR SCHOOLS

Grid Question 1: Are we recognizing God as ultimate over everything else?

Not to diminish the rest of his book, but Rick Warren's most profound statement in his best-selling *The Purpose Driven Life* is found in the first four words: "It's not about you." This statement fits quite well with the implications of the Bible's first four words: "In the beginning, God." For, if God was in the beginning, He's first, which insists that everything else owes its existence to Him. Then, it really isn't about us; it's about Him.

This must be foundational in Christian education: it's not about us, our schools, our students, our teachers, or our parents. It's about God. While I doubt any of us would object to this truth, we need to do a better job of articulating and practicing it.

Don't be Scared of Metaphysics

I'm reminded of a popular YouTube clip, filmed by an amateur videographer who stood near Yosemite National Park following a rainstorm. While panning from side to side, his footage reveals a rainbow, and another, then another. At first, we hear his excitement which turns into unexplainable and rather loud sobs. In the midst of his wander and tears, he warbles, "What does this mean? Why are we here?" I was always intrigued that an encounter with beauty causes a person to contemplate his own existence.

On a few occasions, I've climbed to the top of Clingmans Dome, a beautiful day-hike along the Appalachian Trail and the highest point in Tennessee. On one of these trips with a friend, we found a spot at the summit to unpack our lunches, dangle our legs over a rock, and admire the vista. Amidst a bit of "people watching," we ate and marveled at the surrounding beauty. We noticed that everyone else sat quietly and pondered what was around them, not taking it for granted. Yet there were a few dogs who accompanied their owners; their behavior gave me no reason to believe they even noticed their surroundings. They continued to behave like they would at any other place – a lot of sniffing the ground and hoping to get a bite to eat. It struck me as another distinctive of our humanity: we are moved by beauty. When confronted with the largeness and wonder of the world around us, it gives us pause. Much of that reflection is a contemplation of our own existence.

The French existentialist Jean Paul Sartre once said that all philosophical problems arise from acknowledging that things really exist. Being here immediately forces us to figure out what's behind our existence. Like Sartre, every human throughout history has dealt with this problem. Maybe we're not that different than the sobbing videographer.

Metaphysics is a philosophical category which studies existence and tries to explain where it came from. Or, we might say metaphysics attempts to explain the nature of being, reality, and what ultimately holds everything together. Aristotle said that whatever this "first cause" is must be different than everything else, because something can't be both a cause and effect at the same time. Metaphysical questions typically deal with what's beyond the things of this world, as the word literally means beyond (*meta*) the things of nature (*physika*).

By asking **What Exists? What is ultimately real?** or **What's really out there?** metaphysical questions always work themselves back to the question of whether or not there is a God. Certainly, it could be metaphysical to figure out if the computer I'm typing on really exists. Yet, metaphysics is primarily concerned with existence on foundational levels. What's really out there? What's holding it all together? What's most ultimate? Even when atheists claim nothing exists beside matter and energy, it's a metaphysical assertion, because it offers an explanation of what's ultimate.

Not all metaphysical questions have to sound academic. Everyone asks questions like "Why am I here?" "What's the meaning of life?" "What was here before everything else?" I'll hang out more in the realm of these sorts of questions rather than in the philosophical terms. Have no fear as we jump into answering the question: <u>What's most ultimate?</u>

ORTHODOXY

Moving toward a Christian perspective, it's helpful to consider various ways people answer these questions and systematically break them down to explain why the Christian answer is reliable. From there, we'll consider how the Christian answer affects our educational endeavors. But it's vitally important that we understand the Christian basis for the belief in God, then direct that toward our tasks in Christian schools.

I'll dedicate more to the doctrinal section of this chapter than what you'll see in other chapters, because our answers to this question drive how we answer all other questions. It's necessary to have clarity here, because it lays the foundation for everything else. Don't worry; I won't go nearly as in-depth into the "philosophy" the rest of the way through. Because the strands of the Grid all build on each other, I'll camp out on it more here than what you'll see elsewhere.

Answering the Question

I don't want to get bogged down in lengthy arguments. But I'll attempt to provide a summary of Christian answers, which looks very much like a poor man's summary of Schaeffer's *Escape from Reason*. It's helpful to place the Christian answer to the question within the context of Schaeffer's explanation, because it's important that we see the necessity and validity of the Christian answer.

First, some ground rules:

Rule One: We should expect to see connections between primary things (whatever they are) and tangible things in the world around us. Everything we observe owes its existence to something more ultimate, or even eternal. In other words, how we answer these fundamental questions must align with what we actually see, because something can't come from nothing (even the writers of *The Sound of Music*[38] knew that). If we see beauty around us, whatever is out there must give an explanation of that beauty. If we find a widget, there has to be a larger Something which can account for the existence of widgetness.

Rule Two: This Something needs to be big enough to account for the existence and source of all things while holding them together. This "bigness" also must explain the similarities (unity) we see. For instance, there are laws which seem to govern everything. Einstein furthered this idea with his theory of relativity. We know that living things are generally made of the same stuff, and the universe is made up of elements, which are all composed of the same three particles.

We see common building blocks to the universe. We see common rules in Mathematics. We also see commonality even among humans; generally speaking, humans tend to believe many of the same things, regardless of the culture they grew up in. For example, most humans believe it's not ok to light your neighbor's home on fire. So, whatever is out there must be really big (even absolute and eternal) for this unity and binding principles to hold true.

Rule Three: This ultimate entity must also account for the diversity and personality we see around us. Certainly, we see a lot of commonalities in our experiences, but we also see surprising uniqueness. We see (what appears to be) randomness and disorder at times.

We also notice something shockingly wonderous about humanity. Despite our shared commonality, we are still unique from each other. We have diverse longings, hopes, affections; there's something in us profoundly personal – even, the dignity of personhood. Most people feel that there is a "me" that's more than just our bodies and the sum of our chemicals.

Note that the existence of the first rule is what forces the second and third rule. Because we see unity and unique personhood in our experiences, whatever is out there needs to offer an explanation.

The Natural Answer

Some say this big Something is entirely physical, because there's nothing outside the natural world. As an umbrella term, the person who holds this perspective is often labeled as a Naturalist, because he only believes in the natural world (atheists fit in this category). In this perspective, there is only matter (protons, neutrons, and electrons arranged in various forms), and everything has to be explained somehow materially. Within this view, there is no room for abstract concepts like love, hope, beauty, or ghosts. These all must be explained in terms of an impersonal, material answer. From this take, what feels like love is merely a chemical reaction which we call love.

The Naturalist does have answers to most questions; his answer is "Big" in that everything is made up of something which is in a way beyond us; the entire cosmos is made up of this material. This answer can explain the rockiness of mountains, the heat of fire, and the force of weather. While the Naturalist has an answer which provides unity in numerous areas, there are still problems worth addressing:

- There is a noticeable difference between people and everything else. There seems to be real personhood, and while the Naturalists claim that all these longings are purely illusion, they sure do feel real. The Naturalistic claims seem to go against what we experience; that breaks Rule One.
- If everything is essentially composed of the exact same substance with the same rules, we should expect the great unity we see among the particulars, but it becomes more difficult to account for the diversity, uniqueness, and surprises that we see in our experiences. This breaks Rule Three.
- Finding meaning and value in the particulars of life becomes very difficult. If there is nothing more than the physical realm, making value judgments about the particulars or conversations about dignity (any belief in abstract ideas, for that matter) becomes quite difficult. That doesn't seem to line up with our experience either. Our worlds make the most sense when there is room for both the concrete and the abstract.

I appreciate Chesterton's reflection about naturalism in *Orthodoxy.* Using the analogy of two circles, he says both are complete, but one could be far larger. Naturalism is a complete worldview – it provides answers, but the worldview seems narrow and insufficient. For example, a naturalist can explain why people seem drawn to the spiritual realm. But saying we evolved this spiritual sense to enhance our likelihood or fitness for survival seems to oppose what we feel (It pushes against Rule One).

In short, a worldview committed to the physical world alone is big enough to provide answers and connections. However, it fails to fully fit our experiences, which suggest that our loves, hopes, joys, deep questioning, and moral sense are not evolutionary illusions, but real.

The Supernatural Answer

Because the Naturalistic explanation doesn't adequately meet our metaphysical needs, let's consider Something beyond the physical realm. If there is a supernatural Something out there, the basic three options are some form of a singular god (monotheism), multiple gods (polytheism), or a "life force" (pantheism).

Once again, whatever provides the basis for ultimate reality needs to support adequate explanations for what we see (Rule One). The primary issues which ought to be explained by any answer to the metaphysical question are:

- It has to be big enough to provide real answers and provide explanation for what exists. It should be Absolute, unchanging, reliable, transcendent.
- It needs to provide explanation for personhood
- It needs to provide explanation for both unity and diversity

Polytheism - there are many gods.

Most polytheistic religions (e.g., believing in the Greek gods) explain personhood and diversity because these religions ascribe the uniqueness in the world to individual and diverse gods. These gods have personalities, hopes, and aspirations. But these religions fail to explain absolutes and unity because the gods disagree. These systems struggle to provide adequate reference points because their gods aren't infinite, though supernatural. Also, with multiple gods, it becomes difficult to know which one is the most powerful and should be obeyed above others. There isn't any one standard which makes sense of everything else (Rule Two).

Pantheism - everything is part of God.

Most pantheistic religions provide adequate explanation for the unity we see. Believing the whole universe is alive, this view proclaims that everything is connected; it's all a part of a big, living something (Rule Two). Yet, this view doesn't account for diversity or personhood, because there is no diversity in this "force," nor is the force knowable or capable of having desires, will, hopes, and emotions. It's a similar struggle the naturalist has (Rule Three).

Monotheism - there is only one God.

Most monotheistic religions have answers for personhood, and they have answers for absolutes. Their god is big enough, and is knowable. These religions know what their god requires of them, because this Being has revealed his characteristics. They also find answers for the unity we see among the particulars. Yet, they typically struggle to explain the diversity we see. (Rule 3)

A Biblical Answer

"The mere use of the word god proves nothing. The word god as such is no answer to the philosophic problem of

> *existence, but the Judeo–Christian content of the word God as given in the Old and New Testament does meet the need of what exists ... the existence of the universe in its complexity and of man as a man ... It relates to an infinite – personal God, who is personal unity and diversity on the high order of the Trinity... I would still be an agnostic if there was no Trinity, because there would be no answers. Without the high order of personal unity and diversity as given in the Trinity, there are no answers."*[39] Francis Schaeffer

I've been amazed by this quote for a long time, often having tiptoed around the doctrine of the Trinity, myself. Yet Schaeffer explains that the Christian view of God meets all our metaphysical needs, precisely *because* of the Trinity.

Our metaphysical need requires Something big enough to provide reliable answers and meaning to the particulars. Specifically, this Something needs to be personal, because people are personal. We must have Something higher than ourselves to find real meaning. We also need this something to explain the unity and the diversity we see in the world. Only the Christian view of God gives adequate explanation. God created and sustains the entire cosmos. He is knowable and has revealed Himself, yet there is both diversity and unified personhood central to His very nature. He is an eternally personal God, because of what we find in the Trinity.

When God revealed Himself to Moses at the burning bush, He revealed His name: "I Am." Essentially, God reveals Himself as ultimate existence: yesterday, today, and forever. And, in this same conversation, God tells Moses that He cares so much about His people that He will do great things on their behalf. Throughout the Old Testament, God even defines Himself by His covenantal relationship with Israel. This God is the only God; there is no other. Yet for some reason, He takes great joy in defining Himself by His covenantal interactions with His people to the point where He one day entered that relationship and gave His life to repair and ensure His covenant.

God alone is ultimate; He is knowable; He is Infinite; He is personal; He is Triune.

Metaphysics and Education

Recognizing God as ultimate must dominate our approach to our curricula, lesson designs, assessment plans, and behavioral management models. Too often, our "plans" are not driven by deference to God or a desire to know and love Him more. Rather, they're driven by external systems which already assume what education ought to look like. However, Christians must teach, recognizing God primacy above the teacher, student, or parent by keeping before students the reality that the goal of our educational pursuits is knowing God. This is first. All other answers (while practical and often good) are secondary. This recognition ought to change our motivation and liberate us all in tow.

The primary goal of education is not excellence. It's knowing and loving God. It's not battling racism by reducing ignorance; it's knowing and loving God. The goal of a geometry class is not equipping students to perform on the SAT so they can get into a good college; it's to be transformed to know and love God more through the study of geometry. How we answer the metaphysical question radically affects our approach to school mission and what we do in the classroom.

This recognition upholds the gospel, because it declares God above everything else. Believing this, we need God because we owe existence to Him. The gospel tells us that we're people of need because we're not sufficient. And, the Christian approach to metaphysics affirms this. That's why we ask: <u>Are we recognizing God as ultimate over everything else?</u>

ORTHOPRAXY

As schools look to properly recognize God as God, we must constantly consider who God is and who we are in relation to Him. It's imperative that we take steps to ensure that our commitments to who God is and what He desires to see in us and in our schools. This needs to show up throughout our schools' entire cultures – in what we teach, in our interactions, and in the decisions we make. **Content:** There should be clear articulation of how we ensure that our curricula acknowledge God – who He is, what He loves, and what He has done. It's not unreasonable to expect every teacher, sports team, or school organization to demonstrate how and where this will be done. **Practice:** Our practice is harder to "define" or "control," because these are not necessarily curricular, planned out instances. But our community must be equipped to look for every opportunity to recognize God as God. They may be side conversations, responses to a question that comes up in class, or unspoken drivers which affect the way we choose to treat a student or a peer. In all cases, our schools can leave no doubt that we are concerned about God and His glory above all else. Here are some helpful questions and ideas to consider:

1. Be willing to risk the outcomes of asking God-centered questions and embracing God-centered answers.

Of course, education meets tangible needs and produces concrete benefits. Many statistics suggest strong correlations between education and earning power, and college admission is typically linked to high school performance. However, we need to carefully prevent lesser answers from becoming the primary answers students receive in Christian schools.

Every teacher has been asked, "Why do we have to know this?" Unfortunately, typical answers to these questions don't rest upon the knowledge of God above everything else. I've been guilty of weak answers: "you'll have to know this for the test" or "this will help you on the ACT" or "college admissions offices require two years of World Languages." All these answers are true, and we should rejoice in the tangible results of a proper education. Yet, these answers are insufficient if that's all we give.

Most students have the capacity to recognize the temporality of these answers; if the main reason for learning a set of materials is high test scores, the information loses its value after the test has been taken. Even if we add biblical language like "all for the glory of God," we've still allowed students to surmise that the whole purpose of education is temporary and self-serving.

Whenever we tell a student, "This will help you (fill in the blank)" in response to their questions, we've made the individual the center of our educational endeavors. This will help *you* get a good job. This program will bring *more people* to our school. *You* will have to know this for the A.P. Test. While true, these answers are lesser; they're secondary. I really don't have problems with these responses; I have a problem with these being the primary answers our students and families hear.

However, being God-centered means we start with a pursuit of God. That's the point. That's why our schools exist, even if saying so discourages some from enrolling in our school.

Critique every program, curriculum, and policy through a God-centered lens. This means you might ditch some parts of your school because you can't rationalize how they honor God. I was involved in a discussion to cancel our senior class cruise because it was nearly impossible to connect it with our school mission. We took a lot of heat for it; I wouldn't change the decision.

We all want to be distinctive. What's more distinctive than a school that doubles down on its commitment to honor God in what it does! Do things in your school because you've thought deeply about how and why they're necessary, because your school couldn't honor God as much without them. But don't just keep doing what you're doing and slap prayer on it to functionally make it "Christian."

At the same time, be willing to cancel or radically change whatever can't be supported through this same desire.

We all like our idols. They're shiny. So, when we make changes which threaten what we hold most dear, people get upset. Even in a Christian school, people will be in uproar when we start tinkering with "the way it's always been."

Have courage.

Hold everything in your school under the microscope.

Practically Speaking:

- This may mean you add more chapels than once a week, or you might need to overhaul your chapel program all together.
- You might reconsider some of your marketing material which might celebrate the *creation* above the *Creator*.
- Maybe you need to look in your curricula and lessons and ask where you're talking about God and where you aren't, and try to infuse a more God-centered emphasis.
- Ask your students every day "what did you learn about God today?" Make it a habit.
- Similarly, ask yourself, "What am I trying to teach students about God today / this week / in this unit?" Let this recenter your approach.

2. Do this with the smallest parts of your school – even the books chosen to read in class.

One of my friends' dad grew up in a Midwestern farming community still very connected to its historic, Dutch roots. So, all his vintage tools had the words "Holy unto the Lord" carved into their handles. Evidently, all tools in this community had a similar etching, even the pitchforks and shovels used for manure.

The moment I heard this, I was immediately reminded of Gerard Manley Hopkins' famous statement:

> "It is not only prayer that gives God glory but work. Smiting on an anvil, sawing a beam, whitewashing a wall, driving horses, sweeping, scouring, everything gives God glory if, being in his grace, you do it as your duty. To go to communion worthily gives God great glory, but to take food in thankfulness and temperance gives him glory too. To lift up the hands in prayer gives God glory, but a man with a dung-fork in his hand, a woman with a slop-pail, give him glory too. He is so great that all things give Him glory if you mean they should. So then, my brethren, live."[40]

In Christian lingo-heavy circles (and especially in Christian schools) it's quite normal to hear and see references to I Corinthians 10:31, "So, whether you eat or drink, or whatever you do, do all to the glory of God" as rallying cries for how we're to approach our efforts. Certainly, this is a high calling, and something we should take seriously – so seriously that we might want to reevaluate talking about doing everything for God's glory until we can do a better job of helping our communities understand what that means. Let's not be lazy with our Christianese.

I'll be honest; I'm not entirely sure what it means. But I think about it quite a lot, and that often makes me hesitate using the phrase all together. I do know that *glory* deals with the weight or substance of God. Giving Him glory might be in the ballpark of recognizing His greatness, His worth, His presence. Maybe that looks like giving Him more thanks than we do or seeking to know Him more in these experiences. Pausing. Recognizing that we owe God the recognition He deserves for what comes our way. Maybe playing tennis in a way that glorifies God means severe gratitude for the chance to play, for the lessons learned, for the very sport itself. For these are from God. They're His. In fact, it's all His.

Psalm 19:1 says the skies declare the glory of God. That's pretty big and magnificent, and it's often easy to see and reflect on God's greatness when we behold marvelous wonders. Just as it's often easier to see God's glory in the big things than in the small ones, we also tend to dedicate to God or seek Him in the big aspects of life rather than what we believe to be insignificant.

This is where I'm so very thankful for Tish Harrison Warren's focus on seeing God more in the day-to-day aspects of our lives, which make up the overwhelming majority of our lives. She says, "I like big ideas … But these big ideas are born out – lived, believed, and enfleshed in the small moments of our day … Today is the proving ground of what I believe and of whom I worship."[41] We need to think deeply about the small moments of our day and consider how and where we're God-centered there – where we thank Him, where we see our need more for Him, and where we seek to learn more about Him in those moments. In the education world, it means we need to be far more intentional about the mundane, ordinary, or "less significant" aspects of our school lives.

How often do you ask, "am I doing this because it's absolutely the best way I know of to help students recognize God more?

Imagine you've been tasked with teaching a new class. Let's say it's Medieval Literature. You ask what curriculum is in place. Maybe, you're handed an anthology with excerpts from different Medieval texts and review questions at the end of each chapter. Does that textbook become essentially what you teach? Maybe, you're told what books have been taught in the past but also given freedom to choose what books you want to read. Will you read *Beowulf*? All of it, or just part? What about Dante and Chaucer? Aren't they on the *bawdy* side? How do you choose? How do you determine the amount of time you will dedicate to reading or writing? How do you determine the sort of classroom ethos you'll aim for?

I love these sorts of conversations, and I fear they don't happen enough. Far too often, school curricula amount to little more than what's purchased (therefore, whatever is in the textbook or packet is one and the same with what's taught in class), or the curriculum changes, based upon who's teaching the course. Yet schools need to decide what their curricula will be, and then ask what will best help students know and love God through that discipline.

Some schools dedicate a lot of time to carefully planning out their curricula, and not basing them on pre-packaged models. In that process, where does the question of worshiping God through that content fall?

Work backwards. How will these books help know God more? What themes about God and our relation to Him will these books uncover? What essential questions will guide students toward these themes? What assessments will determine if we've been successful in answering these questions? What formative projects will help students do well on these assessments? What skills and content needs to be taught so that these projects will be meaningful? I could not more highly recommend taking your school through the ***Understanding By Design***[42] process (or something very similar to it). But work into your starting point objectives which direct students toward God.

If we decide to teach Beowulf or Chaucer, to show a Ken Burns documentary to connect dates and facts to images and stories, to allow flexible seating options for our third-grade students, or iPads for seventh grade in a one-to-one format, we should do so because we're convinced this is the best way to help students know, thank, or recognize God more. By the way, that could be said of any of these. Everything can be done as unto the Lord – and should be. Because of this, we cannot idly stand by and abdicate our responsibilities to be intentional about every little thing we do in our classrooms.

Certainly, we should be informed by data, recognized best practices, and parental input, but we should never allow this to dictate first and foremost what we do in our schools. If students take the ERB, dig deeply into what the results tell you. Ask hard questions. If another school in town adds a robotics program which enables students to flourish in new ways, consider what this program could bring to your school. By all means, work to get better, and look outside your school to inform what "better" means in your context. But change, add, or improve what you do only through an unrelentingly, stubbornly, constant, God-centered focus. Your school is a Christian school; make choices through a lens that is most Christian: a dependent declaration over and over again, "For from Him, and through Him, and to Him are *all things.*"[43]

Practically, this should show up in curriculum maps and essential questions for all classes taught. It should show up in philosophy statements for athletic or fine arts programs. It should be front-and-center in communications about changes or improvements – not just to programs, but also to facilities, and personnel. You should never give anyone a reason to believe you made decisions without first considering how it fits with a God-centered commitment.

Of course, this is true of the big things (like mission statements, hiring new administrators, or communicating plans for navigating a pandemic), but it's no less essential when we decide to add cheerleading, require school uniforms, or put Harry Potter books in your school library. The end result might not change for many things, but our community needs to see that we can provide a God-centered answer, because we've asked God-centered questions.

All things! Questions like: One to one classrooms or low tech? Traditional math instruction or problems-based learning? Why should we increase student and faculty diversity? Should we cover more material or go deeper? What's our plan for discipline and classroom management? How many recesses should you have a day? What kind of additional learning services can we provide? What field trips should a class take? When should we talk about sex-ed? How do we become more experiential in our approach to learning?

All things! "Holy unto the Lord"

Practically Speaking:

- Pinpoint in your curriculum where you consciously help students learn more about God. It should be plainly obvious to students and observable by a peer.
    - o If you can define at least one place, use it as a model to infuse that same objective into other areas of your curriculum.
- Do this with your other school programs. Is there a club you started solely for the purpose of proclaiming the supremacy of God or helping your community to know Him more? Build on that into other areas of your school.

3. Rather than asking what we get, consider what we give.

One of my seminary professors often said that we have made our worship services so consumer-driven that we've begun to threaten what worship is. We ask, "what did you get out of the sermon today?" or "did you like the songs we sang?" I'm guilty of this. I don't think we intentionally invert the focus on the worship service, but these sorts of questions essentially put the emphasis on the participant but not the Object of worship.

America's consumer-driven mentality has made it appear normal to think about church services or school life through this marketplace lens. At times, it seems like we are more interested in filling seats than the Kingdom.

If worship is primary, we should think more often about what we bring than about what we get. Yes, we need to communicate well, clearly articulate our mission, have top shelf programs, curricula, and instruction. But not because we are consumer-driven. We do all these things because we love God and what He loves. Timely communication from teachers to parents is expected by our "customers," but that's not why we do it. We should do it, because it loves people well and treats them with dignity.

When a prospective family enters our school or classrooms, rather than telling the family how the school will benefit them, our message should be, "here's how we will equip you to use your gifts for God and His kingdom." Through this mindset, *we're not courting consumers, but empowering worshipers.* Speaking this way also helps students and families recognize that we're mindful of the diversity of gifts and talents in the Kingdom of God. The Kingdom needs all its members to live in flourishing harmony with each other. The individual is not lost; she has great value, because her role is uniquely created by God. Families need to hear this, because the Christian school cannot be a place which caters to the idolatry of self, which is so pervasive throughout our culture.

Maybe, a great way to train our students and families to learn "it's not about you" is to change our language from "here's what you get" to "here's what we will enable you to bring."

Practically Speaking:

- Make a list of some of the idols that are most prevalent in your school. How will you work to see God increase in those areas and your idols diminish?
- Make a list of where God is most worshiped in your school. Where are the obvious places? Where are the unexpected places? Where are the places God is least worshiped in your school? How can you address them?
- Work into your admissions tours clear statements about how your school helps students and families use their giftings to further the kingdom.
- List all the student benefits your school or classroom describes and explore how these very same things can be reworded to describe how you equip students to use their giftings.
- Make a list of the ways your schools help students realize that it's not about them. Add to that another list of areas where you have the greatest untapped opportunities to teach this lesson.

4. Get in the habit of maximizing every opportunity to help students learn that there is Something higher than themselves.

When students join a sports team, they learn the danger of selfishness. They learn that there's something bigger than themselves – the team. They learn that they can't play however they want, but by the rules and according to the game plan.

In Math class, students learn that numbers are bigger than us all. Infinitely so. They learn that repeating numbers will keep going unto eternity. They learn about the discovery (not creation) of Math principles; they're true – not because we have said so, but because God made them so – independent of people.

In history class, students see the infinite number of stories, perspectives, and wonder of events. Properly taught, students should be struck with awe at the magnitude of individual events seen within an overwhelming context of each of the participants and variables at play. It puts our place in history within a recognition that this is part of something WAY bigger. Don't let that opportunity pass you by.

There are myriad ways to get students to see it. Brainstorm how students can face what's bigger than them. And, when they catch a glimmer of it, model for them to respond the way God's people did in the Bible: trembling, fear, amazement, and exuberant thanksgiving.

In that moment, remind them, "And this is why we've been studying what we have." We want to teach whatever will enable students to meet God in their learning. Help them see that these events or ideas could have shown up in a myriad of different ways, but God chose for these to be precisely the way that He ordained them. What can we learn about Him in that moment?

It's good for students to come to grips with who they are in regard to the Infinite One. Not to "put them in their place," but to enable them to wrestle with the scope of what's bigger than them. In these places, they begin to be rightly humbled. They see themselves in relation to the Divine. In these spaces, they can be drawn to wonder.

Also, it's good to employ this way of thinking with our teams and clubs. Though an overused cliche, it's healthy for every member to remember that there is "no 'I' in team." We say this, because we realize how destructive it is when a team is made up of self-centered players. The same is true of clubs. It's true of businesses. It's true of faculties. It's true of administrative teams.

Employ all sorts of groupings to remind students that they are not independent. We need Christian schools to be places where students, faculties, administrators, and parents realize that we are dependent – because it's not about us. Look for every opportunity to springboard the lessons learned from working within groups to drive home the reality that we are finite beings who are not sufficient to ourselves. This should automatically create the context where we talk about the only One who is independent and sufficient unto Himself.

Practically Speaking:

- In Math, whenever talking about infinity, repeating numbers going on forever, or lines on a graph getting infinitely close together but never touching, there's a great opportunity to talk about eternity and what's bigger than us.
- Keep a list in your classroom of things students (and their teacher) don't understand. If you ever get to a place where you are nearer an answer, thank God for it. For those that are still mysteries, praise God for his thoughts being higher than ours.
- Talk openly with your students about mystery. Let them wrestle with it, but don't always try to make sure that you've got answers to the mysteries.
- Science lessons can teach students how much more there is to learn. They can help students see how individual organisms

are parts of larger systems. Much can be learned from ants; the colony and the queen are more important than the ant itself. Yet the ant is still valuable. These can be helpful to enable students to see how they fit into God's Kingdom. It's not about me; it's about God and His Kingdom, but the individual still has worth in that context.

- There will come times when the "team" fails because of the selfishness or mistake of an individual. Maximize these opportunities to talk about the world not revolving around any one of us. Yes, it's about the team, or the organization. But far more importantly, these conversations can be harnessed to talk about the supremacy of God.

5. Look for every opportunity to talk about who God is and praise Him for what He has done.

Throughout the Old Testament, God reminds His people repeatedly to remember what He has done for them, especially the events surrounding the Exodus. It's unmistakable that God wants His people to be defined in recognition of His actions on their behalf.

What has God done for your school? Do you talk openly about it? Are your stories primarily about God's favor? Of course, the simple answer is that God's people and His schools should be most defined by our ability to articulate who we are in relation to God and what He has done for us. That's who we need to be.

We need to celebrate successes. If your school pursues excellence, you will see awards and accolades. Expect it. And successes are great opportunities to talk about God's faithfulness. But be very careful to avoid the pitfall of only talking about God's provision in the context of successes. The book of Job reminds us that God ordains times of both plenty and of lack. So, we need to talk about God's sovereignty and providence without ceasing. A loss, challenge, or trial can be powerful tools to learn more about God's faithfulness.

Our schools need to respond in unwavering proclamation of God's action, recognizing His favor and care in all things.

There are many schools whose Christian teachers cannot talk openly about God with students. Is it possible that this freedom can and has been taken for granted in your school? when we look at the Bible, we see that Israel is most identified as a people who recounts what God has done to enter into a covenantal relationship with and deliver them. Similarly, Christian teachers ought not take for granted the freedoms we have; we must be renewed in our efforts to pause and recount what God has done.

Talk about God. Often. Daily. Give Him the recognition due His name. (Psalm 29:2)

Practically Speaking:

- Develop rituals in your classroom and school where you tell stories about God's provision. Get in the habit of thanking Him on the spot. It's vital for students to realize that these things didn't *just* happen. They are from the hand of God.
- Whenever you ask students for prayer requests, make sure you also ask what they can praise and thank Him for. It's important that students see this as important as our requests are.
- Make sure your literature and website don't minimize the Lord's faithfulness to your school. It would be a tragedy for someone to wonder how "Christian" your school is after reading about it. Our outward facing dependence upon and recognition of God's goodness must be conspicuous.
- Whenever you take students outside, remind them of the blessing it is to be surrounded by God's handiwork. How cool would it be if kids can't imagine seeing God's creation and not automatically say or think, "how much greater and more beautiful is the God who made these things!" These are habits you can build when students are very young.

Why it's Christian

Most every religious system describes its "god" as supreme. However, when we get into the nature of these religions, we see that they're really about people. Muslims say *Allah* is absolute, yet the obedient Muslim ultimately gets paradise with seventy-two virgins. Because the system is a transactional one, if a Muslim follows the five pillars and his good works outweighs his bad works, he *will* go to paradise. It's just an equation; the system is ultimately in charge, not *Allah.*

However, in Christianity the system isn't in charge at all. God is. Yes, Jesus talks about preparing a place for us in the New Jerusalem, but the Bible is very clear; the focus of eternity isn't the things we get, it's the God we get. It's a restored relationship with Him. We know that we're not saved because of ourselves and what we do; we're saved by Grace, through faith, "and this is not of ourselves, it is the gift of God." (Ephesians 2:8)

Recognizing God as ultimate (in an ultimate sense) is uniquely Christian because it proclaims God as higher than us. It confesses that it's not about us; it's loaded with the gospel. This is why we need to double down on declaring that it's all about God, pursuing Him above all else, and living out our philosophies accordingly. *I can't; He can.*

ORTHOPATHY

I have come to imagine/dream about what it would look like if our schools really believed what the Heidelberg Catechism proclaims in its very first question and answer:

> Q: **What is your only comfort in life and in death**?
> A: "*That I am not my own, but belong body and soul, in life and in death to my faithful Savior, Jesus Christ.*

> *He has fully paid for all my sins with his precious blood, and has set me free from the tyranny of the devil. He also watches over me in such a way that not a hair can fall from my head without the will of my Father in heaven; in fact, all things must work together for my salvation. Because I belong to him, Christ, by his Holy Spirit, assures me of eternal life and makes me wholeheartedly willing and ready from now on to live for him."*

I've recited this so many times in church that I've forgotten how shocking it is. The most comforting thing we can know is that we are not our own. This is the foundational truth we all need to hear, and it's our task to harness every opportunity to help students learn that what we do in our schools is primarily neither about the students nor the teachers. It's about God. There may be nothing more radical for students to learn than this, because it flies in the face of everything their worlds tell them.

I've always thought that a graduation service most publicly proclaims what the school values most. As a Southerner, I tend to think that Friday nights are not too far behind, but graduation has a feeling of culmination. It has an air of "this is what it has all been about."

At most of the graduation ceremonies, schools give a lot of data: how many national merit scholars are in the class, how much total scholarship money the class received, how many seniors will attend four-year colleges, and the cumulative GPA of the valedictorian. When recounted, we hear gasps of amazement from the audience. We're far too easily impressed.

We may sanctify Christian school commencements by prayer, singing hymns, and securing a Christian keynote speaker. But were we to consider an on-looker's perspective, I wonder if he would think we've celebrated anything significantly differently than what would be celebrated in any secular school. How did we define success? What seemed most important?

Yes, commencement is an academic event. So, it makes sense to recognize academic achievement. That's to be expected. Considering that this is the final opportunity to let everyone know what the seniors' time at your school has been about, shouldn't we expect more?

I once heard Paul David Tripp say that the most dangerous idols are the ones most easily Christianized. It sounds a lot like Lewis' point in *Mere Christianity* that good things become bad things when we allow them to become *ultimate* things.

We all have idols. I've got lots of them; so do you. I'm most scared of the idols I don't realize I have. We likely don't realize the ones that don't seem egregious. Academic success is not bad. I want my children and students to do well. For some reason, academics and Fine Arts are more acceptable idols than athletics. Shouldn't we still be concerned if we've allowed students to think more highly of themselves because of their academic or artistic success?

Safety isn't bad. Nor is security.

Career success is to be commended.

Winning a state title in bass fishing is incredible.

Earning a full-ride academic scholarship should be celebrated.

Is this what it has all about? Do our Christian schools cater to this? Do we justify that this is who we really are because we've just sprinkled some Jesus Dust on it? Or do we think about the idols of our students' hearts and allow the gospel to do its messy work of revealing and attacking all our idols? What better education could students receive!

Humanity's first sin was motivated by a desire to be God, to be above Him, to live independently of, and to not need Him. If we're honest with ourselves, this continues to be our greatest struggle. It's why the first of the 10 Commandments focuses on putting nothing else before God. If you're like me, the "thing" we most often put before God is ourselves. And when we look at our schools, it's surprisingly easy to put countless things before God: enrollment, success, prosperity, admiration, reputation, a balanced budget, and the list keeps going. Of course, we tend to say we do everything for the glory of God, but our practice often tells a different story. Just like Adam, we are tempted by a desire to be our own gods.

As long as our idols hold our hearts, we will constantly hear, "just try harder." "Do more." "Maybe next time." A school committed to God above all else seeks to rescue students from the rat race by helping them to be enamored by Jesus who came to rescue our hearts. Recognizing our need for rescue requires that we all understand there was a problem, and we are a part of it.

We want students whose hearts are bent away from exaltation of self toward the only place where they'll find wholeness. It's an immeasurably difficult task, but we're not going to get there by just trying harder. We will only inch in that direction by unquestionably depending upon God and seeking our students' dependence rather than their sufficiency. It's peculiar; it turns things upside down; but it's the only way any of us will ever be free. It's also the only way we'll look more and more like we believe the gospel.

In *A Grief Observed,* C.S. Lewis says that reality is iconoclastic, or "idol smashing." If we live long enough, we'll realize that God's agenda and the reality of the contexts into which He has put us can blow up many of our assumptions. Yet we still cling to our idols.

We need taglines and mottos which can be understood by the masses. I want to be in a school whose in-house motto says something like "God-centered, life-giving iconoclasm." If this was first and foremost, I doubt our students (and their teachers) would forget how good it is to need Jesus.

5

COMPASSIONATELY THOUGHTFUL, DEPENDENT LEARNERS

Grid Question 2: Are we modeling and encouraging dependence upon God's Truth wherever it's seen?

In his book, *The Philosophy of Jesus*, Peter Kreeft says that, as soon as children can talk, they want to know what things are. They ask, "What's that?" As they grow in their ability to process, they ask, "Why?" Of course, parents end up getting lots of "Why" questions along the way. To a maddening extent, even.

As seen in the lives of children, it's rather automatic to move directly from talking about "what's really out there?" to wondering how or why we know it. Historically, a person's epistemology has always proceeded from her metaphysics. What a person believes to be ultimate will also be the driving force behind what she knows.

Certainly, we see this in our schools – as students mature, they want deeper explanations. They aren't quite as willing to accept "because I said so" as they once were. This isn't because teenagers are necessarily skeptical, demanding, or rebellious. It's more of a product of cognitive development; as they come to know more information, their developing minds want explanation. Of course, they're affected by the Fall, so their desire to know can be manifested in frustration and even doubt against the authority and boundaries set before them.

Yet, their desire to know "why" isn't a result of moral or intellectual error. Young children ask why, because they truly want to know and believe their parents and teachers are capable of providing real answers. Similarly, before the Fall, Adam and Eve wanted to know "why" and likely asked God lots of questions. Though, they never would have demanded or doubted God's answers. In the end, our desire to know is a product of our finiteness. Even in Heaven, we will want to know; we will never cease in our exploration, as T.S. Eliot says.

Epistemology comes from a Greek root word, *episteme*, which we translate as knowledge or understanding. Plato often referenced this as a higher goal than simple belief or opinion. Epistemology, then, is essentially the study of knowledge or understanding, or the branch of philosophy which attempts to explain how we know.

Schools aim to do more than metaphorically saw off the top of students' heads and dump in information. We want students to know why they know what they do. In fact, it's better for them to know they don't believe God than spout "Christian" claims without knowing why they hold them. We want students to understand their beliefs. It's critical for students to be presented with biblical truth clearly enough that they leave our schools knowing what they know about God, themselves, and why they do.

If they never believe in God, students ought to know why. Similarly, if they claim faith in Christ, they ought to know what it means and why they believe what they do. True education refuses to allow students to "know" things without actually knowing why they know them. Ultimately, it's not true education any other way, and that's why it's so important that we have solid answers to the question: <u>How do we know what we know?</u>

ORTHODOXY

There are essentially two ways people claim to know what they do: independently or dependently. Of course, only God is fully independent. Everything else depends on Him for existence, and all people depend on God for truth, even if in denial about it. That's why I refer to it as a "claim" to independence.

Within the realm of autonomous reasoning, people look to the scientific method, majority opinion, pragmatic results, personal feelings, or authorities deemed reliable. While none of these are inherently flawed sources for answers, the issue is one of trust; the person committed to independence places his trust in finite sources. A Christian perspective recognizes these tools to understand the world; yet they are instruments through which God reveals Himself. But these tools were never intended to be the ground upon which we stand.

Many people who commit to independent reasoning argue for their own objectivity; they are "free thinkers." This is similar to what the *Humanist Manifesto II* argues when declaring that dependence on anything other than human experience, whether it's "revelation, God, ritual, or creed," restricts and is a disservice to our species.

Answering the Question

The person who looks to science or other natural measures puts his trust in what could be wrong or likely to change over time. Pragmatic solutions change routinely; public opinion does too. Despite their best efforts, scientists make errors, and we often have findings which change what we formerly believed to be true. These aren't reasons to mistrust the scientific method or majority opinion; however, they create a problem for the person who places his confidence and trust entirely on the backs of things which could be wrong or change.

Others try to make sense out of life and knowledge while saying there is no standard for truth; this resembles the post-modern or relativistic way of looking at the world. While these people seek meaning through looking inward or by some sort of mystical connection with the world around them, they lose any hope of standards which can be agreed upon. Some claim to be fine with such a world, but we all know the difficulty of interacting with people who ignore anyone else's perspectives. While such a view seems charitable and accepting, it's destructive to living fruitfully in community. For, all societies are essentially held together by some sort of binding commitment upon which everyone agrees.

U.S. currency is inscribed with the phrase *e pluribus unum*, Latin for "out of the many, one." Americans realize a society built upon a multitude of nationalities, perspectives, and abilities. Yet, there must be a "One" … an *unum* which binds us together. *E pluribus plurus* is not sustainable.

It's not wrong to embrace these as tools to understand God's world. Science is a wonderful gift from God which helps us understand His world. It's quite reasonable to make decisions which take into account personal perspectives or experiences we've had. Those, too, are gifts from God, yet it's very dangerous to create standards for measuring truth and knowledge from perspectives or experiences. They should be tools, not the basis for our understanding.

As with the conclusions which arise from non-Christian attempts to make sense of metaphysics, we soon recognize the need to answer the epistemological questions in a way which fits with our own experiences in the world. If we're honest we recognize our need for reliable answers, are not content with not knowing, and we want our knowledge to be based upon something which stands up over time.

A Biblical Answer

When we consider how the Bible speaks about truth and knowledge, it meets us precisely in our need. Biblical truth is objective and absolute; it transcends and judges culture; it's not based on preference. It's universal and eternal; it's not situational.

True knowledge doesn't start with us. In his complaint against God, many of Job's accusations are based on his own experience, but his friend, Elihu, tells him, "I get my knowledge from afar; I will ascribe justice to my Maker." (Job 36:3) Similarly, Solomon tells us, "The fear of the Lord is the beginning of Knowledge." (Proverbs 1:7) The Bible speaks about truth as though it is something which is revealed; it is not constructed by us – only discovered.

The starting point for a Christian epistemology is the **Creator/ Creation** distinction, because a Christian epistemology depends upon God. The biggest problem with a non-Christian epistemology is that its hope rests on what's created. God created good things; they just aren't strong enough to support the hopes we place on them. This separates God from everything else. God alone is infinite, eternal, and self-sustaining. Everything else is finite, dependent, and temporal. It's also not because of the Fall. It would have also been true of Adam in the Garden had he never sinned, and it will be true in Heaven.

Because of the Creator/Creation distinction, anything we know is ultimately dependent on God. So, Christians answer any question of knowledge or understanding by starting with God. Of course, this is very similar to how the Christian speaks of the gospel. In the same way we are dependent on God for knowledge, we also depend on Him for righteousness which is essential for salvation. Therefore, our starting point for faith and belief has to be the work of God. To say we believe in God because of what we see is not a sufficient answer. For, it puts man as the judge and allows a person's perspective as primary, rather than the revelation of God.

On several occasions, I've done epistemological role-play with students, where I pretend to be one of my skeptic friends and ask students why they believe what they do. Because of the books they read, many of my students think they have patented, foolproof answers. They were surprised to discover that the evidence they threw my way didn't automatically wrestle me from unbelief into the light as their books suggested.[44] They thought they were armed with silver bullets which would automatically slay (in the Spirit, of course) the non-believer.

After dismantling their arguments and convincing them of the complexity of dialogue, they felt defeated. Of course, they wanted to know what they were supposed to say. They wanted to know what would help them "win." After I helped them understand that "winning" isn't the goal, they finally got around to asking me, "Then, why do you believe, Coach?"

At first, they didn't like my answer ...

I tend to think there is an epistemological crisis – a crisis of faith – at least, among many of the evangelicals I know. For two reasons:

First, I often hear people talk about faith as a "blind leap." They'll say things like, "we can't know for sure" or "there are just things we can't understand" ... "and that's why we have faith." When we speak of faith this way, it seems entirely irrational to the onlooker. It also suggests there isn't sufficient reason to believe. That's not very compelling.

This is quite unlike Hebrews 11:1: "Now faith is the assurance of things hoped for, the conviction of things not seen." Words like "assurance" and "conviction" don't even remotely sound like a blind leap. Rather, they sound like certainty, reasonableness, and confidence.

Similarly, in *Mere Christianity* C.S. Lewis says that faith is "the art of holding on to things your reason has once accepted, in spite of your changing moods."[45] I adore how Lewis connects faith to reason. Though we've separated them; they weren't so from the beginning. Lewis reminds us that faith is not the absence of evidence; it's an interpretation of the evidence and holding onto that interpretation. That's why it's an art. It takes work. Notice, too, that it's not the evidence or reason that's in question – it's the emotions.

I once heard pastor Les Newsom recall a discussion with college students about what it would be like if Jesus lived among us today. To his surprise, one of these students said, "If Jesus was really here, we wouldn't need faith." That's an interesting response. Les immediately took this student to John 11 to talk about faith. On that day in Bethany, onlookers watched Jesus call a dead man out of a tomb. They all saw it, but John tells us that some believed in Him (v. 46) while others went to the Jewish leaders to plot his death. (v. 53) There was no lack of evidence; people just interpreted it differently. Some took what they saw to conclude that the only way Lazarus could be alive is if Jesus was who He claimed to be. Others didn't like what they saw and accelerated their plot to kill Him.

Faith is not a catch-all term for what we do when we don't have evidence. Everyone has faith in *something*. Even if Jesus still walked among us, we'd need no less faith to believe in Him. His disciples needed faith to believe what they saw right in front of their faces.

Secondly, I hear belief discussed as though it's entirely about evidence. There have been so many times where I've heard people say something like, "The reason I believe in God is because of all the evidence I see around me." I've often heard these sorts of statements from students after they've read anti-evolution books. The absolute wonders of the flagellum or human eye are jaw dropping. Yet, they don't *prove* the existence of God. They do prove that there is order in this world, fine-tuning, and beauty. That's an important point to argue, because some suggest it's all chaos and disorder.

It's dangerous to mount a case for the existence of God from "evidence." There are all sorts of wonders which speak to the handiwork of God or further an argument for the reliability of Scripture. But evidence will never *prove* anything for the same reason onlookers didn't think bringing a dead man back to life was sufficient evidence to prove Jesus's divinity.

What's the goal of this evidential argument? Is the hope to enter into a debate, constructing a mountain of evidence which the opponent will not be able to refute? I see many people go to "evidences" when they try to argue for God or the Bible. Josh McDowell's work is *wonderful*, but no level of "evidence" is guaranteed to convince anyone. What if the other person has more evidence? Does he win? If I have eighty-four evidences for God's existence and my friend has seventy against it, I win, and he must believe in God.

Game. Set. Match. Right?

We all know it doesn't work that way.

If I declare belief because of all the evidence I see in creation, my belief hinges upon my perception; I become Judge. That's problematic because I'm deeply flawed. Seems like a risky basis for belief. Also, I'm in a pickle if the person who responds to my evidential argument by saying, "I only see evidence of pain, suffering, and disorder." Now, we're back to the "who has more evidence" dilemma. This line of thinking puts trust in evidence or arguments rather than dependence on the working of God's Spirit.

My students didn't like my answer, "I believe because God has revealed Himself to me." They ask, "well how do you know?" And, I respond, "because He says so."

"Where?"

"In the Bible."

"How do you know it's true?"

"Because He says so."

"Where?"

"In the Bible."

Sounds like circular reasoning. I've been accused of as much – not just by students, but also by my secular friends. Yes, it's circular. Point taken.

This answer is grounded in an unwillingness to trust myself as the determiner of what's true and what isn't. I also know the danger of the "my evidence is better than yours" argument. Eventually, we'll run into someone who has more. I also realize the inconsistency of saying God is ultimate, yet I'm the one who determines whether or not He exists. I'm dependent on this God. For everything. For my existence and for what I know. Shouldn't my basis for belief be a statement of dependence? If there's a God, He exists on His terms. Period. And He chooses to reveal Himself in the Bible and says it's sufficient.

It's like Jesus's caution about building a house on a Rock vs. sand. (Matthew 7:24-27) The message of the parable is clear: we need to build our hopes and trust upon something which won't wash away. Shouldn't this be true of our knowledge and belief? Our perception of the evidence could be quite shaky. I'd far rather base belief on the unchanging, infinite One.

Yet, we still feel like we need to *prove* it. Like Spurgeon says, I don't know why we feel the need to defend God. Let the Lion out of His cage, and He'll defend Himself. When we start with God as our beginning point for belief, truth, and knowledge it confesses our dependence, it recognizes the Creator/Creation distinction, it aligns with saying that God is ultimate over everything else, and it provides real certainty in our faith. It's not based on ourselves.

When we see God as the Source of all truth and stand upon His Word as our basis for knowledge and His Spirit, we can know have real confidence. This sort of dependent knowledge is consistent with the gospel, it is unchanging, and it confesses God as God. If God is ultimate, our basis for knowledge should hinge on what He has said and done.

Epistemology and Education

I oversaw part of the philosophy paper writing process my former school included in its professional development program. The architects of the paper requirements detailed a standard where teachers had to discuss how the Holy Spirit influences the teaching and learning process. The oversight committee was constantly amazed by how often our teachers wrote about the Holy Spirit only as their Comforter. Yes, the Holy Spirit does bring comfort (Jesus calls Him the Comforter in John 14:26), and we all dearly need One to provide rest amidst the hectic lives we lead in our schools. However, Jesus also calls Him the "Spirit of truth."

A triune view of education requires that we embrace our dependence on God for anything we know. Not only is all truth from God, our ability to comprehend truth is from God as well. We find it easy to think about needing God's revelation to understand Him and His Word. We ask Him to open our hearts and minds to understand "spiritual" things. But we rarely express the same dependence for understanding physical truths like the Pythagorean Theorem. We need Him just as much to understand and remember these ideas. In sin, we think we can manage on our own for the "everyday" aspects of life and what we learn. Our Christian schools should be known for their dependence on God. Where is it seen in your school? Is it one of your distinctives?

Students should hear repeatedly that anything we know comes from God – not just what we know about Him, but *everything* we know is dependent upon Him. This should nurture gratitude; it should nurture a sense of confidence in what we know. It should set us free to explore and discover truth wherever it's found, because it digs deeply into what God has made, and that helps us know Him more. This is why we routinely ask, Are we modeling and encouraging dependence upon God's Truth wherever it's seen?

ORTHOPRAXY

1. Both our schools and our classrooms should be marked by prayer, not to "sanctify" what we do, but to model dependence.

I had a teacher who began every class by asking for prayer requests and took great care to pray for each student in the room.

I typically looked forward to it, not because I was moved by my teacher's heart for us, but because it reduced the amount of time we spent on the actual lesson. From that prayer time forward there was nothing in class which distinguished it from a comparable class in any secular school.

This break in the academic routine wasn't a waste of time, but there are underlying flaws in what she modeled. In ways, the message I received was that there wasn't anything necessarily Christian in the material we studied, so we needed to add Christian content to the class. What better way to do that than with prayer!

Also, I learned it was acceptable for Christian schools to consciously minimize the rigors of academic study for the purpose of making sure we carved out space for the Christian aspects of school. I was trained to think it was acceptable for us to minimally pursue academic excellence, because we needed to sacrifice time for more important things.

Before I go further, I don't want to be misunderstood. I'm not saying Christian schools need to be enslaved by the rat race of keeping up with other schools. It's very appropriate to set the curriculum aside occasionally to take advantage of teaching opportunities which transcend the material for the day. I also don't think it's essential to maximize every spare moment to cover a record-breaking amount of information within a forty-five-minute block. Our classrooms shouldn't resemble *blitzkrieg* – lightning warfare pace.

Often, we try to cover way too much in our classrooms in our attempt to be rigorous. I would far rather see us reduce the volume of things we try to address in our classes and opt for taking time to challenge students to be more thoughtful and deeply understand the content.

It's desirable to move slower through the curriculum for the purpose of nurturing thought-leaders in our classrooms. Far be it from a Christian school which has a right view of truth to ever devalue academic discipline for the purpose of adding a spiritual dimension to class! True things don't need to be Christianized. The Christian teacher can teach physics, geometry, handwriting, or the fundamentals of wiffle ball without apology or feeling guilty for not reading a verse with an obscure, biblical analogy to what's being learned that day. Despite my teacher's loving attempt to include God in class, God was removed from it, because we were taught that there was a separation between the faith part of our class and the truths of the lesson.

In opposition to what was modeled for me, I very consciously didn't pray at the beginning of class for my first five or six years of teaching. However, a mentor challenged me to reconsider and convinced me to change course and start praying at the beginning of class, but for different reasons.

When we understand where we stand in relationship to God and His truth, we recognize our dependence. If dependent, we must approach learning in a way which shows we truly embrace a posture of neediness. What better way to approach learning dependently than by asking the Holy Spirit for help in the learning process? I can't think of one.

In the same way that we have a prayer of invocation at the beginning of worship services, our classrooms should be marked by dependent invocation. Christian schools don't have the monopoly on truth; only God does. We can't even get our minds around the knowledge of God, certainly not left to ourselves. We need God to enlighten our minds and hearts so we can deal properly with His truth. And this is a great testimony to students when they see their teachers stand before them and confess need. But for God's intervention, neither the teacher nor the student will be able to understand the lesson.

This is transparent, and it holds God and His truth highly. It models the reality of our need. It deflates our sinful pride. And that's what the Gospel is all about – not just for our salvation, but for all things. Praying for the Spirit's leading models and demonstrates this way of living; it's also a great reminder of what we fundamentally believe in school. We aren't merely learning things. These are God's truths, encompassing an infinite number of ways we can know more about Him.

Prayer also confesses the power of the Holy Spirit and His ability to help us understand our studies. This confession leads to confidence, not because of our own cognitive abilities, but because of the One at work in the life of the school.

Practically Speaking:

- Pray near the start of your classes – that God would allow you to understand the things you will learn that day – that these truths will be life changing, and that you'll see more of God in whatever you're learning.
- Ask students to pray and train them so they will understand the purpose of prayer.
- Periodically take a moment to ask students why we need God to understand these things. Remember, we never want students to think they don't need Jesus.

2. Treat non-Christian works with the same care as Christian works, celebrating the truth in the works and giving credit to the One who is the source of that Truth.

All truth is from God; and consequently, if wicked men have said anything that is true and we ought not reject it, for it is from God." – John Calvin

Whenever I hear that a school has chosen only Christian texts and curriculum, I immediately doubt the quality of that school. The Lord continues to work on my patience and is tempering how quickly I jump to conclusions. But I can't help believing that these texts are often sub-par in their content, compared to their non-Christian counterparts. Christian schools need to choose the absolute best texts and curricula to meet their educational objective, whether written by a Christian or not.

Because God is the Source of truth, anywhere we find truth, Christians ought to celebrate it. In *The Ballad of the White Horse*, G.K. Chesterton says it is "only Christian men that guard heathen things."[46] This is especially true in our current "cancel culture" world. The Christian school may be the only place where a student will still have access to the full canon of good literature. And we can do this precisely because of what we believe about truth – wherever it's seen. Christianity alone allows people to make sense out of the truth found in all areas of life. And further it. This is why Thomas Aquinas said, "It is impossible for the truth of faith to be contrary to principles known by natural reason."[47]

The truth found throughout the entire curriculum of the school ought to be celebrated. We are not bound to use Christian textbooks alone. In fact, we must read good books written by both Christians and non-Christians, listen to good music composed by non-Christians, and marvel at the art of Christians and non-Christians alike.

Rosaria Butterfield said that she learned about hospitality (which is vital to her role now as a pastor's wife) within the "queer community" she used to be a part of.[48] In his *Confessions*, St. Augustine speaks of learning God's truths, years before his conversion through the writings of Ovid and Cicero who did not worship God. Were not Moses raised in the Egyptian palace where he received a pagan education, would he have known how to write and record what we have in the *Torah*? Were it not for his pagan, Roman education, would the Apostle Paul have been able to relate to the scholars on Mars Hill or quote from Greek poets like Menander (Acts 17:28) and Epimenides (Titus 1:12) to defend and spread the gospel?

I get excited for students to learn more about God by reading His Word. I'm also confident that our students can do so through *all* the books they read in our schools, for as Eugene Peterson says,

"Christ plays in 10,000 places."[49] Believing all truth is God's truth, we recognize how wonderful ideas can be found in the pages of books written by all people. Since they all are created in God's image, we should expect to find truth, beauty, and goodness written by those who don't love Him, as well as by those who do. This is one of the primary reasons we have books in our curricula, our classrooms, and our school libraries written by all sorts of authors. We promote these intentionally selected books, because they're *good* books.

In his *A Theology of Reading* Alan Jacobs says the biblical mandate to "Love Thy Neighbor" doesn't apply merely to our interactions with those standing in front of us. It also needs to shape how we read and treat texts. I'm called to love the author of the book I read, which means I should treat him and his words with dignity – giving him a fair shot. Before I give my students an article to read and ask them to respond to it, I need to teach them how to properly respect the text and recognize the truth they *will* find in it.

Far too often, we tend to think reading non-Christian books, watching non-Christian movies, or listening to non-Christian music through a Christian lens looks like pointing out all the "bad" stuff in it. Why is this a "Christian response" to culture when Jesus didn't walk around the streets of Capernaum, pointing out all the bad things people were doing? He was the harshest toward the most religious people of His day. Today, maybe that might look like Jesus being most critical of Christian books, theater, art, music, and movies.

A commitment to treating authors or artists with dignity and considering their works through a Christian perspective means we will recognize truth, beauty, and goodness whenever we see it. We'll celebrate images of hope. We'll sit with the stories of brokenness and allow them to sharpen our ability to mourn the ravages of the Fall. We don't merely point out where books are wrong, we also highlight where they're *right.*

I firmly believe the Christian school has the greatest freedom to expose students to good works (both Christian and secular) because of what we believe about truth and the nature of humans. We believe in common grace. We believe all people reflect God, because they are created in His image. Therefore, our students should have broader and deeper exposures, equipped with the wisdom to point out errors while becoming better persons because of the goodness they read, hear, or see.

Assuming age-appropriateness, our schools need to more aggressively ensure that our students are given space to have healthy dialogue about the canon of good art, literature, movies, and theater - especially that which is not Christian. Bring on Steinbeck, Degas, and Mozart! This should be a distinctive feature of our schools.

Practically Speaking:

- Always choose curriculum, art, music, or other texts because they're the best you can find – whether they're "Christian" or not.
- Don't shy away from authors who aren't believers. Talk with your students about these authors as image bearers and celebrate how God has revealed His truth in their work.
- When you find ideas that are inconsistent with God's character and nature, allow students to discuss where it's wrong, what they think about it, and ask them why (or why not) it's still good to use that material.
- Whenever you critique material, ask whether your class treats the author or artist with dignity and respect.
- When you find truth in unexpected places, emphasize praising God for revealing Himself even there.

3. Cultivate a culture which embraces asking hard questions.

Not many of my memories in Christian schooling are as dear to me as the year I was able to have one of my atheist friends speak in a high school chapel to explain to the student body why he doesn't believe in God.

We did our due-diligence. Our Headmaster wrote a letter to the school community to explain our reasoning. I also spoke to the students in the chapels preceding the date, hoping to explain that our guest was my good friend who was doing us a service by putting himself and his beliefs on the spot. We also set aside extended time so students could ask questions. They asked him quite a few great ones! I was so proud.

Years later, students still talk about this chapel as one of their favorite chapels ever. We didn't give an altar call. We didn't have dry ice or lasers. There wasn't even a biblical message to speak of. But the students point back to it, because they were engaged. What engaged them? Honest questions. They were forced to think, and they were moved by that.

Another of our successful chapel experiments was less planned. One of our speakers had to cancel at the last moment, so I came up with a crazy idea seconds before game time: I projected my cell phone number on the screen behind me and told the students that we wanted them to feel like our school was a safe place for them to ask their questions. Over the next thirty minutes, I received hundreds of texts from students.

I did my best to answer on the spot. Many were very transparent and painful to read. Because I couldn't answer nearly all, I responded to those I couldn't answer in the chapel with a document I posted in a high-traffic part of the school building. For weeks, students congregated around. They wanted to know; they wanted answers to the questions everyone was thinking, but no one was willing to ask. My answers weren't flawless; I never claimed they were. But the fact that I answered these questions grabbed their attention.

While glad to provide this space for students to ask their questions anonymously, I was also concerned. The exercise showed how deeply students craved answers, and when given the first hint of the space to do it, they poured their questions out *en masse.* This revealed that our students didn't feel free to ask uncomfortable questions of their teachers. Maybe it wasn't the teachers' response they feared; maybe it was their peers.

We shouldn't have to give students an opportunity to ask deep questions anonymously for them to feel safe to ask. Our schools shouldn't be places where students simply walk away with a bunch of rote knowledge; they should be houses of learning. Deep learning. If that's going to happen, students need to feel safe to think with curiosity and honesty.

The Bible is full of people questioning God, and God would not have allowed it to show up in Scripture if it were entirely forbidden. Seemingly, God wants us to ask, even wrestle. Jacob did and is honored for it. It's human to do so. It's real. That's where we meet God. Abraham questioned God, and that's never even mentioned when his faith is heralded in Romans and Hebrews. Habakkuk questioned God, and he's never critiqued for it. Even Jesus struggled in the Garden of Gethsemane – questioning whether there could be another way.[50]

Because we know there are real answers, Christian schools should be educational havens where students feel most free to dig deeply. Yet, the norm seems that many Christian schools are places where students are expected to conform. But conformity often stifles true learning. We want them to love learning, and to get there, we've got to allow students to explore, and ask, and risk.

Yes, risk. A former Head of School, Bryan Miller used to say he wanted a billboard posted on the main street near the school saying, "send your kids to our school and put them at risk." I so deeply wish to have seen it. It's risky to allow students to ask hard questions. How else will their learning enthrall them? How else will you prevent them from becoming Older Brothers?

If we're so committed to intellectual and academic tidiness that we never have students deeply challenged, we have failed. Let's face it, we know students have questions; many have questions they fear to even think. We also know that lasting growth comes from challenge, stretching, and dissonance. Our communities need to be places where students know we're more about growth than answers. Growth may mean students don't *arrive*, and that's quite ok.

Neither you nor your students will arrive this side of Paradise. We will always have more to learn, and that's not a result of sin; it's because God's truth is infinite, like He is. We will always be finite. Even in Heaven. Of course, the Bible clearly says we will live forever with God, but we will still have limitations, because we are the creations, not the Creator. As a result, there will always be more to ask in our exploration. Our schools ought to be safe havens for question-asking. More than any other institution.

Practically Speaking:

- Simply asking "what do you think?" could be sufficient to get some students going. You might need to prime others beyond that. It will be hard for them to disagree, but maybe you could ask, "does anyone disagree with …?" "Does anyone have a hard time agreeing with …?" "Does anyone have a better way of thinking about it?"
- Whenever students offer a different opinion, don't shut it down. Honor the fact that they chose the road less traveled.
- If students ask questions where they truly want to know (not just being difficult), you might need to protect them from ridicule they may get from peers. The best way to do that is to show how highly you regard them. It's not a sign of weakness to express curiosity or doubt, but of strength.
- You might even need to create systems of acknowledgments where you keep track of intriguing things said or questions asked and reward the best one of the week. We want students to be deep thinkers. Deep thinkers ask good questions, and it's important to nurture that environment in all our classrooms.

- With little ones, celebrate the fact that students asked questions as much as they know the answers – maybe even more so. It's much easier to answer a question from something you know than to think, "well what about …?"
- In general, everyone should identify you as a teacher who is more interested in good questions than good answers.[51]

4. Get comfortable with telling your students, "I don't know."

Ryan Dixon is a master of responding to questions he doesn't know the answer to. He is absolutely brilliant, but there are times when students ask him questions he has never considered. His response is perfect: "I really don't know, but I'd love to explore the answer with you if you'll join me." How winsome is that!

We want students to ask questions we don't know the answers to. There's *nothing* lost when it happens. Oh sure, it may hurt the teacher's sense of intellectual authority in the classroom. Maybe we should trash that, or at least bring it down a few notches. If students don't ever ask questions we haven't considered, they either aren't adequately challenged, or they don't feel safe to ask them in your classroom. Both are unacceptable.

It's not the teacher's job to tell students all the things they don't know or be the end-all authority on a subject. It's the teacher's job to help students learn. If students become entirely dependent on their teachers, they might functionally replace God with their teachers – when it comes to understanding and learning. We can't let that happen.

When we allow students to know that their teachers don't have all the answers, it reminds them that only God knows everything. It also encourages students to realize there is always more to know. It may also nurture a bit more of their curiosity, especially if their teacher confesses that the question is new. I'd love to have students feel empowered to learn something because they realize their teacher would actually be thrilled that students know something better than their teacher does. Students might also pursue answers freely if they have a vulnerable teacher who walks alongside them.

It's hard to have this posture of curiosity and vulnerability as a teacher if we try to micro-manage what they learn. If we truly want students to learn, we must allow them to explore – and even surpass their teacher. Many of us might be a bit nervous about being exposed. They might see that we don't know it all! But wouldn't this inspire students to know that their teacher is a human like them who wants nothing more than to walk alongside them in their learning?

Even better, it may be good for students to witness that their teacher is wrong. Yikes! What we do with it is critical. Do I get defensive when a student points out my errors, or do I use these situations as reminders that only God's knowledge is perfect? Do I allow students to see that I'm still learning, just as they are? Or do I try to shield them from my errors so I can continue the illusion of being the "brilliant" teacher?

Practically Speaking:

- Whenever telling students that you don't know, ask, "Does anyone else?" That may mean that students realize that other students might know something you don't.
- Do not avoid conversations or lessons where you feel like questions will come up that you can't answer. It's a great opportunity for students to know that you're learning along with them in their exploration.
- When you must confess that you don't know, capture the opportunity to talk about God knowing the answers, and that our confidence can always rest in Him. Then, tell your students that God may not reveal His answers to you, but it's going to be really cool to pursue God and His truth in this way.

5. Don't be scared of mystery and paradox

My own faith tradition tends to put a heavy emphasis on rationality and celebrates an organized, thoughtful, and biblical theology. I learned my catechism, nailed down the *ordo salutis*, and have a pretty solid grasp of significant confessions, creeds, and my own denomination's *Book of Church Order.* Having a systematic theology is important to many people in my theological camp, and that's not a bad thing.

Only recently, have I started to flirt with a bit of rebellion against my tradition, and I blame G.K. Chesterton. In *Orthodoxy*, he emphasizes the importance of being more concerned with truth than consistency.[52] Consistency is good, but not to the detriment of truth.

In my own tradition, I've seen many attempts to "massage" biblical passages to make them fit within the system, rather than living with the tension of apparent contradictions. But there are multiple things about Christianity that don't fit into tidy systems. There is mystery, and not only is it ok; it's good. It's good, because our world is full of mystery and wonder. Of course, it must be so, because our God will always be higher than us – and full of mystery and wonder. Living in the mystery where we don't force-fit things into consistent answers and systems, it confesses that we are finite and embraces a posture of imagination and wonder.

For example, the Bible tells us that God is in control of all things. There's nothing outside His control, and the Bible is actually quite clear about this. The Bible also tells us that humans are free to choose and that we are responsible for our choices. However, all of us can see how these two ideas can butt up against each other. If God is in control, we must not have real choice. Or our free will is so great that God must not have total control. Rather than living in the tension that both must be true because the Bible says so, we create systems to explain the tension such that it minimizes one of the truths. Of course, it frustrated my students when they asked me which of these biblical truths is truer, and my answer was always "yes."

We don't need to have all the answers; we need to stick to what's true – to what God has revealed. At times, it's easy to see what God is saying. At others, it's not so simple, and rather than giving answers which ignore other truths, don't dodge sitting in the tension and mystery. That's a big part of what being dependent upon God and His truth looks like.

Practically Speaking:

- When you encounter mystery or tension, ask your students how that makes them feel? Your "control freaks" will want solid answers. Use that as an opportunity to embrace the reality that mystery and paradox forces us to recognize how limited we are.
- Talk about why we want things to make sense, that this too is part of our design. God wants us to make sense of the world. Yet, as Ecclesiastes 3 tells us, God puts "eternity in our hearts" to frustrate us and remind us that there will always be something higher than us.
- When possible, it is even good to plan out a lesson that intentionally points the students toward mystery – toward things that we simply cannot understand. I'd argue that mystery is so important, that it should show up in all our curriculum maps. But not just for the purpose of mystery. It should be designated so that these things help us be more amazed by and dependent upon God.

6. Don't forget; there are solid answers.

Recently, I visited with a school's Bible department as they began to overhaul their curriculum. I appreciated that they surveyed their parents, students, and other teachers to ensure their decisions were informed by perceptions and data. One of these recurring themes was that the Bible department was doing "too good" of a job of creating dissonance. In talking with the teachers, it was clear that teachers were pushing their students away from packaged answers, Christian lingo, and "safe" spirituality. Yet, there was no *reassembling*, before the school sent them off to college. Parents felt there should be some sort of capstone class which brought together all these disparate pieces, where they matriculated with a strong foundation.

I admired that this school was smashing idols, forcing students to think, and dragging them out of their comfort zones. However, they are still children. We do not want to leave students with questions, doubts, and uncertainties absent of hope and answers. Yes, I want my students to have questions, and I am often more concerned that they have the right questions than the right answers.

However, students need to know that the Bible's answers are sound and sufficient, providing enough information to stand on. It's unchanging; it's reliable; it's life-giving. Amid all their questions, our students ought to understand the frailty of all other options and to answer like Peter in John 6:68, "Lord, to whom shall we go? You have the words of eternal life ..." In Peter's answer, I don't see lingo. I actually see struggle, but he knows the other options don't work. He has lots of questions, but this does not deter Peter from knowing that Jesus is the only One he can run to.

If a student were to leave our schools like a John 6 Peter, I'd be thrilled. He knows where His hope is. He doesn't have perfect answers. But he knows where to find them. In a way, this is better than the student who thinks he has it all figured out and never sees his continual need. So, we shouldn't fear questions, doubts, and concerns, but we want students to know the reliability they can find in Jesus's claims.

Practically Speaking

- While it may be good to let some questions fester beyond a lesson, class period, or two, make sure you don't leave students there for an extended period of time.

  - Keep track of those unresolved questions and commit to resolving them before too long.
  - Rather than simply giving the students the answer, always lead them toward the answer. This may look like the Harkness or Socratic method.
- When you finally give students answers they can rely on, don't merely provide them as matters of fact. Help students to see why these answers are good for them.
- Thank God for being knowable and providing understanding. Give Him credit for revealing these things to you and your students.

7. Your ability to do Biblical interaction well will be directly linked to the depth of your knowledge of the Bible.

Maybe the most "predictable" thing I can say in a book about Christian education is that we will never grow as Christian educators without a growing knowledge of God's Word. This is truly a non-negotiable. It's not rocket science. We have to know the Bible, the source of the Truth we are dependent upon.

Whenever you get around other Christian educators and talk about school, biblical integration seems to be a hot topic. Seemingly, every school wants to get better in this area, and the simple truth is that we need to know the Bible a whole lot better before we'll see progress in biblical integration.

I once heard a Christian professor who taught at an Ivy League university for four decades say that today's Christian students enter college with less knowledge of the Bible than the non-Christian students did thirty years ago. In a culture which has minimized the discipline of deep Bible study, the trend needs to change. We must know the Bible, and that comes through reading and studying it. It's absolutely critical.

Biblical integration means far more than providing connections between content and a biblical story or teaching. Merely finding allegories or analogies isn't adequate for students. It's an error to assume that biblical integration in Math class looks primarily like creating a problem where students try to calculate how many times five loaves and two fish must be divided in order to feed 5,000 people. That's not integration, even though it could be a fun exercise.

The more I work with schools, the more I'm convinced that biblical integration works best when there's a framework of ideas and questions that teachers and students can routinely return to. That's more reliable than asking teachers to draw analogies to what they find in the Bible, because this creates quite limited outlets for integration.

Yet, we have to know the Bible well enough to meander into biblical connections when they organically arise. It shouldn't be forced, but it should flow out of us. That only happens when we know Scripture.

Obviously, this can easily show up in literature classes, when we see stories with clear overlap:

- When Harry Potter or Aslan come back to life, what a great opportunity to talk about Jesus's resurrection!
- When Hamlet fakes insanity, we can draw connections to David's ruse at Gath.
- When the Joads face extreme hunger in *The Grapes of Wrath,* it's a great opportunity to weave in the Israelites' hunger in the desert and Jesus's words about hunger and bread in John 6.

And the list goes on and on and on. We have to know Scripture so well that it becomes second nature to be reminded of biblical images because of what we find in our curricula. But, if we never get beyond drawing connections between the Bible and curriculum, we lose a great theological and pedagogical opportunity. Drawing the connection is only the spark that lights a far hotter fire. Take them to deeper levels where they can connect both the curriculum and the biblical images to their own lives. Just as important as knowing individual stories in Scripture, it's vital that we know the themes of Scripture and the general placements of events and fundamental ideas of the Bible so well that we naturally see how *the* Story fits in immeasurable places.

What does Aslan's resurrection remind you of? Why is resurrection so shocking? Why do we need it? Why does it create such drastic changes in emotion? Why is it such a powerful igniter of hope? Why do you need hope?

Similarly, when we see biblical connections in Math, Science, World Languages, or History, we still need to take students to deeper questions, because we're always after their hearts. If we reference Paul's metaphor of training to run a race to talk about the Christian life, merely taking students or athletes there isn't enough. We should use these biblical allusions to push them deeper: Why is the Christian life hard? Why do we have to train in order to tackle hard things?

When talking about slavery, take students to biblical images of slavery but also to what the Bible says about the dignity of all people. Certainly, look at the stories of the Jews enslaved in Egypt, but don't stop there. Talk about why slavery is wrong. Talk about the sin in our hearts that causes us to devalue people – not just back then, but today as well.

Practically Speaking:

- Look at your curriculum map, where do you intentionally draw connections to the Bible? Do you have a goal for what a sufficient amount of biblical connection should look like?
- With those connections, always go to deeper questions. Talk about God, ourselves, the gospel. Creation, Fall, and Redemption.

- Make sure you think about biblical connections within the informal curriculum of the school as well. Knowing Scripture better gives you even more context for drawing connections to God's Word – from a conversation with a child in the hall, to a behavior situation, after a hard-fought loss, or when encouraging a peer. Don't just attach a verse, use that verse in dependence on foundational ideas.

Why it's Christian

"You be you." "Tell your truth."

Our modern world tries to convince us that we need to be independent, yet Christians confess that dependence is the only way we'll ever be free. It's the only way to have confidence in what we know, and it comes by basing our knowledge upon the word of Him who is without error and never changes. While Christians humbly acknowledge our insufficiency, we recognize that truth and knowledge are only reliable when found in what the Infinite One has revealed.

Confessing our inadequacy and dependency in the area of truth is gospel-centric, because it recognizes our need for God. It's very good news, because it recognizes God's grace, His action, His authority. It's the sort of Truth that sets a person free.

ORTHOPATHY

One of the worst effects of the Age of Enlightenment is that men openly thought they no longer needed God. In these learned Humanists' perspective, believing in anything higher than mankind does a disservice to us. They didn't arrive at this overnight. The earliest Enlightenment thinkers used their reason to comprehend God's existence. But they declared that God is reasonable because *people* can understand and think our way to belief. Their basis for knowledge wasn't God's revelation, but human perception. It didn't take long before this line of thinking resulted in secular humanists believing that human reason is all we need.

It's good for students to learn that truth is higher than them. So, our curricular choices need to help students come to grips with what they can't do. If our students master everything we put in front of them, we unintentionally enable them to think they have a total handle on Truth, and by default think they have come to its same level.

We don't want students to live in constant frustration by what we're teaching, nor do we want them crushed under the weight of Truth. For Jesus says that Truth sets us free. Yet we must hold Truth so highly that we are unwilling to allow students to put themselves on its level.

In pursuit of their hearts and desires, our handling of Truth should cause students to both see how it's good for them and that it's always going to be higher than them. Psalm 139 wonderfully speaks to the knowledge of God – His knowledge of all things and of us in deeply personal ways. In verse six, the Psalmist says, "such knowledge is too wonderful for me; it is high; I cannot attain it." In these lines, I see awe, wonder, and healthy fear. I see incomprehensibleness. I know it's hard to think that it's good to say there are things we can't do. Yet this is truly good for us. We can only flourish when we see ourselves in full dependence upon God – not just for salvation, but for everything.

This should be a result of what we teach. If students leave our school with puffed-up knowledge and over-inflated perspectives of what they've obtained intellectually, we've failed. It's one more way we've allowed them to believe they don't need Jesus.

6

THE RADICAL NOTION OF EDUCATING WHOLE PERSONS

Grid Question 3: Are we honoring the full image of God in all members of the school community?

One of my friends recently stepped into a new administrative job at a large Christian school. After a few months, a group of seasoned teachers entered his office to express concern; they had a mounting suspicion that he was too "pro-student." They hoped their confrontation would convict him and change the trajectory of his administrative tenure. It didn't encourage them when he admitted to being unapologetically pro-student. He did follow it up with saying that he's also "pro-teacher," because they aren't mutually exclusive statements. Unfortunately, the damage had already been done.

For whatever reason, there often seems to be a chasmic divide between students and teachers, as though some still function like they're teaching in the 1950's.[53] I remember one of my first teaching mentors advising me to avoid laughing or smiling for the first semester. I didn't last through the first day without throwing the advice in the woodchipper. I was having too much fun.

Successful teachers realize that the best way to connect with students requires stepping outside the outdated models of teaching. It requires engaging students' wills, not just their minds. We're teaching whole persons, and teaching whole persons needs an in-depth consideration of who these learners actually are. As a result, much of what we see in modern education comes down to beliefs about the nature of students.

Nearly every philosophy or system of thought has an articulation about what it means to be human. This stems from the reality that all people question who we are, where we came from, and what our purpose in life is. A religion or worldview is incomplete without an explanation of these fundamental questions. Since all humanity seeks answers to these questions, having a clear articulation of what it means to be human must be central to our educational commitments. In the same way a religion or philosophy is incomplete without these answers, our Christian schools are philosophically incomplete if we have not paid special attention to the question: <u>what does it mean to be human?</u>

ORTHODOXY

Of the worldview questions we've covered so far, the question of anthropology typically has the most direct effect on a culture, because it hits closest to home. Though, this doesn't elevate the third question above the ones we've covered so far. It's impossible to arrive at an orthodox view of humanity without a foundational view of God and His Word. While each of these questions is vital to the life of the school, it's important to see that there's an ordered process to them. This is one of the reasons it's mightily important to address *all* these questions and see them in an order which starts with our beliefs about God and truth.

Answering the Question

Throughout history, people have been all over the map in their search for a definition of humanity. It's not been easy. If our definitions rely too heavily on physical attributes, we run into problems. For various reasons, some humans don't have two arms, two legs, or two working eyes. Most people agree that these physical handicaps don't make a person any less human. On the other hand, a robot which might have all these physical components is far from human. On a personal level, it becomes very difficult to base human dignity on physical attributes when they can so easily change. Similarly, it's hard to focus on mental capacity, because many people argue quite vehemently for the dignity of loved ones with mental handicaps.

When cultures have struggled with these definitions, their confusion often resulted in gross atrocities. We're all aware of many of these. Without clear definitions, it becomes very difficult to ascribe value to people in reliable ways.

Nearly all my secular friends ascribe tremendous value to people. They believe that humans have dignity and rights, and their perspectives and freedoms should be honored. Yet they often struggle to ascribe to humanity any kind of intrinsic value which distinguishes people from other species. My friends are smart enough to know the implications of such statements. Secular Humanists ascribe extreme value to mankind, but lack basis for their assertions, so they cannot hold to unchanging, timeless claims.

From a naturalistic perspective, people have extreme value because they are the most complex of the animal kingdom, but this view gives people value *as long as* they demonstrate complexity. This explains why many humanists may endorse abortion or euthanasia when a person has significant handicaps.

Other thinkers who view humans entirely through a naturalistic lens have articulated the danger of ascribing greater value to people than to animals. Praised Princeton philosopher Peter Singer suggests that it's a form of speciesism to grant voting rights to invalid humans above monkeys who could make a choice between candidates on a ballot. I appreciate his consistency. If nothing gives humans absolute value, it's discriminatory to prioritize humans above other species.

To go even further, some have applied Charles Darwin's evolutionary theories to mankind. In his book *The Descent of Man,* Darwin points out that humans are the only species which take care of their invalids and allow their weakest to reproduce. A farmer seeks to improve his herd by prioritizing reproduction among animals with the most desirable traits and prevent the runts of the herd from siring young. Margaret Sanger (founder of Planned Parenthood) goes even further in her perspective and suggests that birth control and eugenics are the "pivot of civilization," because this ensures our future preservation by those fittest to survive. Many fascist governments built upon this thinking, decreeing their races as supreme. By reducing the humanity of other races and people with handicaps, these governments performed well-documented horrors against men, women, and children.

Certainly, most naturalists vehemently oppose crimes on the scale of the Holocaust. Yet saying that the Nazis didn't seek to execute Darwinian naturalism to its most aggressive, logical extreme ignores history.

Other non-Christian systems minimize human dignity, but not because of naturalistic leanings. Some argue that all people are part of god or some kind of spiritualized concept of nature. While ascribing divine connection to humanity sounds dignifying, it reduces the value of individual humans, because each person is only a part of a larger force or energy in constant motion, reanimated with each new life.

Anthropology and Education

We don't need to go much further than to look at two "fathers" of American education to see how their naturalistic views of individuals affected what we see today.

John Dewey, the twentieth century educational theorist, proposed pragmatic education with no ultimate end. In *Democracy and Education*, he writes, "We have just pointed out the futility of trying to establish the aim of education -- some one final aim which subordinates all others to itself." This statement undercuts the dominant historical view of the purpose of education. Ironically, Dewey replaces the notion of an intrinsic purpose to school with acquiring and sustaining a job. He suggests that in "the change from an oligarchical to a democratic society, it is natural that the significance of an education which should result in a person's ability to make his way economically in the world, and to manage economic resources usefully instead of for mere display and luxury, should receive emphasis." Dominant in many secular schools today, this view is not the biblical picture of education, because it replaces the knowledge of God with mechanical skills or what it takes to get into college.

Further study of American education quickly uncovers the massive influence of BF Skinner's introduction of radical behaviorism into our modern educational theory. In *Technology of Teaching,* he acknowledges the failure of most teachers to produce desired results because they wrongly assume students make choices. Because he has no room for personhood in his answers to ultimate questions, he claims that students (and we as teachers) have no personhood either. Therefore, we must understand that students are driven only by internal or external conditions.

This probably sounds like much of what is taught in many education classes, because modern educational theory is so highly influenced by Skinner. By the way, much of Skinner's theory "works" because we are, in part, physical beings who are highly influenced by our environments. Of course, we're also more than that. While there's truth in some of Skinner's conclusions, we must consider why his most influential book is called *Beyond Freedom and Dignity.* He believes students have neither freedom nor dignity; There is no person – only his actions. That's why he says, "give me a child, and I'll shape him into anything." We ought not be surprised; he's simply consistent. If there's nothing more than matter, this minimizes how we view students. They are only highly complex, material organisms who will be taught most effectively by those who understand the power of conditions.

Neither Dewey nor Skinner believed in anything transcendent. They were both naturalists who reduced people to the complexity of their elemental makeup. As a result, they were only concerned with what is outwardly verifiable, because that's all there is.

We shouldn't be surprised that many students and their parents view the educational process sort of like a factory. There's a desired product to manufacture. That's the goal. The product is a tangible outcome, and the process is geared toward ensuring that.

But what if the desired outcome is more than acquired skills and knowledge? What if the desire is to see *changed persons* because we believe that true education seeks the knowledge of God and transformed lives?

A Biblical Answer

God's Word describes humans as the highest of all creation, and Psalm 8 paints a beautiful picture of our place under God in relation to the rest of the world. This psalm declares that we're less than God, but still of incomprehensible value to Him. This baffles the psalmist to consider how God appreciates us. Though, the writer understands the implications of this value: everything else is put under our feet.

When looking at the creation account, we see that God put men and women in the world, giving them certain responsibilities. This provides two bases for understanding ourselves: **Who are we?** and **How ought we live in the world?**

First, the Bible tells us that we are created in the image of God. (Genesis. 1:27) I imagine we use the phrase quite a lot in our school communities as it's one of the biblical concepts which most distinguishes Christian schools. Outside Christian circles, saying we're created in God's image could mean many things, but we probably need to do a better job of defining what we mean by it.

Being created in God's image doesn't mean we "look" like God. Many religions have anthropomorphic representations of God, and many Christians unintentionally do as well. If our physical attributes are what make us in God's image, there are a whole lot of people who aren't in His image due to whatever deformities they might have. Similarly, an unborn child wouldn't yet be an image bearer.

Most Christians use this concept to refer to what makes us uniquely human and distinguishes us from all other species. I can't provide a perfect definition of all it means to be image bearers, but I'll focus on five categories which seem to gobble up most of the different ideas I've found. Like God, Human beings are:

<u>Rational</u>. All animals have brains, and they use them for amazing purposes. Yet humans are unique in the logical processes we execute. Being rational means more than merely knowing or remembering things, which is certainly part of it; it focuses on our capacity to reach the terms on the higher levels of Bloom's Taxonomy – application, analysis, synthesis and evaluation. Like God, we make plans according to desires and purposes, connecting ideas together according to those plans. Many animals can be trained to perform tasks, which suggest process, but humans have capacity to generate entirely new and unlearned processes.

<u>Relational</u>. God's only negative statement about His creation was that it wasn't good for Adam to be alone (Genesis 2:18). At the core of His nature, God is relational; He has existed eternally in loving affection among the Father, Son, and Holy Spirit. When God created a relational partner for Adam, He created a woman of the same substance, value, and dignity, but different. Together, they are one flesh. For this reason, we shouldn't be surprised that one of the greatest of all punishments is solitary confinement in prison. In that space, a person is separated from an aspect vital to humanity.

Similarly, personal feelings of loneliness are some of the most painful emotions any person can suffer.

A biblical view of humanity reveals primary categories for our relationships. Of course, our primary relationship is with God. Genesis 2:25 wonderfully helps us see these relationships working together. Adam and Eve were in the garden together with God. We see intimacy and transparency with each other. We see personal wholeness, because Adam and Eve lived in right relationship with God. So, their relationship to each other, to themselves, and to the natural world flourished.

Spiritual. We are physical beings, but like God we are also way more than that. We have souls (or spirits), which will exist eternally. This is also the part of us that is most "us." It's the "Noahness" of me. We have a desire for what's spiritual, all knowing we were made for more. In *Mere Christianity*, Lewis says, "If I find in myself a desire which no experience in this world can satisfy, the most probable explanation is that we were made for another world."[54] This is part of what Solomon means when he says God has put eternity in our hearts. (Ecclesiastes 3:11) Being spiritual also means we have capacity for connecting with and are affected by the spiritual world; we're even tempted by Satan's work. We commune with God through prayer; we're often prone to worship (both rightly and wrongly).

Moral. Like God, we know the difference between right and wrong and make free choices with that knowledge. Some say that men and women didn't have this knowledge until they sinned. God hasn't sinned – does He not know the difference? It's foolish to say that sin is what enabled Adam and Eve to become like God. When Satan first tempted Eve, she resists because she *knows* what she's supposed to do. Granted, our senses can be dulled over time, but all people know; even little children do. Animals do not, even though they can be trained to do certain things and fear consequences when they have violated their training. Yet, humans uniquely know something is wrong or right, regardless of consequences.

Creative. In *The Everlasting Man,* G.K. Chesterton says that art is the clearest stamp of the divine upon people. Like God, we desire to create simply for the purpose of joy in creating. Animals build things, but their "art" is almost entirely for functional purposes. Humans have the capacity for taking what's in their mind and painting it on canvas, acting it out on stage, telling it in a story, putting it to the tune of a song, or expressing it through humorous analogy. All people are creative, and our ability to create brings us joy. It makes us feel alive; we feel fulfilled when we create.

By design, these five attributes are cohesive. There's tremendous overlap, as image bearers are supposed to live out all of these at the same time. We are moral in our relationships, creative in our thinking, and spiritual in our relationships. No attribute would be more pronounced than the other had sin never entered the world.

In education, we tend to focus primarily on the rational nature of the learner (especially as students get older). In doing so, we both minimize the power of education and diminish our students' inherent value. In *Orthodoxy,* Chesterton says that "the madman is not the man who has lost his reason; the madman is the man who has lost everything but his reason."[55] By focusing on one dimension of our "image bearerness," we minimize the value of our students and fail to target their full natures. We puff up one aspect of students' humanity, while ignoring the rest, creating an imbalance. Madness.

Of course, this raises many questions in regard to our classrooms. How ought we teach, considering we're all image bearers of God? How ought we treat our students?

Because our students are created in God's image, they are the pinnacle of God's creation, and have the utmost value. The Westminster Catechism states that man's chief end is to "Glorify God and enjoy Him forever." As educators, we ought to engage our disciplines according to our chief end, while pointing students to see how pursuing our disciplines can further help us both glorify God and enjoy Him.

Above all else, our students must see, hear, feel, and know that we are *for* them more than we are for our curriculum. By "curriculum," I mean all aspects of the "teaching" or "coaching" process: lesson plans, assessments, lesson content, teams, programs, or clubs. The reason we must prioritize our students above our curriculum is that they are of greater value. While I know we believe this, if you're anything like me, you need the reminder.

While our curriculum is most often based on truth and correspondingly good for students, our curriculum is not created in the image of God. But our students are. While the preparation we've often put into our curriculum is good, and we want to honor that work, our curriculum is not the goal. Honoring God and those made in His image is.

Maybe we should start each day by praying that God prevents us from prioritizing what's lesser (what we teach) above what's greater (who we teach).

How Image Bearers Engage the World

God rules His creation through divine fiat; he also rules it indirectly through people as His viceroys. In the Bible, we find clear standards for understanding who we are as image bearers as well as a framework for how we are to live in the World, according to the three-fold offices of Prophet, Priest, and King.

It's relatively normal to see schools recognize their students as God's image bearers, and some have taken steps to develop what this means for the mission of their schools. But I haven't come across too many which give the same attention to the implications of the offices of prophet, priest, and king. Yet, this is just as important to developing a school mission which reflects a robust, biblical philosophy of humanity.

While given to people to use and delight in, we have clear responsibilities toward Creation. We cannot take the world for granted, because it's good; it has value. We've been given responsibility over God's handiwork. (Genesis 1:28, 2:15) From this "creation mandate" we see God's expectation that we take care of His creation, to engage it by employing all it means to bear God's image, and to improve it. As agents of God's work in the world, we are called to improve the creation around us. This must be at the heart of what we do in our schools. In *The Advantage*, Lencioni says that healthy organizations' purpose statements should be lofty statements like "making the world a better place." There's a cosmic nature to the task. Having a developed understanding of the offices of prophet, priest, and king helps us in this endeavor.

We link the theology of these offices to two very important biblical characters: Adam and Jesus, the second Adam. In Romans 5, Paul mirrors them to help us see their similarities. In both cases, we have perfect men whose actions had colossal effects on the rest of humanity. The first Adam's act of disobedience brought death and the second Adam's obedience brought life. (v. 18-19) Clearly, Adam was created exactly as God intended; he was perfect, but he fell from his original state. Jesus was also perfect, and came to restore humanity and the rest of Creation to its original intent.

When we consider the role of the **Prophets** in the Old Testament, they didn't merely tell the future. They spoke God's truth to the community; they directed the attention of the people toward God's law – to both hear it and obey it. Prophets were in fellowship with God, and they communicated to others based on what God shared with them through direct revelation. They were given the task to speak the mind of God (His Truth) to God's intended audience.

Priests were given the responsibility of tending and working the Temple, to preserve the holiness of God and His law. They also represented the community before God and God back to the community. Obviously, a big part of that was through performing sacrifice, once sin entered the world. But this was a mechanism of performing their primary function: to mediate righteousness and holiness to the community as representatives.

Romans 13:4 tells us that earthly rulers are God's servants to do good. **Kings** are intended to rule with justice and to bring about faithfulness to God's covenant. We see this throughout the Old Testament - those kings who were most successful were those who were not only personally faithful to God's covenant, but also those who nurtured faithfulness among those they ruled. Kings are anointed by God to bring about order, safety, prosperity, and shalom – full, flourishing wholeness.

Adam

Adam served in these offices, as the ruler over all Creation with a clear mandate to take care of the Garden to bring about order and beauty and expand its borders to the rest of the world. He regularly communed with God. Therefore, anything he spoke, he did as the first prophet – whether to his wife, or even in the naming of the animals – would have been seasoned with the truth that proceeded from fellowship with God.

I'm thankful for John Fesko's reflections in *Last Things First,* where he suggests that the Garden was far more than a prehistoric farm. Rather, Adam tended the first Temple, for God was present there. Also, there are tremendous similarities between the Garden of Eden, the Temple which God had Solomon build, and the Temple city that John describes in his visions of Revelation 21. This is another wonderful example of the grand story of Scripture – Creation, Fall, and Redemption. So, Adam took care of the first temple as a representative of all Creation. We know this, because we see how clearly his actions affected the history of the world.

Even though Eve was the first to give into the Devil's temptation, Scripture routinely blames Adam for sin entering the world, and it's not much of a stretch to say that he sinned by failing to faithfully execute the offices of prophet, priest, and King. In his book, *The Silence of Adam,* Larry Crab points out Adam's failures, starting with his passivity amidst his wife's temptation. He was there with her (Genesis 3:6), but he chose not to speak up and remind his wife of God's commandments (Prophet). In fact, as king, he should have expelled the invader (the Devil) from the Garden, but it would have to be the second Adam who would crush Satan's head. (3:15) Also, when God confronts Adam and Eve about their sin, Adam should have taken the blame that both he and his wife deserve (Priest). Instead, he blames her – and in a way God, Himself, for putting her there. (3:12)

Jesus

It doesn't take nearly as much work to see how Jesus fulfilled these offices, for we're told far more about Him. The book of Hebrews ties together many of these themes which can clearly be seen throughout the rest of the Bible, but Hebrews so enables us to see Jesus's fulfillment of the types and shadows in the Old Testament, starting with the connection between Jesus and Melchizedek.

Like Tom Bombadil in *The Lord of the Rings,* Melchizedek appears on the scene in Genesis 14 and disappears just as quickly. Yet his importance can't be overlooked; the writer of Hebrews suggests that he was even greater than Abraham. (6:16 and 7:4) He was king of Salem (often identified with Jerusalem) and priest of the true God, which is rather profound, considering that the Jewish people didn't even exist yet. The writer of Hebrews says it's important to identify Jesus with Melchizedek, rather than Aaron, because His priesthood is royal, greater than the Law, and indestructible (7:16). By identifying Jesus with the greater priestly line, the writer of Hebrews shows how Jesus fulfills all the priestly responsibilities, sacrificing Himself on our behalf to restore our broken relationship with God. It's not difficult to see how Jesus is our high priest.

Like Melchizedek, Jesus is also a King. When Dionysius Exiguus restructured dating methods around the life of Christ during the 6th century, he categorized everything after the life of Jesus as "A.D" or *Anno Domini*, which we translate as "in the year of our Lord." It was rather common for societies to chart time around the reign of the monarch. We see this in Isaiah 6, when he says, "In the year that King Uzziah died, I saw the Lord." This pinpointed a definitive year; it's historical. By dating every day after Jesus's life as *Anno Domini*, Dionysius made a remarkable worldview statement: King Jesus reigns today. Therefore, it is His. Jesus reigns, and the Bible gives plenty of images of Jesus's rule. The book of Revelation places Jesus on a throne, and gives Him rule and a crown.

It's also not difficult to see how Jesus fulfills the role of prophet, for everything He spoke was true and proceeded from His fellowship with His Father. Sounding very much like the prophets of old, Jesus says, "For this I was born, and for this I came into the world, to bear witness to the truth." (John 18:37) He came to call people to repent and believe in Him (Mark 1:15) as well as give hope in our pardon and forgiveness of sin. (Colossians 1:14)

If the two perfect men in the Bible held offices of the prophet, priest, and king, it's not a stretch to believe this is the original intent for all people. The framework of Scripture also often applies these images to all believers – referring to God's people as a "kingdom of priests," "royal priesthood," or "priesthood of all believers."

This provides mandates for how we are to engage the world around us. Like Adam, we are to tend and take care of the world, but not just for agrarian purposes. Like kings, we are to seek and bring about justice. We would never consider a man to be a good king if he were overcome by the disorder of the world around him. When trouble comes, good kings engage it.

Prophets stay in fellowship with God's truth and speak it with boldness, focusing primarily on a call to repentance and offering the profound hope of the gospel. God was angry with Jonah for his unwillingness to speak of both to the people of Nineveh. At the end of the book, he ends up speaking about God's judgment, but doesn't seem to be too excited about God's mercy. Yet we are to speak God's truth by holding His holiness and expectations with the highest regard, while championing His forgiveness and mercy.

One of my mentors often insisted that Jesus's articulation of the Greatest Commandment drives the Christian school to be ever mindful of our Head, Heart, and Hand. He artfully spoke of how this inspires what we do as educators and what we want from students. As I've considered his words and the implications of the offices of prophet, priest, and king, I see direct overlaps. As prophet (Head), we hear then speak to the truth of God to all creation that others might know Him. As priest (Heart), we intercede with God, taking the burdens of others on ourselves as we live sacrificially in the world. As king (Hand), we are called to engage the world, to tend it, care for it, and in covenant faithfulness fight for justice and order.

Head, Heart, Hand
Upward, Inward, Outward

Because God created people in His image-bearers and gave us the task of living as prophet, priest, and king, all people have profound dignity and purpose. In *The Weight of Glory* Lewis says,

> "It is a serious thing to live in a society of possible gods and goddesses, to remember that the dullest and most uninteresting person you talk to may one day be a creature which, if you saw it now, you would be strongly tempted to worship, or else a horror and a corruption such as you now meet, if at all, only in a nightmare. All day long we are, in some degree, helping each other to one or other of these destinations. It is in the light of these overwhelming possibilities, it is with the awe and the circumspection proper to them, that we should conduct all our

> dealings with one another, all friendships, all loves, all play, all politics. There are no 'ordinary' people. You have never talked to a mere mortal."[56]

Our students are not mere morals. They're not ordinary, nor are their teachers. They bear the image of the infinite, personal, triune God. They're young kings. Prophets. Queens. Priests. Priestesses. Considering who students are and how God designed them to live in this world, we have a profound task to educate them in a way which champions their profound value. This profound task requires that we ask, <u>Are we honoring the full nature of God in all members of the school community?</u>

ORTHOPRAXY

Before I get too far into this section, I should lay my cards on the table. Our schools are schools. They're not churches. They're schools, and we need to be crystal clear about that.

Some might think all my focus on the image of God and prophet, priest, and king could suggest a greater interest in teaching church doctrines than rigorous, academic curriculum. There doesn't need to be a dichotomy; we don't have to pick between doctrine and educational best practices.

We'll only enhance our educational practice by strong biblical doctrine about humanity. We don't set aside pedagogy for the sake of human dignity. In fact, teaching toward our students' full nature increases their capacity to learn in innovative, life changing ways. With growth in biblical orthodoxy, we become better educators, validated by the lasting change seen in students' lives. Charlotte Mason says, "Our crying need today is less for a better method of educating than for an adequate conception of children."[57] If we view students as we ought and consider how that reality affects what we do in our schools, we'll see the fruit we hope for.

There will be things in this section which many teachers already do. I don't want to change your practice. However, I hope to affirm you in what you're currently doing. Often, good teaching is good because it connects to biblical implications of humanity, whether or not the theorist and practitioner knows it. If I mention things you're already doing, I hope my ideas can bolster your commitment to them or that you'll feel renewed in your attempts to experiment with best practices.

1. Teach students like you believe they are image-bearers …

I could read Chesterton's *The Ballad of the White Horse* every year and still not get everything out of it. I often feel like it's his attempt to bring the philosophy of *Orthodoxy* to narrative via an epic, poetic myth. It's a glorious retelling of the story of King Alfred's defense of Christian England against the onslaught of the pagan Vikings in the 9th century.

In one of the chapters, a group of pagan Danes sit around a campfire singing songs. In each song, Chesterton weaves the philosophy of modern worldviews. Guthrum, lord of the Danes, sings a song of hopelessness, where only violence brings him comfort. Alfred responds that a worldview void of mystery and wonder leads only to great sadness and emptiness, there really is hope and joy, and that Christianity alone enables us to make sense of the world.

Far too often, we treat students as though they are primarily rational beings. This is especially true the older they get. In younger grades, teachers tend to do a better job of enabling students to connect their learning to hands-on, creative experiences. I'm routinely amazed at the way elementary teachers target learning to a very tactile, vivid activity; I watch as students participate in activities while listening to their teachers explain what the students will learn. Often, students simply have a joyous time engaging the activity; they're not even aware of the lesson, curriculum, or great amount of *work* it took for the teacher to construct the activity.

Because we believe students are image bearers, we need to consider how to maximize the various aspects of what being image bearers means to the learning process.

Rational

Because we're often guilty of overemphasizing the rational components of students' natures, we could think, "Ok, we have this one down. No further work needed." I wish it were that simple. In my own practice, I have undervalued students' rational capacity, and I imagine others have, too.

Do we teach students as though they are sponges which simply absorb information, only for us to squeeze it out when required of them? Far too often, we can teach students like they are less than rational. We could even say that we treat them like parrots. Maybe that's less offensive, because they're more active than sponges.

Think about the average college lecture hall where a professor covers vast amounts of information that students are expected to retain. I've been guilty of throwing information at students in expectation that they merely memorize what they're told. If we're honest, this form of teaching doesn't require the teacher or students to be physically present. It could just as easily be a recording that's watched by the student. If this is all that happens in class, I fully endorse an online option. Unfortunately, I've observed many classrooms where I felt like I was watching a robotic lecture – performing instructive tasks but preventing students from demonstrating the fullness of what it means to be rational.

Rational beings follow processes of connected ideas, far more than merely regurgitating information. When we talk about advances in "artificial intelligence," innovators aren't describing computers' ability to handle more complex programming at faster speeds. "A.I." means that a computer learns and creates new ideas based upon its programming. In a similar way, believing that our students are rational beings means we recognize intelligence which draws connections, builds on ideas, and seeks to understand. It's good to teach in a way which allows students to question and follow a rational process, and it's a crime against their rational natures to prevent their freedom to learn in ways which exceed memorizing required answers.

"Higher Order Thinking Skills" are great starting points to access some of what it means to view students as rational beings. Certainly, they can absorb volumes of information; it's amazing what people can retain. But memorization is at the bottom of Bloom's Taxonomy for a reason. Because students are complex, rational learners we should take great care to enable them to own their learning, so it lasts.

We don't want students to merely know; we want them to know *why* they know, and we want their learning to ignite something within them. Once again, we're not just after students retaining bits of information so they can succeed on standardized tests. With a far grander view of learning, we want students to make sense of themselves and their world. To do so we need to get them to evaluate, synthesize, create, analyze and apply. Not just because it's what the "educational theorists" suggest, we pursue this because it treats the students as though we really believe what the Bible says about them as image bearers and prophet, priest, and king. Here, we return to the first two categories of the Grid, as we consider the goal of learning. Are we "teaching" or are we helping students "learn"? Those don't have to be mutually exclusive, but I'm saddened by how often I've seen such a wide gap between the two.

In general, what we'll find is that many of the things educational theories and studies find hold water, not just because researchers happened to stumble onto an idea or studied at length. These methods often work because they target specific aspects of a biblical anthropology. All the more reason to ask how we can better our practices in ways which targets who students truly are.

We should also be mindful of what we're accomplishing with piles of assigned worksheets, especially if we know it's primarily a space-filler – "busy work." Having students do "work" is not the same as having them learn. Obviously, we should focus on the later, and the former should always have the later in mind. Busy work reduces nearly all image bearer aspects out of the student.

Relational

Growing up in a very self-centered culture, I understand the tendency to read the Bible as though it's about "God and me." God cares for a *people*; Jesus came to save His Church, of which individuals are a part. However, it's very common for us to overlook the dominant theme of Scripture that we are part of a community (a Body), and things go poorly if we try to isolate ourselves from the importance of that community.

Learning is not a one-directional activity. The learning process is so much more than a relationship between the teacher and student where the teacher says information and the student memorizes it. Certainly, this is an aspect of the learning process, but it's tragically myopic to stop here.

Many schools with robust faculty development cultures have harnessed the power of professional learning communities. They know that teachers who work and learn in relationships with other teachers are most likely to grow. In a similar way, there's extreme value in allowing students to learn in community with each other.

When I explained this to some of my teacher friends, a very senior teacher said, "Oh no; you're talking about group work. Aren't you?" I smiled.

Group work has gotten a bad reputation. It's hard for teachers to "control" what's learned and who does the work. Rubrics are difficult. They're not tidy. But let's not allow our idols of tidiness, safety and predictability become obstacles to transformative learning.

Constructivist educational theorists like Piaget and Vygotsky take things a bit too far to question the absoluteness of Truth, but they're onto something when they suggest the importance of being able to connect experiences through social interactions. From the outset of Creation, God said that it wasn't good for Adam to be alone. Why, then, do we try to isolate the students in their learning? They need more than the teacher. Adam had the Source of all truth, and he still needed another human being as he interacted with the world around him.

In a similar way, students will flourish in their learning if we release our tight grip on what and how they learn and allow for exploration, where their learning exists within conversation with their peers in a variety of ways.

This takes work and more preparation. It also means teachers might see themselves as facilitators, guiding activities where students learn from each other under the watchful and directive care of the teacher. This is one of the best aspects of implementations like the Harkness Method. Done well, students learn how to ask good questions – not just of their teachers, but also of their peers.

One of my teaching friends assigns reading communally, where students are given sections of a text to read with preassigned roles to play when they come back to class. Some of the students are assigned to read for plot and details of the text. Other students are assigned to read to consider the application of the text to life. The third group is given the responsibility to read the text with the purpose of guiding the conversation the next day, assuring that each student's voice is heard and that the class stays connected with the text. From the outset, students understand that they aren't learning or reading on an island.

Directing such a class means that ideas may surface which the teacher never predicted, and that's both beautiful and scary. It also means that teachers may have to be willing to engage heavy topics. In this context, students realize that their individual voice has value in the class. Their dignity is recognized, because they are part of the community.

I have another friend who says that our current age of immediate information requires that teachers see themselves less as authorities of information and more as brokers of it. This view sees the teacher as a guide through all the information that's out there, but it also allows for the students to learn in a way which recognizes that the student isn't learning in a vacuum.

We need to teach students in constant consideration of the community in which they learn and give them avenues for learning from their peers. Not only will getting them off their islands enable a more holistic and broad learning experience, it will shape their hearts for life as they realize their own finiteness and their need for others.

Moral

Many behavioral theorists argue that students don't make choices; they simply respond to stimuli in predictable ways. Because our students are physical beings, they are affected by external and internal conditions. It's extremely important for teachers to be aware of the conditions which influence students' abilities to learn. However, students *do* make choices, and we need to view the educational process as a moral endeavor.

Students aren't just learning information, they're being shaped as persons. They're forming habits of discipline, faithfulness, care, trustworthiness, thankfulness, and patience. Teachers need to keep in mind that the information we teach has profound value, but the learning process is also a vehicle of shaping their moral lives. We ask students to be the sorts of people who submit to authority, who recognize that they are dependent on others for what they learn, who realize that they don't know everything, who work hard when they don't understand, who accept correction.

We will likely forget much of the content we learn throughout elementary school, secondary school, and college. I don't want to minimize the importance of what we teach, but we need to remember that we're engaging the entire person, and their moral natures are very important dimensions of their learning.

Spiritual

A brilliant high school Calculus teacher, Claudia Allendar routinely welcomed her students on the first day of class by saying, "we'll start by worshiping." Then she would pause while her students would get silent and prepare to be "spiritual." Once having everyone's attention, she would say, "Get out your Calculus books." It was no trick. For Claudia, studying Calculus was an act of worship, because it reveals the character and nature of God in ways only complex math can.

In his 2005 commencement address to Kenyon College, author David Foster Wallace (who was not a Christian)[58] said,

> "In the day-to-day trenches of adult life, there is actually no such thing as atheism. There is no such thing as not worshiping. Everybody worships. The only choice we get is what to worship. And an outstanding reason for choosing some sort of God or spiritual-type thing to worship – is that pretty much anything else you worship will eat you alive."

In his song, "Gotta Serve Somebody," Bob Dylan also suggests as much. In his book, *Let the Nations be Glad*, John Piper says, "Worship is what we were created for" and he argues that worship must be primary above everything else.

Considering that our students are worshipers, much of the task of the Christian school is shaping and directing their worship. We will find something to worship; it's what we do.

A few pages ago, I referenced the song of the Danes in *The Ballad of the White Horse.* One of the pagan songs talks about growing up and hearing the fables and tall tales of childhood, but adulthood requires that we put those behind us. We often think this is much of what it means to grow up; we stop believing in Santa Clause and the Easter Bunny. Now, I'm not saying that we should think there really is a plump elf who shimmies his way down our chimneys, but we must war against a worldview void of mystery and wonder. Chesterton suggests that we need to have a sense of childish wonder, and because we believe our students are spiritual beings, we need to harness every opportunity we have to nurture their wonder. We want them to think the world is amazing, because it is.

Because they are worshippers, we need to make sure we properly direct their awe. First of all, we need to make sure they don't take their learning for granted, and when they are prone to wonder at the world around them, we need to harness it and direct it toward the One who has taken great joy to reveal Himself the way He has.

On those occasions when teachers see that students are acutely aware of this wonder, pause and take a moment to nurture that. This is an appropriate time to offer a word of thankful prayer. Or, maybe it's a great opportunity to allow students to journal or voice their appreciation. In *Desiring God* John Piper says that our wonder isn't made complete until we can voice it in praise. To bring students to a point where they truly grasp the weight or amazement of what we're teaching and not take that step to allow them to voice it is a lost opportunity.

In his book *Everyday Apocalypse,* David Dark mentions how poignant it would be to carry around a book of stickers which says, "Insert Soul Here" and put them wherever he goes. Our souls are always being engaged. We need to be constantly aware of the fact that students are prone to worship and that they long for spiritual connection. This needs to season our lesson preparation, our interactions with students, and our curricular decisions.

Creative

It's no coincidence that "Create" is the highest level of Bloom's Taxonomy, considering that creativity is a dynamic which most distinguishes humans from animals. Madeleine L'Engle says, "In art, the Trinity is expressed in the Creative Idea, the Creative Energy, and the Creative Power—the first imagining of the work, then the making incarnate of the work, and third the meaning of the work."[59] To create anything requires the ability to master a subject by assembling knowledge, drawing connections, and applying it to something new.

At times, we might reduce creativity to aesthetic aspects alone. Certainly, use of colorful pictures and graphics or playing sounds may pique their imaginations and get their "creative juices" flowing, but we need to think about our students' creativity as their desires to design, build, create, author, and investigate.

I've witnessed many teachers construct assignments which target students' creativity:

- Requiring students to write original sonnets demands that students understand the boundaries of sonnethood.
- Assigning students to build trebuchets in physics class requires mastery of mathematics and physical concepts.
- Asking students to draw what they think Atticus Finch looks like expects them to have paid attention to Harper Lee's descriptions.
- Blocking out time for students to draw pictures to explain how 5+4=9 empowers students to demonstrate that they connect the meaning of numbers to real objects.

Each of these examples accesses our students' creative capabilities, and these are not just good ways to pass the time in class, but the imaginative work required to assemble original ideas targets this profound aspect of what it means for them to be human.

Because creativity is vital to humanity, it's critical that Christian teachers be both creative in their teaching (to model that for students by thinking of new ways to convey information) and consider ways which require them to employ their creativity in the learning process.

It takes time and intentionality for their creations to connect to the desired learning objectives, and the results may not perfectly match what we hoped for, but it incorporates who students are into the learning process. Teaching toward their creativity shows that we value this aspect of who they are as learners, and we've not adequately engaged them until we consider how to access their creativity. Because we often don't, it's easy to understand why so many students find school "boring." I've gotten to a point where I'm no longer willing to point the finger at the students, blaming their apathy and lack of engagement. Maybe, the problem is that we haven't taught them in the way we should. Be creative. Let them create.

Practically Speaking

- While it's possible to design lessons that incorporate all these dimensions, it may not be the norm that you're able to pull it off. That's fine. However, we need to be mindful of all five of them – so much so, that we intentionally emphasize the different dimensions of being image bearers across our days, weeks, and units.
- Don't be surprised if this requires you to teach outside your own comfort zone at times. Be of good cheer, though, because what isn't natural to us becomes far easy the more we work at it.
- Lean on your peers to determine which are most adept at teaching towards students' relational or creative natures (for example), and go watch them teach, learn from them, and experiment with trying some of the things they're doing.

2. And Prophet, Priest, and King as well …

We should also look to find ways to bring out the three-fold offices that will enable students to engage the world according to God's design. There will be some overlap here with the image bearer categories, but we need to both fulfill these offices in our roles as teachers and look to find ways to target these offices in their lives.

When we teach, we must think about our calling as prophets. This should affect how we handle truth in our classrooms – humbly, because it's not our truth (it's God's), but confidently, because we can stand on the solid ground of His truth. We need to approach our preparation and delivery with the recognition that we are called to be truth speakers, and this needs to season our interactions with students and peers. It's a high calling, indeed.

We're also called to be priests, which means that we should intercede and advocate for our students, bear their burdens, and live sacrificially before them. We should pray with and for them and walk with them as they navigate the effects of sin both in their own lives, but all around them. We must care for their hearts and constantly look for ways to present Jesus to them.

In our offices as Kings, teachers need to physically engage our callings by promoting security, order, and justice. Certainly, this starts with having clear classroom rules, strong management skills, and willingness to be consistent with correction and celebration. As sovereigns within the spheres of our classrooms, we have significant amounts of control – curriculum, lesson design, and developing an ethos within the classroom environment. Good kings are not overcome. They don't retreat. They engage and enter in to provide structure, clarity, and leadership in physical ways.

Head, Heart, and Hand.

Not only do teachers need to be mindful of our callings as prophet, priest, and king, we also need to teach our students, being mindful of their responsibilities in these same offices. We need to engage their minds, hearts, and bodies – another reason we should hold onto our commitments to teaching the "whole student." We must take care to recognize who they are in these offices by making sure we create space for them to learn through their heads, hearts, and hands. This teaches toward their nature.

We also need to teach toward the direction of their calling by empowering and emboldening them to live as prophet, priest, and king. If we have concern about lasting change, we need to teach them in a way which challenges them to be truth speakers, to live sacrificially and emotively, and to engage the world to bring about justice. Regardless of what we teach.

Practically Speaking

- Always give students the ability to experience, to get their hands engaged, to own, and to have responsibility over their education – it's part of their "king" calling.
- Not only do students need to see their teachers intercede for them, but we need to model for them how to intercede for each other, both to our Heavenly Father, but also in the day-to-day interactions. We need to praise them when we see them bearing the burdens of their peers.
- Whenever students see us put others before ourselves or when we encourage students when we see it in them, we emphasize their calling as priests.
- Having students recite in class or do public speaking or presentations equips them to develop the skills of truth speakers
- At times, playing the "devil's advocate" in class to train students to recognize error can further equip them to live as prophets. It's important that we train them to distinguish truth from error and develop the habits of voicing what they see.

3. And assess them like you believe this.

Because instruction can't be separated from assessment, we also need to consider that our methods of evaluation reflect these same commitments. Unfortunately, our report cards lack a full picture of what we want students to learn. This is especially true as students get older; we leave the "moral" or "spiritual" components off their report cards. We talk about "educating" the whole person, yet our report cards don't give the same picture we say we're fundamentally about, especially in high school.

Some of my philosophy students truly hated that "classroom participation" was a significant part of my summative evaluation. Half of their grade was based upon their ability to talk to each other both in class and in an online classroom discussion board in fruitful ways about the content we were discussing. It wasn't a "fluff" assignment or a buffer grade to pad their overall average; I constructed a rubric for scoring them and defining my expectations. Several were even more frustrated that their exam was a timed conversation that they needed to have with each other in groups. But I wanted them to reflect that they understood how the ideas we were discussing are fundamentally a conversation with other ideas.

We need to build assessments – both summative and formative – which challenge students to be rational, relational, moral, spiritual, and creative. We need to design assessments which access their calling as prophet, priest, and king. All of this takes work, and it starts with correct design, where we consider how our content will access these categories and build backwards from there to create the assessments and lessons which reflect whether the students accomplished what we desired.

I had a teacher who gave us a prayer journal assignment as a major part of our semester grade. Just because the assignment dealt with spiritual matters, our teacher didn't automatically emphasize spiritual natures. It didn't necessarily prompt us toward awe nor nurture our hunger for the other. Similarly, just because we have students highlight their notes with different colors doesn't mean they're doing something creative. Yet, these are all beginning attempts to target the whole student.

Several years ago, I divided students into groups and assigned them the same passage of Shakespeare's *Much Ado about Nothing.*

In the scene, two characters lob insults back and forth at each other for several pages of the script. The groups were told to "translate" the scene into different American stereotypes. I don't know if I've laughed as hard as I did while listening to students put a "redneck" twist on some of Benedict's lobs at Beatrice. To this day, the students still remember that scene – not just their translations, but Shakespeare's actual words, because they were having to access their rational, relational, and creative dimensions. A larger chunk of their whole person was engaged.

Practically Speaking

- Within each unit, figure out how you're going to target students as rational, moral, relational, spiritual, and creative learners. It doesn't have to be all in one assignment. However, the more of these dimensions you can engage in an assignment, the more likely you'll find that students will demonstrate deeper understanding.
- Don't be afraid to experiment and be open with your students about what you're attempting to do.
- Students will need to be encouraged to see how it's good for them to be assessed in a more whole-person way. They will primarily want to be assessed where they feel most comfortable, and very few students would be comfortable with each of these dimensions.

4. And build lesson plans and behavior management plans with these same commitments.

If we believe that students are rational, relational, moral, spiritual, and creative beings who are intended to speak truth, bear each other's burdens, and engage the world's problems, this must affect our class rules and the sort of lessons we put together.

When you decide what information you intend to impart to your students, how will you target what it means to be an image bearer? If you target only certain aspects in a given lesson (which will most often be the case), you should be mindful of how you plan to target the other dimensions in later lessons. In an overarching curriculum map, you should be able to reflect where you've targeted these different dimensions.

I've found tremendous value by simply asking myself the question when making plans for the week: Do I focus on the creative components alone? How do I access their spiritual dimensions? Have I emphasized their relational nature enough in the plan for the week? Have I given them enough choice? Have I nurtured a process of thinking which intentionally connects ideas? It's possible to get at all five of these attributes in a given lesson, but it's more likely that you'll find yourself looking at larger units and trying to make sure you're encouraging certain emphases.

Also, classroom management isn't just rules, structures, and consequences for violation of them, it's a rhythm of a classroom culture. If our management plan and general rhythm for a day, lesson, or class period only accentuates one of these dimensions, we should expect to see students failing to engage the way we want them to. Students are most likely to be fully engaged if there are rhythms of our classrooms which engage them creatively, relationally, morally, and spiritually – not just rationally.

Practically Speaking

- Look at each unit and identify which student dimensions you're targeting with your lessons and activities.
- In a typical class period or lesson, how much time is spent with you doing most of the talking? If it's a significant majority, you'll likely see the other dimensions of what it means to engage the whole person diminish significantly. Students need to talk – both to their teachers and to each

other. They need to connect what they learn to different experiences – spiritually, morally, creatively.

- Try bringing different media into your classroom to engage students creatively. Regardless of the discipline you teach, there are always opportunities to incorporate art, music, or film and to allow for students to create as well. Look at your routines and rhythms and see where you do this and figure out how you can do it more.

5. We should be at the front of the line in thought-leading advances in addressing different learning styles and needs.

It's embarrassing how often parents must take their children with unique learning needs to the local public school because the Christian school can't provide adequate support for this child's needs. Shouldn't it strike us as odd that the public schools (which don't believe that students have God-given dignity) have dedicated greater programmatic, personnel, and financial resources for *all* students than schools like ours who are philosophically committed to recognizing the image of God in these students?

The cost associated with such programs and personnel commitments is substantial, but the Christian school should make this a top priority of any strategic planning process – not because it allows us to attract more students, but because of our theology.

In lieu of having the resources for such commitments, the Christian school should still take active steps to equip its teachers to enable students to flourish with these different needs.

I had a student who taught me a great deal about this need. If you visited my Bible class to observe him, you would assume he was an above average to excellent student. He asked good questions, gave insightful answers, and his non-verbal cues suggested that he was very interested in class. He tracked with what both I and his peers were saying.

If you evaluated any of his written assessments, you would conclude that he was not connecting at all. Taken at face value, his answers suggested that he had not paid attention to anything; *everything* was wrong.

How could a student seem to "get it" in class then do so poorly on a written assessment? I looked at his grades in his other classes; English, and history were also really low. I asked our learning specialist if this student had any sort of evaluation on file; there was no record of it. Somehow, we had a tragic record of assigning him low grades without thinking twice about what was going on.

After I gave our next assessment, I asked him to talk with me about his test. Before I even looked at his answers, I went through the questions with him and listened to his *spot-on* answers. As he spoke, I made notes to inform what grade I thought he should get. I went back to his written assessment and noticed an enormous gap between the quality of his spoken answers and his written ones. I didn't know what to make of it, but something was getting in the way when he attempted to write his answers down. Even though he knew what he wanted to say, it couldn't make its way onto paper. Our learning specialist helped me figure out what was likely going on, but the students' parents were resistant to getting him tested. But for the rest of the year, he and I talked through his quizzes and tests after each one.

When I talked with my peers, a few were critical.

"That's not treating everyone the same."

"That's not preparing him for college or what he'll have to do in the workforce."

True, I didn't treat everyone the same. Guilty as charged. Grace doesn't treat everyone the same. Also, believing in the unique dignity of individuals will often result in treating them according to their individual needs.

If none of my essential questions asks whether a student can respond to questions with pen and paper, why is it a non-negotiable that students must do this in a Bible class? If it's not a stated goal, shouldn't we allow all sorts of techniques to determine if students know what we want them to know?

This is an example of an overlap between the second and third categories of the Grid. If I believe that the truth we teach students is actually good for our students and that they have profound dignity, we need to be comfortable embracing all sorts of methods to determine whether they really are learning. If it's truly good for them, we should celebrate *however* students can reflect that they know it. If we believe that God created them with profound dignity, we should flex around how they learn. Because Christians have a firmer starting point for celebrating students' dignity, we should do everything we can to access their dignity and long for truth to penetrate their minds and hearts.

Practically Speaking

- If you're a school administrator, reflect deeply on whether or not your school is adequately resourced to walk alongside students who learn in different ways.
- If you're a teacher, it's wise to simultaneously consider both potential learning deficiencies and student preparation when we notice trends where they struggle.
- Be quick to reach out to school resources when you see trends; they may notice things you don't.
    - At times, interventions and accommodations can feel disruptive to teachers. It's healthy to always approach these by asking whether these extra initiatives allow and encourage image bearers to reflect what they've learned? If they do, we should want to see this growth.
    - If they only allow and encourage a different grade rather than learning, it's justified to work with the specialist to find better solutions.
- Invite learning specialists to come to your classroom to see if there are ways you can adjust aspects of your teaching to give more students more success in your classroom.

6. Embrace school programs which increase student capacity to flourish in the various areas of their giftings and utilize the fullness of God's intent for humanity.

I tend to feel most comfortable in larger Christian schools, not just because that's been where I've spent most of my time in Christian schooling. While we need to rethink aspects of the traditional brick-and-mortar model of Christian schooling, I also think it's the larger Christian schools which have an advantage for targeting the image of God and prophet, priest, and king in ways where smaller schools might struggle.

It's rare that I come across a school that doesn't want to grow. Many of them have great reasons, and some desire growth for financial benefits or prestige. Yet, the greatest reason for any growth should be the resources needed to provide more offerings for the members of the community – not just to keep up with what other schools offer, but because of a commitment to recognize our students' full-natures.

Many schools have jumped on the bandwagon of developing STEM programs, and I certainly see the need. But there's a far greater reason to offer these programs than competing with other schools or because of the financial options it generates for students who will pursue these fields in college.

Programs like STEM can target new ways to help students flourish. STEM provides practical application of what's learned in our math and science classes. This very much gets at the office of King. Students need both the theoretical and the applied and tangible. We should also revisit the classes like home economics or shop class, which can be very hands-on ways for students to apply the things they've learned. The same thing to be true for service-learning programs.

Many schools have started to offer robotics programs as an off-shoot of their STEM emphasis. This is a wonderful example of creating programs which allow different students to flourish. I've watched students who would have been marginalized in my own school experience thrive as part of a robotics program. There are students in our schools who will flourish as parts of a robotics team but would never fit with a football team. I've seen a lot of "computer geeks" (I mean that as affectionately as possible) find a home in groups like this. Growing up, these sorts of students never seemed to fit. Yet not only have they found a place to feel connected, their giftings are being brought out, and the whole community benefits as a result. This celebrates their dignity.

Similarly, schools ought to investigate offering other programs which enable students to use their hands, to connect to the world and each other in varied ways. Once the trend of being "college preparatory" became the norm, schools have reduced the sorts of things they offer, but we should return shop class[60] or "home-ec" (or a version of it, maybe something like culinary arts) to our offerings. Why can't a child be successful without attending a four-year college? There are far more ways to enable students to use their gifting than one approach alone.

Practically Speaking

- What are some of the clubs your school could create to better engage students on the fringes?
- Is there a way to add something to a lesson that's specifically intended to grab a student whose passions and strengths are different?
    - Talking about a video game example for math/science – or even to use it as an example of storytelling for reading/literature.
    - Looking at lyrics from a rap song as a way to connect to what you're discussing in class. Why not build a club for poetry, spoken word?

- Where do students who don't seem to "fit" find themselves fitting in your school? Who pursues them? Is there a way to find what their passions are and build something to give them a greater sense of belonging?

7. Work to steward a healthy, theological commitment to being a community of diversity.

Zora Neale Hurston once said, "Nothing God ever made is the same thing to more than one person." This should be one of the primary reasons why Christian schools should be profoundly committed to becoming more diverse.

We live in a time when schools are very concerned about their diversity. It shows up in their admissions literature. School websites reflect pictures intentionally staged to show diverse skin colors. It's even built into many financial aid strategies. But it seems as though many schools run after diversity for the sake of greater diversity, believing that greater diversity will make us more appealing to onlookers. In worst case scenarios, schools "recruit" families of color for the purpose of using students to accomplish pragmatic ends, like winning football championships.

This treats families like mercenaries.

However, schools should run after all forms of diversity for the purpose of knowing God more and knowing more about how He has revealed himself throughout human experiences. Diverse skin colors, neighborhoods, socio-economic status, worship styles, learning styles, gifts and talents, languages, hopes, and longings. All these uniquenesses, brought together will teach us about what it means to live in the kingdom of God. Schools with means should not give financial aid to needy families solely because they want to help those with needs (while, yes, we should be generous). The "haves" need the "have nots" in their lives. They need to hear the voices of those with different experiences; they need to be shaped by those who have different struggles. Otherwise, those with privilege look down on those they help.

I will discuss this far more in Chapter 11, but the school which is committed to God above all else and has a high view of humanity will seek diversity in order to have a deeper and richer view of God and a broader appreciation of what it means to be His children. Otherwise, increased diversity will most likely bring harmful, unexpected factions into a school. Yet, when we seek greater diversity so all members of a community can know more about how God is at work in myriad ways, it strengthens us.

It's easy for us to have a narrow view of God and of what it means to be human if we are never forced to look outside our own experiences. Yet when we allow our lives to be shaped by the different experiences of others, it even broadens our capacity to live as prophet, priest, and king in the world.

On the heels of the events of 2020 and 2021, many private schools scramble to address issues of racial diversity. It has moved to the top of strategic plans; schools have created new policies and administrative positions to address them. "Diversity and Inclusion" show up as key buttons and articles on website homepages. Interestingly, Christian schools seem to be just as interested in keeping up with this cultural push, even though most of us don't embrace the same LGBTQ+ inclusions in that push.

While many schools pursue diversity for diversity's sake, Christian schools should be driven by a theology of difference. A Godly understanding of difference causes us to see how it affords the opportunity to see God and His world more fully. It furthers our capacity to love Him and others. It deepens our appreciation for who He is and better allows us to see our place in the world.

We should think about the ways reckless diversity initiatives or fears of diversity both inhibit our movement toward wholeness. Both extremes cause fragmentation, but a Christian approach models for the world God's original intent and His plan for the restoration of all things.

We should have curricula and programs that provide both mirrors and windows for students. Mirrors allow students to see themselves in the curriculum, so our black children should be able to see some of their experience in library books and in the lessons taught. Windows allow students to see the experiences of others through the curriculum. So, a student can learn to see the perspectives of others. Windows and Mirrors break down the fragmentation of the Fall and bring about the restoration we crave to see in students' lives.

Practically Speaking

- Work toward making your school more welcoming to a more diverse population by considering your curricula and books in your library
    - Do the books provide both windows and mirrors?
    - Does your curriculum allow for multiple perspectives?
- When you talk about diversity, speak first to the need for the whole community to have those different perspectives.
- While building racial diversity may take time, you can work to build a culture which doesn't just tolerate difference, but seeks it out and celebrates uniqueness.

8. Give students more agency in your school.

There are countless studies, articles, and books[61] which suggest that there's a direct link between student choice and passion for learning. The research is so compelling, we might as well say there's "causation." Choice in the classes they take, choice in the books they read. Choice in class projects. Choice in the performances students put on for the community. Jon Eckert says that students need to feel in control and that "giving them options creates this perception - whether it is illusion or reality is irrelevant."[62] What is most relevant is that students have choice.

Good educators commit a great deal of mental horsepower into figuring out what's best for their students. We've thought holistically about curricula and programs. We've considered the best materials, assessments, and instructional techniques. So, we shouldn't entirely abdicate those decisions to the students. As the "experts," we should make such important decisions. But this expertise also means we need to recognize what's most likely going to "stick" with our students.

If you pay even slight attention to studies or theories about best practices, you'll see that differentiation and student agency are important factors toward positive student outcomes. Of course, we want students to do well. We want them to learn, grow, and flourish. Considering all the common grace insights and research out there, we have compelling reasons to give students more choice in the learning process – even if we're mere pragmatists!

Our theology gives us greater reason to pay attention. Far more importantly, the Christian educator recognizes students' profound dignity as image bearers. And because we see their dignity, we look for avenues to harness it.

In healthy organizations and communities, strong leaders don't control others. They empower those they have responsibility over. That's where growth happens. Sure, there's some risk there, but the best leaders trust the people they lead and respect and accentuate others' giftings.

We can think about in terms of a risk/reward proposition. Delegating greater responsibility is riskier (for you, the other person, and the organization), but it has a higher chance of reward for all involved. Similarly, when we choose to take the path of lower risk (lower chaos, lower messiness, greater control), we decrease the potential of reward. In our school context, we minimize the depth and richness of student growth.

God has will; He makes choices. He has control. When He made man, He chose to give man freedom and choice. In no way, did this compromise God's sovereignty. Yet, by granting freedom to man, in a way, it put God at risk[63] – so much so, that it required Him to enter the world and die for it. Certainly, God was never scared of the risk. Maybe the "risk" was worth it to Him. Maybe the risk should be worth it to us.

From the outset of his creation, Adam was instructed by God to make choices. He was told to name the animals. God didn't micro-manage Adam. But He also wasn't abdicating His control by giving this task to Adam. In fact, I can't help thinking that God delighted in watching Adam go through the naming process.

Considering that students bear the image of the infinite, personal, Triune God, they need to be given space to choose. They need to be given areas of responsibility. Dutch Reformers often refer to this as "Sphere Sovereignty" – little kingdoms. Every student needs to be given little spheres to "rule."

If everything is dictated to our students, we ignore what's most likely to bolster their learning. We also minimize the wonder of who they are as image bearers.

Provide more elective courses. Let students teach components of lessons. Give them voice in how they're going to be assessed. Allow them to play a part in deciding the pace and rhythms of classes. Risky business. But when they own aspects of their learning, students will care more about it. I promise.

Practically Speaking:

- Try giving students the choice of seating options – not just their location in your classroom, but the type of seating too. Of course, with that choice comes responsibility, which the child could lose if they can't handle the consequences of the choices they make.
- Consider a mix of assigned readings and options that fit what you're trying to accomplish. The next level of agency

allows them to choose something that's not even one of the options but still fits within parameters you set.

- I've seen some teachers assign different levels of assignments – where certain work can achieve more credit, but that gives the student the choice to determine how much work they're willing to take on.
- Let students "teach" some ideas to their peers. Mix it in as a rhythm of your classroom, and hold the other students accountable for what they learned from their "teacher."
- When introducing a new unit, ask students what they might want to learn about in that unit and tailor some of the lessons to things they said they'd like to learn about.
- Think about "co-curriculars" in this same vein. Give students more ability to shape clubs, and have greater ownership.
- An "entrepreneurship" type of class is naturally geared toward helping students have ideas and see them carried through to fruition.

Why It's Christian

All other systems, whether religious or not seek to make their "gods" in their own image, or to their own likeness. Humans do this, because we can control the outcome. It's normal to shape our ultimate authority to our own liking.

Rather than shaping God in our image, Christians alone declare that we have been shaped in His image. It's such a beautiful doctrine, giving us a profound source of dignity and value while also providing greater understanding of what it means to be human. It gives meaning to our abilities, desires, and interests. It provides both structure for who we are and direction for what we do with our lives.

A Christian anthropology is unique because it ascribes deep significance to individual persons, but it's not because of something we declare about ourselves. It's what God has declared about us.

That recognition confesses God as God; it proclaims that His plan is higher than ours. It recognizes our need for Him in order to find meaning. We also have a clear picture of how we should be, because we both know our original design in Eden, but also because of the Redeemer who came and lived as a man to both show us how we were meant to be and what we one day will be.

ORTHOPATHY

In his 18th century hymn "Come Thou Fount of Every Blessing," Robert Robinson penned "Prone to wander, Lord, I feel it, Prone to leave the God I love." A biblical anthropology requires that we think deeply about what it means to live as image bearers in the offices of prophet, priest, and king. But it also means that we also recognize that all people are deeply affected by sin – both our own sin, and the sinfulness of the world in which we live. We know who we are, yet we also know that we so often go in a different direction. The prophet Isaiah's image is perfect: "All we like sheep have gone astray. Each of us has turned to our own way" (53:6). However, we must be mindful of who we are and teach toward that, creating space to lament when teachers and students alike don't live according to our design.

I'm familiar with the simple reminder for teachers: "Hook, Book, Took." Something has to draw in the student – to hook them in. Like a well introduced sermon, lessons need to draw initial connections. Often, educators refer to this as an anticipatory set. Next, we provide the content: what's in the "book." Then, we consider what students can apply from the lesson: what the student "took."

It's very similar to how my former pastor Richie Sessions concluded each sermon in application. He'd provide a couple main points from the text, then his last point would always be the question, "so what?" I loved the rhythm. I also appreciated that

Richie made sure we didn't just learn some biblical truths but that we were challenged to consider how those truths mattered to our lives. By asking "so what?" Richie urged us to think what difference God's Word makes in our lives.

Similarly, we teach to our students' full natures because we seek lasting change. We want them to be shaped by the content of our classes, and they are most likely to be moved when we access all that they are. Because we believe their natures and calling say something about how they are to live their lives, our teaching must be seasoned with application, where we challenge them to live considering the truths we teach, especially since we are prone to wander, calling them to live how they were always designed to be – which has always been in a state of needing Jesus.

7

TRY? THERE IS NO TRY; ONLY GRACE.

Grid Question 4: Are we cultivating a culture of grace-prompted Obedience?

Ethics. Morality. Behavior. So, we're talking about rules. Right?

Well …

Despite my apprehension toward behavior modification, it's foolish to ignore the ethical dimensions of Christian schooling. Yes, there's a potential conflict here: how do we uphold the ethical commitments of Christian education while not stumbling into militarized moralism? Of course, we must address behavior because actions reflect what's produced in our schools. If we target students' desires, beliefs, and values, we must realize that their behaviors are good indicators of whether it's sinking in. Thankfully, the gospel provides a blueprint.

The step from Epistemology and Anthropology to Ethics is fairly simple. When we start with Metaphysics, we ask the question, "What's ultimately out there?" From there, we ask "How do we know?" and "Who am I the knower?" The next question flows right from it: "How should we live with this knowledge?" This is what all ethical questions seek – to determine how we're supposed to live considering fundamental beliefs.

It's helpful to understand the similarities between the way our metaphysical views inform our epistemology and anthropology and how our views about knowledge and humanity radically influence our ethical views. If we claim dependence for knowledge, whatever we depend on will ultimately establish our standard for interacting with others. If we believe we are independent, we look to something we can control: what culture defines, some form of data, or personal preference. If we have a temporary view of mankind and minimize his intrinsic value, it will also affect the standards by which we treat others.

Like many teachers, I have a fondness for the movie, *Dead Poets' Society* (1989), wishing I could inspire students the way Mr. Keating does. Despite the beauty of the film and Robin Williams' genius, it's unfortunate that the overall messages of the film are so discouraging. For that reason, I've been more prone to show clips from *The Emperor's Club* (2002) to students. In ways, it's a poor-man's *Dead Poets' Society*, achieving a similar feel. Yet I typically don't arrive at the closing credits with the same frustration I get from *Dead Poets' Society.*

In one of the climatic scenes of *The Emperor's Club*, Mr. Hundert (played by Kevin Kline) confronts the pragmatic depravity of one of his (now adult) former students and responds, "I failed you as a teacher." Elsewhere in the film, Mr. Hundert clearly articulates that education is not a cognitive exercise alone; it's an ethical one as well. I'm always moved by this scene, because I'm reminded how the task isn't merely shaping minds alone but the sorts of persons they become.

Socrates believed that one of the primary goals of education was to ensure that free people become good persons; the goal of their education was to enable them to have "the good life" which he couldn't help but see as a life of virtue. Most educational models hope students will graduate with more than knowledge alone, but moral or ethical excellence as well. However, if the basis for the ethical standard is flawed, it will produce flawed persons. We shouldn't be surprised, because the reality of our "flawedness" is something the gospel hinges upon. All the more reason to have a clear answer to the question, What is our standard for right and wrong behavior?

ORTHODOXY

When we consider historical attempts at behavioral standards, we can certainly glean healthy principles. As far back as records go, civilizations have tried to establish rules and standards for right behavior. Every culture, philosopher, or employee manual has tried to establish a way people are supposed to live together, and it animates school conversations every day.

Answering the Question

Most every Ancient and Medieval moral standard stood upon a belief in transcendence. Plato and Aristotle argued that there were primary virtues to be sought above all others: courage, justice, prudence, and temperance. These four virtues were not created by humans; they come from the spiritual world. Many of these philosophers hoped to construct a system which would guide men toward *eudaimonia*, the good life, which was shaped by a life of virtue.

This is the basis for Aristotle's Golden Mean,[64] a great tool to pursue right behavior. To him, virtue is always the middle point between two vices – a vice of deficiency and a vice of excess. For example, courage (the virtue) is the mean between cowardice (a vice of deficiency) and reckless pride (a vice of excess). We should consider our own propensities toward either of the two vices and move in the other direction. Or, we should consider which vice is more destructive to society and err in the other direction.

Similarly, Medieval philosophy also assumed transcendence. Church thinkers like Aquinas argued for a natural law which binds everyone's conscience. In this view, men are naturally rational beings who should conform to our rational nature which knows good and evil, because God has decreed them to be so. Because God defines goodness and evil, we inherently know these things in our rational nature.

Modern attempts to provide moral standards have tried to provide moral regulations without transcendent or absolute boundaries. I remember auditing a philosophy class at a state university where the primary topic was human ethics. After receiving the syllabus, I noticed that none of our readings came from any pre-Enlightenment thinkers. When I asked the professor why we weren't considering ancient writers like Aristotle, she responded curtly, "because they start from a position of absolutes." Seemingly, there was no room in her framework for considering a standard for goodness or evil.

Francis Schaeffer said that this leaves modern thinkers with no footing for deep conversation about morality. Without clear boundaries, modern thinkers have no sound basis from which to build an argument. They also have no clear direction to guide the trajectory of the argument. As a result, Schaeffer argues that modern ethicists know neither where they came from nor where they are going.

Throughout history, people have promoted various other standards, but most of them have failed because they didn't stand upon something which could never change or err. As a result, many societies haven't provided adequate contexts for determining how people should live. More critically, all these models assume people can solve our ethical dilemma. We feel a sort of moral obligation, yet know that somehow our behavior is unacceptable. All models outside Christianity put the burden on people and what we need to do in order to achieve a level of ethical appropriateness. There is no grace in these models.

A Biblical Answer

Much of my failure to understand the grammar of the gospel stems from the way I was taught (by teachers in both formal and informal roles). I regularly heard that we aren't saved by works, so my teachers weren't consciously leading me astray. Their problem was that they didn't understand the urgency of keeping me from myself and my sinful works-based tendencies.

In *The Disciplines of Grace,* Jerry Bridges suggests that our post-Fall default setting (what we always revert to) is believing we can do enough to become good. It's up to us to meet God's expectations. James Montgomery Boice routinely said that the doctrine of justification by grace is offensive to this default setting. While, what we most need is grace, we often war against it. We live as though we don't need it.

One of my favorite theologians, Bono, gave an interview with Michka Assayas in *World Magazine* quite a few years ago where he contrasted karma and grace, and the content of this conversation is very similar to the lyrics of U2's song "Grace." In the interview, Bono says karma is at the center of all non-Christian religions. Even secular worldviews believe in a form of karma.

Whether religious or not, we assume that good things should happen to good people. Muslims expect to go to paradise if their good works outweigh their bad works. Similarly, most people expect to get promoted in the workplace because of their production. This is typically how the world works. It's all about merit. Yet, Bono argues that if karma is true, we're all in big trouble. Because, we can never do enough things to have good things come our way. This is especially true if we are held responsible for our thoughts, because we all know we have quite condemning thoughts. Yet we continue to think we can *do* enough.

Scripture promotes a radically different approach to ethics. It demands a standard we can't possibly meet. Throughout the Old and New Testaments, we read that God expects us to be perfect. It's not a suggestion, either; it's a command. Not good; Perfect! Even, Jesus reminds us in the Sermon on the Mount that we are to be like God. It's not good news.

In the same way the Bible defines what goodness is, it also defines wrong behavior. Sin. It's a violation against God's nature. In his *Confessions,* Augustine interestingly defines sin as trying to get good things in bad ways. Even our attempts to obtain good things are tainted in countless ways.

The Westminster catechism says that sin is "any want of conformity unto or transgression of the law of God."[65] In other words, sin is either directly violating God's law or failing to meet it. This becomes far more staggering when we consider that the Greatest Commandment requires that we love God with all of our mind, body, and strength. Moment by moment, we fail to meet what this command expects of us, and this is not a lesser rule – but the *Greatest* Commandment! It's serious.

Others have explained this by saying that we struggle with sins of omission and commission. I find it especially interesting that we tend to spend more time talking about sins of commission when Jesus spent more time talking about sins of omission. That seems to be much of the lesson of the Sermon on the Mount.

This is the springboard for the gospel. We need God. That's why Jesus came. We cannot meet God's standard; we cannot fix our problem. Yet Jesus came to bear what we rightly deserve and in the place of what we deserve. Instead, God gave us His covenantal grace. When we look at the story of Scripture, we notice that Grace always precedes law. We see it in the creation story. We see this in the flood account and in the calling of Abram.

The context of the Ten Commandments is especially revealing of this relationship between grace and law. This condensed list of God's moral law shows up in two places – Exodus 20 and Deuteronomy 5. In both occurrences, we see a preamble or introduction to the commandments which essentially says, "I'm God, and I've saved you." This comes before the list of commandments. In essence, it tells us that God has already done His work on behalf of His people. Obedience to His law, then, becomes a response to God's action.

However, we often view the Ten Commandments as though the statement of salvation appears at the end of the commands, as though God says, "if you keep these laws, I'll show you favor." This is Judeo-Christian karma. Even though we know we are not saved by works and that God's laws come to us within a context of His pursuing grace, we still revert to this feeling that we must earn His favor. We believe we can control our lives on some level by being good. Yet, the gospel says we can never do enough good for good to come our way. That's why Jesus came.

Christian educators recognize that outward obedience doesn't make us good. Our position as teachers doesn't put us in the right. Our students' conformity to school policies doesn't make them good kids. On the other hand, our failure to comply doesn't make us any worse. Our problem is sin; it's severe. Christ alone makes us right. Yet, we still find it easy to focus on externals. It's difficult not to focus primarily on that behavior, because it's seen. If we believe the gospel, we have to consider that the standard God set is far beyond what we can meet, and that's precisely what it would take for us to become "good."

We are called to educate the entire person and recognize that, being made in the image of God, we and our students are moral agents. Therefore, we must understand how ethical questions are always before us, even in the classroom. While we typically focus primarily on the content learned, we are ultimately concerned with their wills – we want students whose desires are in line with truth – *not just their answers.*

We want their loves to be what they should be. When we start talking about students' desires, we begin to get at their wills, and this forces us to realize that our educational task is an ethical one. We want the desires and intentions behind their efforts to be right. As a result, we must resist the tendency to engage in tasks which accomplish little more than behavior modification. Gospel-faithfulness requires that we consider students' hearts, recognizing that their wills are always engaged. This is why it's vital that we routinely ask, Are we cultivating a culture of grace-prompted Obedience?

ORTHOPRAXY

1. Be very careful how you define "goodness" in your school.

In my early stages of building a high school student leadership program, I relied heavily on teacher recommendations to decide which students to pursue, especially with rising ninth graders. I didn't know these students; I needed the perspective of middle school teachers. I asked them to recommend a dozen or so students who demonstrated leadership potential. After a couple of years, I realized that I either wasn't asking the right questions or wasn't properly defining terms. Maybe both were true.

Almost all the recommendations were of students with high GPA's and who never got in trouble. They were like clones of me when I was in school! Yet, very few of these students were leaders; they couldn't look over their shoulders and see others following them. Very few had the ability to shape the culture of the school, which is what I was hoping for, because I wanted *leaders.*

I wasn't surprised. This is often how we classify "good kids." These are the sorts of students who keep their shirts tucked in, who turn their work in on time, and who know the right answers. I'm not quite sure how these are traits of leadership, but I can understand how teachers felt that these were the sorts of students we wanted to represent the school.

This is expected in most schools. Don't we want the "most presentable students" in the positions of recognition? It makes sense. But should it in a school committed to the gospel? Christian teachers don't intend to make Christianity fundamentally about rules, rigidity, and conformity. Yet in our fallen tendency to reduce Christianity to performance, we need to do a substantially better job of preventing students from thinking that outward goodness is what defines Christianity.

When the Rich Young Ruler calls Jesus, "Good Teacher" in Mark 10, Jesus challenges the man to understand that the gospel upends our understanding of what goodness is and that this misunderstanding often keeps us miles away from experiencing God as we ought. God is good. We are not; that's why we need Jesus. Far too often, students leave our schools having categories of good and bad students or good and bad Christians. As a result, many end up wounded or having warped ideas about the gospel. The goal of our schools is not to produce good students, it's to point students to Jesus through the program and culture of the school.

Take a hard look at what you might be doing to allow people to think you're categorizing students as good or bad. Strongly consider repurposing those areas with the goal of pointing students (and your peers) toward Jesus, rather than toward these categories.

Also, work tirelessly to prevent grades from being seen in ethical categories. Our grades should reflect mastery of skills and content – not behavior. We need to find other ways for reporting behaviors than factoring them into grades. When we confuse the two, it can easily cause students and parents to equate goodness with content mastery. They're not even in the same ballpark.

Practically Speaking

- Take a hard look at how you define "good" in your school and classrooms. Is it primarily external? Does it include desire to change, habits of repentance, recognition of need for Jesus?
- Pay attention to what you praise in students. Does your practice cause students to feel pressure to conform to a standard many of them may not feel they can meet?
- When you establish your classroom expectations at the beginning of the year, does your list focus only on externals?
    - If/When you talk about this list, make sure to follow it up with a clear statement of the gospel – that following this list doesn't make someone good, and not following it doesn't make someone bad. It exists to promote a learning culture.

2. Do everything you can to prevent a culture of blind conformity.

My ten-year high school reunion was painful for me. Many of my former classmates were hurting. Many have walked away from the church and resent their Christian school experience. Over the weekend event, I heard many jokes about "playing the game" at school, and how freeing it was to get outside of that environment.

One of my female classmates was particularly bitter. She had lived with the consequences of some poor decisions and now holds her upbringing responsible. When we talked about her anger toward our alma mater, I asked what she would have me do, considering I was then teaching there. She looked at me before walking away and said, "Love the bad kids first." I've never forgotten her words.

It's very easy to give accolades to the students who do things well. While we should celebrate excellence, we have to recognize the many eyes watching what we're doing and determine that the best way for them to get the same recognition is to be like the students who seem to do everything right.

There are several problems with this. Maybe the main reason certain students perform well is primarily a genetic one. For them, learning comes easy. Focusing in class is not a struggle. They may have a mild or compliant disposition. But, what about the students who don't have those same advantages? What about those who consciously struggle in their efforts, because they truly *want* to do right? Shouldn't we actually reward those students more?

It's also problematic to have a culture which nurtures conformity, because it either leads to self-righteousness on the part of those who think they're meeting the standard, prompts anxiety on the part of those who are red-lining to try to keep up, or leads to anger and despair on the part of those who realize they can't meet the ideal before them. Eventually, they adopt the persona of being the failure, the rebel, or the one who nobody notices.

What would happen if we truly "loved the bad kids first?" Now, I don't think my former classmate was creating moral categories; she was just referencing those who are not as easy to love. These are precisely the sort of people Jesus pursued: the woman at the Samaritan well, Zacchaeus, lepers, the deaf and blind, prostitutes, and the uneducated fishermen who made up his inner-circle. It must have liberated many onlookers to see this great Teacher seek the invalids – people who had no social capitol.

I have to honestly consider whether or not I and my colleagues have pursued the outsiders. We may talk like it, but what would the true outsiders say? Would they say their school has done anything to make them feel any less disenfranchised? Has our student culture been that much different from what's seen in any other school in America?

Plus, we amplify the high expectations which exist at every other high performing school by adding the "Jesus" dimension. Students are supposed to meet high standards *and* be good Christians, too. This is a heavy burden to put on students – a lofty goal to meet which likely puts an unbearable amount of pressure on developing minds and hearts.

Jesus said that He came to set us free. Yet many Christian school graduates speak about their experiences with shackling language. We should allow our alumni to speak transparently toward their own experiences so we can determine if we're encouraging conformity or nurturing transformation. If the former is true, we need to take a hard look at and change our school ethos, so students are set free in our schools.

Practically Speaking:

- Reconsider tangible awards that may further a works-righteousness model of goodness.
- Look at the sorts of alumni and other people you point your students toward. Do you ever recognize that it's not reasonable for every student to attain those standards?
- Always be mindful that your school's definition of success doesn't push students toward being Older Brothers.

3. Structure your classroom and school programs around a "grace proceeds law" model.

What does a student have to do to earn your favor? How do you demonstrate to them that you are overwhelmingly on their side and that you are pursuing them with love? Do students know that you are rooting for them to succeed? Do students know that they can blow it (either academically or behaviorally) in your classroom and that you are still there to teach, support, and encourage them?

This point is very similar to the previous two. That's intentional, because it's overwhelmingly critical that we go out of our way to embrace the grammar of the gospel, rather than our default moralism. Just as God's laws are encased in His covenantal love, our students need to see that we are more interested in our commitment to them than in their obedience to us. It's good for students to be called to obedience, but it's far more important for students to see our unmerited favor than our expectations. In fact, they're more likely to embrace our expectations if they see our favor.

I use "embrace" intentionally. While we can so often become pragmatists who focus on the immediacy of what's before us, we all know that life-long change is far more desirable than instantaneous obedience. Ethical change is about a change of the will – not merely an action. Like the Older Brother, they may obey but resent doing it. That's not at all what we want. Sure, it may make for a quieter classroom, but these very same students may look back on their schools years later and be turned off toward everything about Christian education.

Do you want a quiet classroom or changed lives? You may ask, "Noah, can't I have both?" Maybe you can have both. But you really need to ask yourself this question, because it will help us keep the main thing the main thing. If we are most concerned about our students' life-long heart change, we'll begin to become more about grace than the law. The expectations and rules will become secondary, and ultimately that's the way it should always be.

Practically Speaking:

- It should always be said of you that you're looking to praise and show affection to students rather than being the one "out to get" them.
- Often remind them that it's not their obedience to you that causes you to care for them, it's because they are your students.
- When having to hold them responsible for violation of your expectations, they need to also hear "this doesn't change your standing with me."

4. Design all classroom procedures and school programs to be "pro-life."

Still pursuing the same point …
In *Engaging God's World*, Cornelius Plantinga says,

> "What God carved at Sinai was a recipe for freedom … sin traps people and makes them wilt; godly obedience liberates people and helps them flourish. The 10 Commandments are guides for a free and flourishing life. They say, 'do this and you will thrive.' Or else, they say, 'Don't do this: it'll kill you.' God's commandments are all pro-life."[66]

God has never given an arbitrary law. His laws show us who He is and restore us and point us toward the good life – a flourishing, whole life.

We have to establish classroom expectations to provide structure and boundaries necessary for a learning environment. Do we choose these expectations and structures around what's easiest for teachers or meets personal preference? Or, do we choose them because of a desire to help students thrive?

If we ask whether our expectations point students toward flourishing and whole lives, we may arrive at the very same structures we already have in place. But the language we use when introducing them might change. Or we might find that these rules don't enliven students, but restrict them.

If students will ever embrace rules and expectations, they need to trust the one who establishes those rules. This happens when students know we are unapologetically committed to them. They also need to see how those rules are good for them – how these expectations enable them to live life to the fullest.

Help students learn to see how your classroom rules aren't just good for *you*, but good for *them*. Bring them into the conversation where they see the benefit of the structures and expectations you put in place. Are your consequences punitive? Or, can you discuss them in a way which helps students see them as pro-life?

Practically Speaking:

- We need to ask ourselves (or let a peer we trust do it) how our rules and expectations actually help students flourish.
- When we tell students what our rules are, they should never see them as arbitrary. It's essential that we walk them toward seeing why these expectations are "pro-life."

5. Uphold[67] absolute standards while pursuing relationships and restoration.

With increased relativism and cries for independence, sports seem to be one of the last holdouts for firm standards. In sports, the out-of-bounds line is the out-of-bounds line; there's really no argument. Instant replay may prompt a debate about whether an athlete stepped out of bounds, but there is no debate that, if he is out of bounds, he's out of bounds.

If a basketball player wants to dribble a basketball five feet outside the baseline, she is welcome to do that. But she is no longer in the game. It's not debatable. While she may argue otherwise, she's most free as a basketball player when she plays inside the boundaries of the court, not according to her own terms.

Using the same analogy, I've also watched a soccer game in a driving blizzard, and because the players weren't absolutely convinced where the sidelines were, they were extra cautious to go nowhere in the vicinity of where they thought the lines might be. Not knowing the location of the lines inhibited their freedom and reduced their field of play.

It's overwhelmingly necessary and freeing for students to have absolute clarity about our boundaries. It only harms them when we aren't consistent with our rules. If we have dress codes, teachers need to hold students to the standards with extreme consistency. If our rules are all pro-life, we have even greater reason for being serious about our boundaries and rules. It doesn't benefit students when they see leniency more often than follow-through when it comes to upholding expectations.

Some of you may ask (or you've had parents throw this in your face): "what about grace?" That's a misunderstanding of grace. Grace doesn't change rules. Mercy doesn't either. Both of these deal with consequences. When we talk about grace and mercy, we enter into inconsistent interactions. We may be inconsistent in our handing out of consequences because of our desire to show grace or mercy, but we cannot be inconsistent in upholding the boundaries and expectations of the school or classroom.

When students overstep boundaries and expectations, our discipline must never be punitive in nature. It needs to be restorative. The Bible tells us that God disciplines those whom He loves to bring us back into relationship with Him. In a similar way, our love for our students should direct our charge to hold them accountable and the consequences that we choose in each situation.

Practically Speaking

- Where are you inconsistent when it comes to enforcing your school's or your own class's rules? Make a plan for improving your consistency.
- What are some boundaries that tend to exasperate students? Do they need to be there? If so, talk with them about their frustrations. Help them understand why the rules are what they are.
- What are some boundaries that could help your students flourish more? Are there steps you could take to introduce this boundary in a way so it's not merely another one added to the list, but there to help them?

6. Nurture gratitude wherever possible.

In his book *Educating for Life*, Nicholas Wolterstorff says that gratitude and lament are intrinsic ways of responding to experience and living in the world. He goes on to say, "The fundamental response on our part to God's good gifts is gratitude, grounding even faith itself. Gratitude lies at the foundation of Christian existence. From this, everything flows. If the Christian school is to educate for Christian life, it must educate for gratitude."[68] G.K. Chesterton also says that gratitude is the greatest of all Christian virtues. Wolterstorff goes on to say, "Gratitude [is] basic. Obedience [is] an act of gratitude rather than, the other way around, gratitude being an act of obedience."[69]

I want my kids to say "thank you" whenever they receive something; it's what I require of them now. I hope to shape them, so they begin to automatically and habitually respond in gratitude – not because it's polite, but because it's a declaration of what they realize is done to and for them.

People who believe the gospel realize how little they deserve. They realize that they deserve God's righteous judgment, and little else. As a result, there's little room for entitlement or fascination with rights or fairness. In a gospel-saturated perspective, anything good we receive is not deserved, and it should make us very thankful. This same gratitude should be at the heart of our desires to do what God calls us to. Above other virtues, gratitude might be at the top of the list for what we want to see in our "portrait of a graduate."

Considering this, one of the best ways to determine whether our school communities are shaped by the gospel is to study how grateful our communities are. How thankful are our teachers? Students? Parents? If it's hard to see, it's likely safe to say that we might not be as close to the gospel as we'd like to believe. Entitlement and the gospel are in stark contrast.

As is the case with any other teaching we do, students are most likely to develop practices of gratitude if they see it modeled by their teachers. Do students see teachers willing to flex, submitting to what their supervisors require of them, covering for co-workers without hesitation, or staying late because a student needs extra help? My willingness or unwillingness to do any of those things is always directly linked to how thankful I am. When students see teachers motivated by thankfulness, it models for them how they should live as well.

Practically Speaking

- What would it look like to put something about gratitude in your mission or portrait of a graduate?
- Thank students for their answers; thank them for their efforts; thank them for being in your life.
- Whenever you can, take opportunities to thank God for all of His goodness.
- Tell your own children (or students you're exceptionally close to) to thank their teachers after each class and maybe it will trickle over into the other students.

7. Love God; love others

I've already called attention to Jesus's teaching about the Greatest Commandment. He says the entire Law can be summarized in saying that we are to love God and love others. Our failures are directly linked to our inability or unwillingness to love God and others as we ought.

Any expectation we put before students needs to be filtered through questioning how it will help students love God and/or others more. Does your school have a dress code? What's the purpose of it? Have you thought about the ways student uniforms further students' abilities to love God and others?

Uniforms and dress codes should never be moral issues in and of themselves. How a student responds to a dress code, though, brings about moral issues. Yet, we need to make sure that moral expectations in front of students have been held up to the Greatest Commandment. For, our goal should always be to love God more, and the goal of our expectations should also aim at loving Him more as well. Behavioral expectations, rules, or boundaries which do not aim at helping people love God and others more will likely cause them to love God less.

Moving in this direction may not require a total upheaval of your expectations. But sit with them and consider whether they can point students toward loving God and others more. It might mean that the language you use to surround or explain your rules is the only thing that needs to change. If we don't do this, though, we'll likely continue to encourage conformity, rather than transformation.

We should also reflect on what we mean by Love. Loving my wife isn't just doing what she tells me to or staying married to her. It also doesn't mean that I associate with her. Similarly, loving God doesn't merely mean doing what we're supposed to or identifying with Christian culture. While all of these are good, they don't presuppose love. I could despise my wife or God internally and externally do *what I'm supposed to.* Christian conformity or moralism for the purpose of having a better life isn't love; it's karma.

Loving my wife means that I want to be with her, to be around her, to have my heart made full because of her in my life. It means wanting to see her more wonderful tomorrow than I do today. Similarly, loving God or others means that our hearts are bent toward them. We care more about them than ourselves. We want to make much of them.

Practically Speaking

- Consider your expectations and ask, do these help students (and yourself) love God and/or others more?

   - If the answer is "yes," double down on that and help students understand how that expectation accomplishes this.
   - If the answer is "no," obviously you should probably get rid of it.
   - If the answer is "I'm not sure," you might want to suspend that rule while you explore it with a peer you've invited to look at it with you.
- At all times, talk about expectations, goals, and objectives – especially when a student asks "why are we doing this" – in a context of how it helps us love God and others more. Students need to understand how our actions are not mere actions, but they fit within our relationship to God and to others around us.

Why It's Christian

When the entirety of the world runs on transactions, an ethic driven by grace at its core is wildly unique. It's natural to want tidiness and conformity; that's what most of "traditional" school models look like. Rules. Order. Structure. That's the model for success.

We're not after success – at least not as the world defines it. Of course, we may find it along the way, but that's not what we're aiming for. While it's rather normal for independent schools to say that their goal or vision is to become the best private or Christian school in the city or nation, I admire schools like Priory Catholic all boys school in St. Louis which simply proclaims that they want to graduate godly young men. I imagine that many of Priory's graduates have seen substantial "success." But that's not what the school is after.

Nor should our schools. We should "Seek first His Kingdom," and then all of these things are added unto us. God's Kingdom is a Kingdom of grace. It's a Kingdom of changed people; that's what we're after. So, our ethical standard must be driven by something far different.

Yes, we have a standard that's reliable and doesn't shift with the preferences of the day. That in itself is unique. But, what's even more unique about grace-prompted obedience is that it's not driven by what the teacher or student gets out of it.

No, a Christian ethic is driven by the glory of Christ.

ORTHOPATHY

Many years ago, the final seconds of a college football game ticked away with my favorite team missing a game-winning field goal against a higher ranked and deeply despised rival. I remember thinking, "if I had only obeyed my mom this morning!"

Maybe you haven't gone so far as to think that the outcome of a football game depends on you, but a lot of people insist on wearing *lucky* jerseys for games (or other superstitious traditions). Where does this line of thinking come from – that somehow a person wearing a certain shirt several hundred miles away can alter the outcome of a game??!!

Yeah, but that's foolish superstition. It's not Christian.

Well ...

Have you ever blamed a bad day on missing your devotions? Starting the day in prayer, meditation, and reading God's Word can calibrate our approach to our day. But what people mean when they blame their day on a missed quiet-time is often driven by a transactional view of God. I didn't do what I was supposed to do, therefore, God didn't show as much favor today.

Transactions – this for that. Karma. It's hard to avoid this thinking, because nearly all our interactions are driven by transactions. It's almost natural to think of God in a transactional way which eventually trickles into the cultures of our schools and classrooms.

Students work hard and get correct answers; we give them good grades. Students do what they're supposed to do; we show them favor. Students break the rules; they face consequences. While there is absolutely nothing wrong with logical, rational processes and laying out expectations before students, our schools need to seek transformations above transactions. We can't be pro-gospel while driven by transactions.

At every turn we need to consider whether we're seeking transformation, rather than transactions. This is at the very center of the story of the Prodigal Son. The Older Brother missed it, because all along he was thinking transactionally. As a result, he was a cynical and entitled son. It's painful to see the dumpster fire of the younger brother's choices, but we also see eventual transformation. We want to see lives changed. It's what we want to see in any good story.

If students graduate with little more than a bunch of transactions, how are we any different than our non-Christian counterparts? Hearts aren't changed by mission statements, curriculum, or great lesson planning. They're changed through relationships seasoned by grace, gratitude, repentance, forgiveness, and hope. And that's where transformation happens.

Micah 6 is one of my favorite passages describing how relationships properly contextualize Christian ethics and behavior. Longtime pastor James Montgomery Boice said that the fundamental question all people ask in various roundabout ways is, "How do I become right?" How do we become whole? At peace? Enough? Acceptable? The prophet Micah asks the same question, "With what shall I come before the Lord, and bow myself before God on high? Shall I come before him with burnt offerings?" (6:6) His question follows God's indictment against Israel's rebellion. In response, Micah asks what God requires from him personally. Is there *anything* Micah can do?

As Micah processes his own dilemma, he asks whether God would be satisfied with vast numbers of sacrifices: Bulls? Thousands of Rams? Oil? His own son? While extreme suggestions, they demonstrate Micah's understanding of the gravity of his situation. He's not right with God and deeply wants to know what God would have him do.

All people long to know the answer. It's behind the world's countless religions; it also supports the $10 Billion secular self-help industry. This question keeps books on best-seller lists and drives the popularity of life coaches' blogs and social media feeds – all because people know we *aren't* right. We aren't whole.

If God were a transactional God, His answer might sound something like "The more sacrifices you make, the more plentiful your life shall be." Or, to put it in modern language, "the better person you are, the happier I'll be with you." Follow the program. Get out of it what you put into it. Try harder. Do more. Be better. Just do it! The gods will be satisfied.

Dr. Seuss once said, "Children want the same things we want. To laugh, to be challenged, to be entertained, and delighted." Similarly, St. Augustine said all people roughly aim at the same things, but just go about it differently. In a way, all schools seek the same things, too. They want students to grow, to learn, to be prepared for the awaiting world. But saying we're all after many of the same things doesn't mean there aren't significant differences.

There's nothing neutral about education because all programs have specific ends in mind. However, only a God-centered mission is truly life-giving for students because we either labor to increase our own kingdoms or God's. The former nurtures selfishness, discouragement, or anxiety, while the latter enables a person to flourish because it seeks restoration to God's original intent which drives God's answer to Micah's question: "He has shown you, O mortal, what is good. And what does the Lord require of you? To act justly, and to love mercy, and to walk humbly with your God." (6:8)

While Micah's question seeks to detail the *program* he must keep, God's answer describes the sort of *person* He wants Micah to be. God is not as interested in our performance as He is in the condition of our hearts. (Psalm 51:16-17) So, He outlines for the prophet what He wants. Surprisingly, it's not a system to follow.

Parents and teachers alike want our children and students to be good, and we work to point them in the right direction. We explore which program will most likely produce our desired results. This is part of what's behind school choice. However, "goodness" apart from the gospel leads to either discouragement or self-righteousness. What God describes in Micah 6:8 drives us to Himself that we "may have life and have it abundantly." (John 10:10)

God loves **justice**, and so must we. His people should pursue what is right and fight against injustice when we see it, and the Bible gives clear guidance for what this looks like. The boundaries God establishes for us show how life works best. They're not arbitrary or confining rules, set in place by a transactional God. Acting justly helps us to taste "the good life." It's how we flourish in our relationships. It's the first aspect of what God tells Micah He desires.

It's also good for us to love **mercy**, which seems to be at odds with justice. Justice and mercy don't fit together, because justice primarily means giving people what they deserve. Mercy often means *not* giving people what they deserve. When God says that it's good for us to act justly and love mercy, He calls us to a life of tension.

Part of the reason we should love mercy is that we don't act justly; therefore, we need mercy. That's humbling. We don't do what we ought, and if God's justice was demonstrated toward us, we would reap the consequences of our sin. Of course, the reason God can show us mercy while not compromising His justice is that the full measure of His justice was met by Christ's sacrifice on our behalf. The only way we can be for both justice and mercy at the same time is by embracing Jesus and His gospel.

Consequently, loving mercy means that we love the gospel because we need it. We love to receive forgiveness and to show it.

Certainly, everyone wants to receive forgiveness and mercy. But, lovers of mercy also delight in seeing it shown to others, especially to those who don't "deserve" it, for that's precisely what mercy is.

God also prescribes a goodness which welcomes us to **walk humbly** with Him. Spiritual and secular self-help programs keep God at a distance and minimize both His supremacy and the weight of the problem. They're "give and take" transactional arrangements. Gospel believers realize that we can't ever do enough for this arrangement to work in our favor. We aren't right, and we know it. That's why we need God. We need His mercy and His grace.

That's why it's so very beautiful to consider that God calls us to act justly, to love mercy, and to walk humbly with Him. He wants us to love what He loves and to be with Him. The image of walking with God is life-giving. It's safe, secure, personal, and familial. God welcomes us into His presence - not once, but in regular nearness.

From the outset of the Creation story, we see that God walked "during the cool of the day" in the garden He made. (Genesis 3:8) We could assume that Adam and Eve had the privilege of participating in this walk, for the language of Genesis suggests that this was a regular occurrence. So, the notion of walking with God generates restorative images – *reCreational* walks – back to the way we were always supposed to be. Rather than calling us to performance, God calls us into a transforming, relational walk. A pro-life walk. A life-giving walk. A walk where we're reminded of how good it is to need Jesus.

The moment we forget our need, our ethics become twisted by performance. We want our students' desires for what is true, good, and beautiful to flow from a rich need for Jesus. Yes, we want them to do what's right and make good choices, but of far greater concern, we want our students' hearts to be bent toward what's better – not because it makes them better, but because Jesus is better. Rather than driven by a longing for merit or sufficiency, we should be motivated by a longing and need for Jesus.

8

ECHOES OF EDENISTIC EDUCATION

Grid Question 5: Are we pursuing, celebrating, and resting in God's original intent?

For quite a while, I've imagined that we are still surrounded by reverberations of the creative shock and harmonious joy described in Genesis 1 and 2. So, when I heard of Jerram Barrs' book on literature and art, *Echoes of Eden*, I was compelled to read it. Having savored Jerram's book, I couldn't help but audit one of his seminary courses on George Herbert, John Donne, Gerard Manley Hopkins, and T.S. Eliot. It was life-giving.

Jerram's class was an embodiment of his book's case for literature and the arts. While we didn't talk much about the Garden of Eden, we talked about poetry in a way which more fully enabled us to view all life through the lens of Paradise. This is the resounding theme of Jerram's book – beauty returns us to the Garden, because it's what we were originally made for. Beauty, rest, and recreation are *Re-Creational.*[70] In his book, Barrs goes on to say, "we will find ourselves longing to make known the beauty of life as it once was in Paradise, the tragedy of its present marring, and the hope of our final redemption."

After I'd been teaching for five or six years, I wrote an article for an upstart academic journal entitled *Fiat Lux as* I was becoming enthralled with the Garden of Eden, wondering what life would be like had sin never entered the world. Ever since, I've been fascinated that we have a clear picture of how things once were and of how all things will be when Jesus makes all things new. (Revelation 21:5) Not only does the discipline of asking these questions detail a past and future, but it also gives a model of how we're supposed to live today.

Christian schools should be Romantic. We should champion and aim toward ideals, because we believe that there really are standards and absolutes we work toward. They're real, because God is real, and He had an original intent for everything He made. That original intent, which we all hear in the echoes, provides a standard to pursue. It's how we and everything else should be. We should know where we're aiming, and it's not based upon the whims of trends and gimmicks.

This is the question the Creation category seeks to answer. We're not primarily asking how things were created or where they came from, even though this is naturally part of the conversation. Yes, Christians believe that God created everything that exists, that He created out of no pre-existing material, and that He didn't create out of need or by accident.[71] When we study the biblical creation story, we find stark contrast between it and its contemporary accounts: there's order, love, and purpose. These are all fundamental truths Christians hold dearly. However, the Christian worldview seeks to take these truths and apply them to the way we make sense of the world. We study the creation account to learn more about God and to establish a foundation for God's original intent.

The Creation category is concerned with the nature of the world and of humanity within the world. It gives us a set of norms for understanding ourselves and our world in light of Scripture's revealed intent. The Creation category forces us to consider how learning should be. How *ought* teaching be? How *ought* athletics be? How *ought* music be? How should all things be?

ORTHODOXY

As we move from the more philosophical Grid strands to those of a biblical framework, it's significant to point out that every worldview answers these questions as well. Everyone struggles with this question. We all function as though we believe there is a way things should be. When a tragedy happens, people are quick to say, "it's not supposed to be this way." Though we all have these thoughts and questions, most people don't take the time to step back and pry into what's behind them.

Why do we feel like pandemics, natural disasters, or job losses should never come to us and our family? Where do we get the notion that these things should not happen – at least *to us*? Even questioning "why" suggests an explanation or meaning; it assumes answers.

Because Eden still echoes, we're all hard-wired with an understanding of and desire for an "ought." When we lose sight of it, we're hindered from being able to properly diagnose errors and have a standard for what we want our "fix" to look like.

Answering the Question

Throughout history, many people have failed in their attempts to create Utopias. Many of these efforts were appealing because they spoke to something deep inside humans. For instance, communism appeals to a belief that people should live in community with each other, sharing our gifts without class division. Yet communism assumes this would be possible without anything higher than mankind. It places the State above people, which hasn't been able to sustain the hopes and dreams of communist ideals.

Consider the many movies themed around attempts to create perfect societies. They tell the same story where everything falls apart because of some flaw in the utopian design. These movies suggest that humans have a compulsion to make things perfect (because we know it's supposed to be that way), but we continue to fail in our attempts, because we try to do it on our terms. Yet, we still make these movies, because the portrayal of a perfect world resonates with our longings. It's a movie recipe that sells.

The writer of Hebrews says this "perfect" is like shalom. It's a rest that still awaits us, but it's God's rest. (Ch. 4) Jesus says it's a rest for our souls – at the center of our being, that's only found in Him. (Matthew 11:29) The fact that we long for it proves that we know such a thing exists. Lewis expands this idea by suggesting that we only have appetites for things which exist. We have hunger, because there is food. We get thirsty, because there is something to quench thirst. We want better schools, because there really is a standard we should aim at. We desire a perfect world, because there is such a thing.

While considering that the smashed hopes of a perfect world creates a type of separation anxiety, it's still good that there is an original intent. It matters to us today, though, for multiple reasons, but I'll focus on two of the most crucial:

First, if there never was an original intent, *this* is the way it's supposed to be. Everything you and I don't like … well ... stop complaining, because that's just the way it is. There is no ought; there is no should. What you see is what you get. Theologically, this creates significant problems too, because it assumes that God approves everything as it is. Marinate on that one for a while. If that's true of God, we have the right to be angry.

I have a friend with six toes on one foot; it took some time for me to get used to it. We're struck by physical abnormalities, because they aren't "normal." I have five fingers on both hands. I doubt that makes anyone uncomfortable, because it's normal. But not every single person has five fingers on each hand or even two hands. While it's extremely common, it's not the absolute norm.

What's more absolutely common to the human condition than death? Most people have working ears. Quite normal, but not everyone does. Everyone dies. *Absolutely* normal. Yet I don't know anyone who's completely ok with the idea of death. Death might be one of the most common things to the human condition, but we struggle with it, because we all know we're not supposed to die! Where do we get that knowledge?

Let me introduce you to the creation category.

Because of the creation category, I'm justified to go to a funeral with clenched teeth – angry because it's not supposed to be that way. This is part of the anger we see from Jesus in John 11; apparently, we see his fury over death. His beautiful creation marred.

Secondly, knowing the original intent directs our efforts and hopes. Doctors spend countless hours studying how the human body is supposed to work. It's essential that my doctor knows that a person's normal body temperature is 98.6°. If he doesn't, he won't treat me well. Similarly, it's vital to know the standard which governs any aspect of human life if we're ever going to properly engage it. Without a clear, creational understanding, we are greatly inhibited in our ability to make sense of our worlds, as Nancy Pearcey says in her book *Total Truth,* "Beginning with sin instead of creation is like trying to read a book by opening it in the middle: You don't know the characters and can't make sense of the plot."[72]

Knowing the way God designed things gives us a pattern for engaging the world. It gives us the capacity for diagnosing what's wrong. More importantly, it provides an absolute standard for how life and the world should be. If we're going to try to make things better, we need to have a clear idea of what "better" is. Otherwise, our efforts and hopes are in vain.

A Biblical Answer

Nearly every ancient culture has creation stories within their communal mythologies. Most of these stories speak of creation as a chaotic event with uncertainty, struggle, and violence driving creative forces. There also isn't a clear separation between the deities and what they make. For example, it's often difficult to see distinctions between the god of the ocean and the ocean itself. Hearing these stories, ancient societies had a general idea where everything came from, but they also had uncertainty and fear in their relationship to the world around them.

Yet, the creation story of Genesis 1-2 is very different. We see purposefulness, order, harmony, and a clear distinction between God and what He has made. Any listener to these stories had a very different view, because he heard God's recurring pleasure in what He made. There's confidence, structure, and a clear articulation of how life should be.

Christians stand on the firm ground of clear creational norms which flow from consistent Christian answers to the other Grid questions. The entirety of God's creation reflects who He is, we read that "God saw all He had made, and it was very good." (Genesis 1:31) We understand this to be true because God Himself is the source of all goodness.

Francis Bacon understood that all Christians could know more of God through studying his "two books": the book of God's Word and the book of God's *works*. The fact that God *created* and that His creation reflected Him motivated men like Bacon, Newton, and Kepler to explore the world. Studying God's creation requires us to understand the norms He set in place. His creation reflects order, law, beauty, and love**.**

Since God has created *all things* and pronounced them good, we have a responsibility to engage His world with a new perspective. As educators, this means all our disciplines are rooted in learning more about those things created as *good* by God. As Schaeffer says, "There are no neutrals." Bible class is not of a higher station than Economics, for example. Economics seeks to understand systems, order, and employ reason in its study of those things. These were created by

God as part of His world. We must pursue them as though they too are good. In his book *Teaching Redemptively,* Donovan Graham says, "To discover and live by the creation norms is good also, for in so doing we reflect God's character and display the truth in His universe."[73] God also put Man in the world that He had made and gave him certain responsibilities.

In his book, *Engaging God's World*, Cornelius Plantinga says that shalom is the framework knit throughout God's creation. Shalom means far more than peace, but "full, flourishing wholeness." In the Garden of Eden, we are given an image of all things as they are supposed to be – flourishing plants, animals, and people. They're whole. They're full of life. There is joy. Harmony. Vibrancy. Peace. Love.

"Oughtness" In Education

One of my favorite ways to start the school year has been showing contrasting clips from two cult-classic 80's movies: "Ferris Bueller's Day Off" and "Better Off Dead."[74] Both clips take place in high school classes with male teachers, but the similarities stop there.

The Ferris Bueller clip is well known for Ben Stein's dead-pan recitation of the roster and questioning his students about Ronald Reagan's "Voo-doo Economics." The clip shows students bored out of their minds. One student even sleeps on his desk with a puddle of drool next to his mouth. I show this clip, simply to say "this is not what we want this year."

In contrast, I show a clip from the second movie to show what class ought to be. The scene shows all students having completed their geometry homework with great pride and zeal; they beg to answer questions and yearn to demonstrate their work on the board. They even laugh at their teacher's weak math jokes. They have great energy, interest, and curiosity. Of course, this is what we all hope to see in our classes.

The "Bueller" clip sticks in our minds because it's a caricature of our own experiences. Far too often, school is seen as boring – or like a chore which must be endured. Yet it's the task of the Christian school teacher to make learning exciting – not just because it's the best way to keep students engaged, but because this is how learning was always supposed to be. As Sir Ken Robinson says, "Children love to learn; they don't always enjoy education and some have big problems with school,"[75] so ought we think of the realities that students naturally want to learn; it's part of their design. Yet we all know we've structured some dimensions of our school with the assumption that they don't want to learn.

Because of our sin, we can't even get our heads wrapped around what Adam's life was like in the Garden of Eden. Adam and Eve learned, and they had God as their teacher – maybe sometimes directly during God's walks through the Garden and at other times indirectly, where they learned something new and realized that it was from the mind of God.

This is the most staggering difference between Adam's learning and ours. Adam wasn't necessarily a genius; being perfect didn't automatically mean he had superhuman intellect. However, there were no flaws in his knowledge. He didn't know everything, but what he knew, he knew correctly. For, Adam recognized himself as totally dependent. Everything he learned came from God, and he never overlooked that reality. Everything he learned taught him more about God. "For from Him, and through Him, and to Him Are all things." (Romans 11:36) Never once did Adam learn something and take it for granted. That would be impossible for a perfect person – impossible, because sinlessness would mean he always recognized God and everything in connection to Him. He was God-centered – not in common Christian lingo terms, but in plain reality. Because he always thought about God, his approach to his learning was always correct.

When Adam learned a new concept or idea, he would have been thankful and would have considered what it taught him about God. He would have pondered how this new understanding enabled him to further the creational mandate.

He would have wanted to know things, because they would show him more about God. While all disciplines may not have been his genetic giftings (e.g., he might have been more bent toward the humanities than math and science), he never would have been disinterested in what he could learn. Never apathetic. He never would have given up because something was difficult to figure out. He would have been wildly curious in his exploration, because each new fact showed him more about who God is and about himself (because he's created in God's image).

The following application points seek to answer the fifth question of the Grid: Are we pursuing, celebrating, and resting in God's original intent?

ORTHOPRAXY

In the "Man of La Mancha,"[76] Don Quixote says, "Maddest of all is to see the world as it is, rather than as it should be." This quote has become one of the theme quotes for my life because it speaks to the Romantic in me and points to a far more hopeful view of life. When things aren't as they should be, it's heartbreaking to be someone who pursues what's true, beautiful, and good. However, we can't have hope for the future without a clear idea of the ways things should be.

While the Bible provides so little detail about Adam and Eve's learning, we can properly assume certain aspects of their "education." For, we know they were perfect, and this gives us enough of a starting point to imagine what learning would have looked like for people who were not shackled by the entanglements of sin. So, let's consider ways we can pursue school as it should be.

1. Teach to both satisfy and nurture awe, wonder, curiosity, and discovery.

My all-time favorite chapter in any book is "The Ethics of Elfland" in Chesterton's *Orthodoxy*. His view of the world is on vivid display – a view full of wonder, a view we all need. I'd likely quote far larger chunks of it, but one part moves me every time I read it:

> "People feel that if the universe was personal it would vary; if the sun were alive it would dance. This is a fallacy even in relation to known fact. For the variation in human affairs is generally brought into them, not by life, but by death; by the dying down or breaking off of their strength or desire … The sun rises every morning. I do not rise every morning; but the variation is due not to my activity, but to my inaction. Now, to put the matter in a popular phrase, it might be true that the sun rises regularly because he never gets tired of rising. His routine might be due, not to a lifelessness, but to a rush of life. The thing I mean can be seen, for instance, in children, when they find some game or joke that they especially enjoy. A child kicks his legs rhythmically through excess, not absence, of life. Because children have abounding vitality, because they are in spirit fierce and free, therefore they want things repeated and unchanged. They always say, 'Do it again'; and the grown-up person does it again until he is nearly dead. For grown-up people are not strong enough to exult in monotony. But perhaps God is strong enough to exult in monotony. It is possible that God says every morning, 'Do it again' to the sun; and every evening, 'Do it again' to the moon. It may not be automatic necessity that makes all daisies alike; it

> may be that God makes every daisy separately and has never got tired of making them. It may be that He has the eternal appetite of infancy; for we have sinned and grown old, and our Father is younger than we. "The repetition in Nature may not be a mere recurrence; it may be a theatrical *ENCORE.*"[77]

What if the repetitive and mundane aspects of our lives happen because there's a heavenly encore behind them all? Amazing! They're intimately linked to the living God who is both wonderfully transcendent and mysteriously immanent.

Children have a desire to experience pleasures over and over again without getting tired of them, and we can't help thinking "they'll grow out of it." If growing up means we're no longer amazed by the wonders of the world around us, we all need to become more like children again, that makes me rethink Matthew 18:3.[78] Let's all stay young.

I used to live in Southern California in a home directly on the beach. During my first few weeks, I simply stared at the ocean every day. After a while, my daily routine changed. I got dressed, walked to my car, and headed off to work without even glancing at the Pacific – because I was used to it. Since pre-Fall Adam wasn't affected by sin and was radically in love with and thankful for God, he didn't take the Garden of Eden for granted. Ever. When he passed by the same tree for the hundredth time, he would have given God thanks for it and recognized that God had put it there for Adam and Eve to learn more about the One who made that tree.

As a result, Adam would have wanted to learn more about the world he was surrounded by. He would have been curious – both intellectually and emotionally, because everything he learned would have taught him more about who God is. The fullness of educational eagerness on display. He would have wanted to understand his world, and when he learned something new, he would have been thankful for it.

Lamentations 3 tells us that God's love and mercies are new every morning. That suggests intentionality on God's part. Things don't just happen. There's never a meaningless second and no little people, as Francis Schaefer says. If there's a God and He made all things, as Abraham Kuyper reminds us, there's not a "square inch" over which King Jesus doesn't say "this is mine." Because all of it is His, every bit of God's world can teach us about Him. What a great enticement for learning! To discover. To be full of wonder. To be amazed.

As a result, we're tasked with doing whatever we can to make education and learning wonderful, engaging, amazing, and new. Yes, these are ideals all teachers want. However, there are days when we're not feeling it and students aren't either, and we let slip out of our mouths, "I know that this isn't very exciting, but..."

We've just conceded to the Fall.

Oh, it's immensely difficult to labor for excitement and wonder, when we see apathy before us. It's a struggle to keep a lesson fresh when we've taught it several times before. But we can't give in, and we need to do whatever we can to help students hold onto their youthful wonder. We cannot lose sight of what education and learning were always designed to be. Good teaching isn't new or revolutionary. It's reformational. It's re-creational.

Start by committing to weave something awe-inspiring into a lesson once a day. Maybe it's not the content you're teaching for the day, but figure out a way to encourage curiosity, wonder, amazement and enthusiasm. It's absolutely critical that you do so consistently. We want our students to get so used to it that they can't imagine learning absent of wonder. I still love poetry and literature, not because I had a natural bent toward it, but my A.P. English teacher cried while reading to us the words of John Donne and Francis Thompson. Seeing her moved grabbed ahold of me, and I was forever shaped by that wonder.

Practically Speaking

1. How you plan to nurture wonder should show up in curriculum maps, be somewhere on your walls, and be ready at your disposal to answer.

2. It should be one of the first things you say when you describe what you're trying to accomplish in your class:
   - "In this unit, I can't wait for students to learn about the power of water as we look at watersheds, see how civilizations have been created around water, and to see its destructive abilities. I'm going to let students witness its power, and we're going to touch it and see it, and we're going to think even more deeply about Jesus's words when He claims to be the water of life."
   - "We're going to look at the power of beauty of words and see how they can paint vivid images and inspire a full array of emotions, and I'm so excited for my students to see how amazing language is and be humbled that God gave this gift to us."
3. When you approach essential questions, units, and lessons, ask "How will I use this to see student wonder and curiosity expand?" It may not be in every lesson, but it should be something you can regularly point to.
4. Don't even hint that content "just isn't that interesting, but we have to learn it anyway." I say this, because I remember teachers saying things like it and I might have said it, too.
5. Pray for a posture to be quick to remember to thank God for the gift it is for you to learn the things you are.
6. Let the students know where you are amazed. They need to see it *in you*. Regularly.

2. Dream about school without sin and work toward that.

In his book, *The Four Loves*, C.S. Lewis encourages us to envision an unfallen rose – and even more than that, with unfallen eyes. Teachers and school leaders need to dream; imagine what "school" would look like if sin had never entered the world. I know it's easier to not ask that question, because sin actually did enter the world. And frankly, who has time to dream! We need to teach the students immediately in front of us.

Give it a try. What would schools look like if there were no sin? I tend to think there would be some form of schools, because even perfect individuals need to be taught. There's always more to learn, and people would have different giftings, and some of those gifts would be teaching. We'd have teachers in an unfallen world. My dad thinks that our callings are eternal in nature, so for those who are called to teach, maybe we will teach in the New Jerusalem, too. Certainly, it's worth considering this question – both in terms of the structures of our schools and in the practices of our classrooms and programs.

Here's where our dreaming comes in. Consider what should prompt a student to go on from one "grade" or level to the next, assuming sin never entered the world. Shouldn't it be mastery rather than the fact that they're just one year older and stepped over a pretty low hurdle? Would sinless teachers in an unbroken system allow a student to progress simply because of good behavior and diligence? If I were a teacher in a world without sin, why would I ever let a student go on to the next level without being sure that a student really grasped a concept? Would I ever say "well, you didn't really learn what I was hoping you would, but it's time to move on"? Sinless teachers working with sinless students in a sinless system would never allow that to happen. Oh, I know it's idealistic to even ask the question, and I know our system of doing things makes it really hard to embrace those ideals, but why don't we at least try to move the needle a little closer toward how it should be?

Of course, this would really change the way we do things. It would mean we either have more fluidity between our grades, or that teachers do radical differentiation in their instruction (and lots of assessment remediation) to make sure the class is where it needs to be before moving on to the next level. Because we believe what we do about Truth (Grid Question 2) and students (Grid Question

3), schools should take a hard look to structure our practice more so we don't leave students behind and pass them along when we know they shouldn't be passed along. There's a theological reason why we must work against this trend.

Let's stop being dictated to by structures, systems, and programs which are shackled by the Fall. Yes, we need to be practical. However, we should be driven by our philosophy and mission (which are ideals), then figure out how to stay true to our beliefs, given the realities of the Fall. Instead, we too easily give in because "that's just the way it is."

I realize that I just pulled the pin out of a grenade and rolled it into your school's strategic conversations; that's not my goal. I'm not concerned just with grade level matriculation, but with every part of what we're doing and asking how things should be and working toward that. Even when it could blow up much of what we've done for generations, even.

Believing what I do about habits and rituals, let me suggest starting with something small. Maybe your school isn't capable of tackling the really hard structures which will be difficult to change. Start with some creational dreaming and Fall analysis. Then address how long you give students to pass between classes. In time, your school might be willing to wrestle with more complex structures if you've created some comfort with and habits of change by addressing smaller things that surface in your analysis. Whatever you do, don't settle, because that's just the way it is.

Practically Speaking

- Make a list of things you know about your school and/or classroom that are manifestations of things not being the way they should.
    - Ones that you can change on your own, design a plan to repair them

- Share more complicated ones with a peer to refine ones that you can be hopeful about changing and make a plan to share that with your administrators.
- With those unlikely to change (e.g., that you have eighteen students in your classroom for only forty minutes at a time), brainstorm about ways to make them better or how you can inch them closer to what they should be.

- Make a list of things that thrive within the realm of how things should be, and embrace them, fight for them, and thank God for them.
    - Put the list in a place you can see and look at it regularly to remind yourself so that you keep the main things the main thing.
- Train students to think along these lines with a "does it match" exercise. When reading a book or learning about history, you can ask them to talk about where things "match" God's original intent of how He would want things to be. You can also ask them where it doesn't match up.
    - As students get older, don't just have them point these things out, go to the next level by asking what we can learn from it. Or, you can ask them why things match or why people would do things differently from how God would want it.

3. Remember that learning is an eternal endeavor.

In his Epistle 53, St. Jerome said, "Let us learn those things on Earth, the knowledge of which continues in Heaven." St. Paul's School in New Hampshire adopted this as its motto, because it properly contextualizes learning. Students aren't *merely* learning facts, equations, and skills. Because God is the source of all truth, any truth they learn teaches them more about God, who is eternal. So, we should think about our curriculum as though it's preparing students for more than college and life, but also for living in the New Jerusalem.

Yes, our broken system requires that we prepare students to do well on the ACT, SAT, and other standardized tests. We want them to go to college (if that's what God has for them) and pursue their callings with passion and a strong intellectual foundation. We shouldn't hamstring students by ignoring the structures of the world they live in. This inhibits their capacity to fully live out Jesus's command to be "in the world."

Not being "of the world" in an educational sense means we should constantly ask how our curriculum and practice is eternally focused. Yes, there needs to be a recognition of temporal reality, but our curricula, schools, teachers, and students won't be here forever. God's Kingdom will. With this in mind, we need to keep the larger task in front of our teachers and students. How does this prepare us all for eternity? Not only should this inform how we teach, but it should also guide some of what we decide to teach, not just formally in the classroom – but in the various ways we teach in our schools.

It's also important to constantly remind ourselves that education is not a result of the Fall. While some of the things we'll learn are responses against sin's ravages, many of them aren't. Learning has always been part of God's original intent; it's part of what God wants for us; and He always will.

Practically Speaking

- When you pray as staff or when you pray personally for your work, ask God to bring you reminders throughout the day that these students will spend eternity in one of two places, and ask Him to use that reality to shape your approach to your students that day.
- Sift through your curriculum by units and lessons and ask, "which of these things will students still need for eternity?" Rejoice in those things and teach them without restraint.

  - For example, math facts, physical laws, language, storytelling, art, music, etc.
  - Ask students the very same question and let them wonder at the thought of using language in the New Jerusalem.
- When opportunities arise, talk with your students about their joys, passions, and giftings, and encourage them to explore the sorts of things they might be doing eternally (e.g., I hope I'll still be teaching) and consider how their experiences equip them for that.

4. Never undervalue the need for deep relationships in the learning process.

One of the primary reasons any new knowledge would have been so dear to Adam is that God is the source of that knowledge and was Adam's teacher. As Adam learned more, he would have developed as a person, but what made his learning so desirable is that it deepened his relationship with God and with the rest of the world.

In the same way, teachers need to be constantly reminded of the relationships our curriculum calls students into. We should teach them in a way which seeks to enhance students' capacity to relate to the world, to their communities, to their past, to their futures, and certainly to their teachers.

I cannot put enough emphasis on the need for healthy relationships between teachers and students. I once had a professor who lectured with exhaustive knowledge of the subject for the absolute entirety of the class time. There was never a wasted second. Obviously, he put in hours of preparation. He briefly answered questions when students had them. But he never lingered after class to talk to any of us. I don't know whether he knew our names. He seemed like a nice man, but I doubt it would have mattered to him whether we were there or not; it likely wouldn't have changed the class dynamics one bit if he lectured via a screen at the front of the room; it could have even been pre-recorded. I've had other teachers and professors who lacked his scholarship, but I was more shaped by them, because they invested in me. Or, they allowed me and my peers to get to know who they were as humans.

Other highly effective teachers may not have been as gregarious, but their lessons stuck with me because of their insistence that students apply what we learned. These teachers creatively thought of ways for us to draw relationships between the curricular content and the world around us. They helped us to understand how and why it mattered to us.

The best teachers build relationships; they don't merely impart information. For, this was always a goal of education – to strengthen the relationship between the Teacher (God) and the student (Adam), but also to grow Adam and Eve's relationship to each other and to the world around them. Because humans are relational by nature (Grid Question 3), we need to find ways for our teaching to be relational as well.

Let students into your lives. Connect what they're learning to their lives and yours. Connect it to other things they're learning. Connect it to their world. Connect it to stories. Let them tell their stories. Relationship must be one of the unmistakable non-negotiables of our classrooms and schools.

Practically Speaking

- Maybe your school needs to take a hard look at size - both of your school and your classrooms. Can you have rich relationships in a classroom with 25 students? What about a school with over 100 students per grade? We need to be honest about our ability to be deeply relational before making decisions about size.
- Explore ways to cultivate both formal and informal mentorship/discipleship groups in your school. It's worth the schedule disruption.

- As teachers, be willing to let the students into your lives. Tell them your stories, just as you encourage them to tell their stories.
- Teachers, coaches, and staff, your students should know that you care about each other, are for each other, and enjoy spending time together. Tighter adult communities automatically trickle down into healthier school relationship culture.
- Work to establish a mutual relationship between teachers and students where you know each other well enough to know what your hopes, joys, and passions are.

5. Encourage continuity across the disciplines.

One of my two favorite high school classes was a pilot class; I had the same teacher for History, Literature, and Bible in back-to-back classes. We didn't have history or literature tests, quizzes, or papers. Our assessments covered the content of all three disciplines, and we got the same grade for each on our report cards. It was a really hard class. The teacher was known for being exceptionally smart. However, because we spent so much time with him and learned to see connections between all these disciplines, we flourished. As we talked about historical events, we read corresponding texts and discussed theological concepts and associated Church history. We were given wholeness.

My children's school has a very thoughtful, integrated curriculum. Last year, my son was a third grader, and their curriculum followed the arc of ancient history. So, when they studied ancient Egypt, they learned about Egyptian history. They learned about their food and cooked some of it. In Bible, they focused on the Exodus. They also talked about monotheism and polytheism. In Literature, they looked at some of the Egyptian myths. In Science, they learned about the ecosystem of the Nile; they also embalmed a chicken and buried it. No joke! In Math, they learned about pyramids: their volume, dimensions, and calculated how long it would take to make them. In Nature Journaling, they learned about scarab beetles and drew pictures of beetles they had found outside. In Art, they made recreations of Pharaoh's headdresses. Because the curriculum was built for students to make connections, their thinking was geared toward wholeness, rather than fragmentation. No doubt, my son *really* has a grasp of Ancient Egypt.

Earlier, I said that *shalom* was a dominant fabric and framework of the Garden of Eden. Full, flourishing wholeness. But, our current model for secondary education pushes students toward fragmented learning. Students leave their history class and have to pivot and start thinking about mathematics, literature, or fine arts. Throughout the day, they have to toggle between different subjects, teaching styles, and expectations. There's value to having teachers who are scholars in their fields imparting knowledge to students; in doing so, we've often lost continuity in this knowledge.

If you teach elementary students, continue to do everything you can to help students see how their studies fits together. Build units around common themes, and challenge students to see overlaps. If you teach secondary students, work with other teachers from other disciplines to align themes, contents, and big ideas. But don't just stop there; think of how you can help students see connections throughout their school day. Work with other teachers to align units, teaching styles, individual lessons, field trips, projects, and assessments. Sin causes fragmentation. Creational, Christian educators seek to unite all learning under the lordship of Christ.

Practically Speaking

- If you teach in middle and high school, talk with your peer levels to see if you can find or create overlaps and try to teach them at the same time, so students can see connections between them.

- If you are willing to overhaul your curriculum to bring about more overlap and integration, establish unifying centers - like the hub of a wheel that the other areas can rotate around like spokes. Typically, history is a good place to start.
- If you teach in the elementary grades, explore where there are parts of your curriculum which seem disjointed and work to bring things more closely together. Whenever possible, help students see connections in their learning across disciplines.

6. Integrate Faith and Learning Restoratively

"Integration of Faith and Learning" has become commonplace in Christian educational circles. Far too often, this means that Christian schools seek to unify faith and learning. Of course, we want to see vibrant faith knit throughout everything our students learn. However, the wording of this phrase suggests that faith and learning are separate, and Christian education tries to bring them together.

My problem with this is that faith and learning were originally unified. There should be no distinction between the two. Of course, sin causes us to separate them, but the two are not disparate ideas which need to be creatively married together. Considering that a creational view of education would incorporate faith in everything learned, we should actually say "reintegration of faith and learning" if we feel compelled to use the phrase.

If by the phrase we intend for a unifying principle in our learning, I'm all for the idea of integration. Integration is a holistic endeavor – not fragmented. We need guiding principles where faith is saturated throughout learning objectives. This brings about comprehensiveness and coherence throughout the curriculum, consistent with a biblical perspective. Creational learning calls us to champion both alignment-integration and reintegration where things are fragmented.

Integration of faith and learning does not mean we try to find faith principle and connect them to what is learned. That treats them as separate entities. Our faith should be woven throughout – sometimes in glaring ways, sometimes less conspicuous, sometimes in the various nooks and crannies and unexpected aspects of the learning process. We also don't need to "force" God into where He already is.

Practically Speaking

- Make sure that "integration" in your school is always seen as organizing and unifying principles rather than add-ons.
- As you build out integrated units, don't focus on where you can connect Bible stories. While you may find Bible stories to connect with your units, it's better to ask fundamental questions (like the ones of the Grid) and use the unit to drive out foundational ideas.
- The "owners" of your curriculum need to be able to articulate how your curriculum celebrates flourishing wholeness between faith and learning.

7. Figure out ways to promote human rest.

A few years ago, I began looking for the perfect school day schedule. I consulted no less than a hundred different schedules, trying to diagnose solutions for a schedule which was constraining much of our ability to "dream." Our students seemed to rush throughout the day, they were regularly exhausted by the end of their class periods, and they were often bored by the same routine every day. We also couldn't add more electives for students because of our restrictive schedule. Christian schools should be bound by our philosophy and mission, not by structures which could be thoughtfully liberated.

I found a schedule at a school in Grand Rapids, and it caused me to break the tenth commandment. I was drawn to the variety resulting from a rotating, modified block. Even more appealing was all the space in the schedule – room to breathe, where students could be *human.* Longer passing periods. Strategically placed breaks of varied lengths throughout the day and week. Extended time at lunch. Office hours for faculty where they're available to answer questions during student free time.

With so many breaks, how did they get anything done? When I looked at the school's academic profile, I didn't see any dip in student standardized test scores. In fact, their average SAT and ACT scores were a bit higher than my own school which tried to cram as much "teaching" into the school day as we could.

My last sentence should create pause. Do we try to cram teaching into our school day, or try to cram learning into our school day? Unfortunately, if the goal is teaching and covering material, it's no surprise that students are mentally exhausted by the end of the day and week. We've all seen how poor student learning is when they're exhausted. We shouldn't be surprised; it's not rocket science.

Our need for rest isn't a consequence of the Fall; it's a pre-Fall ordinance. Before sin entered the world, God instituted structured rest for mankind. We need to rest if we're going to be fruitful in our work.

Rest is also a necessary part of growth. I had a fairly significant amount of success as a track coach – not because I ran athletes to death in practice, but because I was very strategic about rest. It's not the training that makes someone faster or stronger; it's the recovery that comes after it. Muscle fibers need time to repair after being torn during a hard workout. If athletes aren't given time to recover, they won't get stronger. I've witnessed many students who got injured because of constant stress on their bodies; I've seen even more who burned out, because they weren't properly coached.

How could the same principle not be true when it comes to school? If the demands and rigors of the day stay at an extremely high level all day without reflection or a chance to pause, eventually we'll see breakdown. Exhaustion. Apathy. Surrender. Careless mistakes.

If we want students to perform well, we must be mindful of their need to breathe, rest, focus, and be human. If we imagine how learning should be, we would naturally agree that it wouldn't be exhausting or overwhelming. It wouldn't cause students to feel like their hair is on fire with the many things they need to stay on top of.

Yet there is so much we must teach! How do we get through everything? If learning is the goal rather than teaching, we should consider their need to breathe. If we don't, we'll max them out and diminish their capacity.

I'm not saying that learning shouldn't stretch the students. We absolutely must challenge and have high expectations for them. But, if we're going to push them, we must grant them the space that's required for there to be a growth-response, which only comes when they can rest and reflect.

I realize that I have focused primarily on the students here. Teachers also need rest, because there's "no mission without margin." If we never have the space to rest, there will be no reflection or contemplation. Without those, there's little chance of growth. Our schools need to dedicate significant time to consider how we find more margin for our staff.

We also need to respect the Sabbath. I tell most every school that I've worked with that they need to institute a moratorium on school emails on Sundays. Or we should reconsider scheduling a major meeting on Monday morning when we know it will cause those in the meeting to prepare for it or be anxious about it on Sunday. Similarly, maybe we shouldn't schedule major assignments or major assessments for Monday morning, because we know students will be working to prepare on Sundays.

I recognize the difficulty of these commitments, but they manifest what it looks like to live in the overlap of Grid questions 1 and 5. If God is ultimate, we should hold what He desires above what we think is best. And we'll find that it actually is what's best for us.

Or get really crazy and do what Dayspring Christian Academy in Colorado has done. They have a four-day school week. Their days are a bit longer, but they get through as much in four days as most schools do in five. This leaves Fridays open for staff development, meetings, clubs, getting caught up on student work, grading, and lesson planning. And rest!

Practically Speaking

- Make a list of both small and big things you could do to reduce the anxiousness of your school day and make plans for which one you want to tackle first.
- Where are your students overwhelmed? What are you doing to do to address it?
- Maybe you could build space into the day where no "formal" learning is happening, just so there's more room for everyone to breathe.
- If you don't have boundaries around the volume of work you expect (and when you expect it) of your students to do at home, you need to move in that direction.

8. Remember to keep the school in its right place

When it comes to training children, the Bible never mentions the school; it does mention the home and the Church. Those two are primary; the school is secondary. As a result, the Christian school has a very clear mandate to partner with families and with churches in confidence that the work of the school strengthens God's kingdom. So, the school can't be so myopic that it overlooks its place within the larger story of what God is doing and His primary vehicles for training children. I realize that students tend to spend more hours at school than they do at home or in their church, but we still can't make the mistake of thinking that the school is primary.

As a result, we need be very sensitive to whether our actions cause students to think that their school responsibilities supersede all others. Of course, it's frustrating when families make decisions which seems to get in the way of learning, but we need to think deeply about what seems like punishing children for doing what could deepen family relationships.

We also need to make sure that we protect students' abilities to be "home when they're home." One of my personal soapbox speeches is that we need to be much more careful about homework loads. How can students have quality time with their families if their normal homework load requires them to put in multiple hours of work each night? It's not difficult to find numerous studies about the emotional health of children correlated to time spent with their families (even around the dinner table). Granted, we cannot force students to spend more time with their families when they are home, but we certainly shouldn't prevent it.

In a similar way, we should be sensitive to protect and encourage our students' and staff's involvement in their churches. I've known many students who were told that they had to choose summer workouts over involvement with their youth groups, if they were to have any hope of playing. When I was in high school, I was benched for a basketball game because my dad held me out of a Sunday practice earlier in the week. There's no way something like that should ever happen in a Christian school.

On the flipside, I know multiple schools that have created homework/test policies to protect involvement in Wednesday night and Sunday church programming. Granted, this is counter-cultural for a school to put policies in place to encourage students going to church. Christianity is counter-cultural, though, and encouraging students to be more involved with their churches may minimize the immediate amount of work a student can do, but it's eternally minded.

Practically Speaking

- Consider building bridges with churches to learn how your school can do a better job of partnering with them. Listen to them.

- The same goes for our families, a regular survey should explore homework loads and other school programming by asking specifically whether it creates obstacles.
- Explore classroom and other school policies and procedures to ensure that students are never discouraged from their homes and churches.

Why it's Christian

We live in a cultural moment of great confusion. Many people who claim to be Christians argue that God's statements about marriage are cruel, or no longer relevant to today. I'll be honest, there are some things in Scripture that don't automatically fit with how *I* think they should be. As Tim Keller says, if everything God did or said perfectly aligns with the preferences of our cultural moment, he certainly doesn't transcend time. He's not God.

The reality, though, is that God does have an intent for everything He made. And that intention is beautiful, and it's a pro-life picture of the harmony of shalom He loves. But, it's His plan. And, when Christians stand upon His intention, our foundation is not moved by cultural shifts. It's firm. Getting there, though, requires that we relinquish our autonomy and submit to His design. When we do, we'll both find the uniqueness of our position and that there's no better place to be.

ORTHOPATHY

I'm so thankful God gave us tastebuds. He didn't have to, but He did. Eating could have been little more than an activity necessary for survival, but God chose to give us joy in it. Beyond the pleasure we find in food alone, food also provides an avenue for creativity, exploration, and experimentation. Food also is one of our greatest contexts for relationships with others. Even more reason to longingly await the eternal *feast* God has in store for us.

Food is one among many aspects of our human existence that should call forth overwhelmingly thankfulness, because God didn't have to make our lives this way. He gave us countless reminders that He wants us to delight in our world. Like a parent who delights in seeing his children's joy, God loves giving us the gifts He has.

Gifts excite us. We like receiving them. Have we treated the ideas and skills taught in our curriculum as though they're gifts? Our learning should be rooted in the eternal truth that God wants us to find joy in our experiences, and He wants us to find joy in seeing Him in our experiences. So, the goal of our curriculum must be more than mere preparation for what's next (the next grade, college, or a career) – but for greater joy.

In his book, *Educating for Life*, Nicholas Wolterstorff says that "human beings are creatures for whom education is inescapable."[79] As finite beings created in the image of God, there will always be more to learn. Because we were made for Him and to live actively in the world He made for us. When we live according to our purpose, our lives are much richer. Since learning is essential to our God-ordained existence, our educational endeavors should make students and teachers feel full. Complete. Whole. Alive.

Do your students have joy at school? Would they say their education brings them fuller lives? Would your alumni say that? If we find that our students aren't thriving, but rather grinding through and tolerating their school experience, we must address our approach toward learning in our schools.

Most importantly, our schools should be places where students live joyful, thriving lives because they've found the fullness in God's provision in their learning. If we have allowed God to be an add-on, or an idea, rather than a joyful and loving Provider, students will conform to what we ask of them and use the right lingo. But they likely won't have been transformed. Yet when we pursue learning according to its original intent, we are far more likely to see lives changed by joyful thanksgiving for all we have in God's sustaining and restoring work.

When we point to learning as it was meant to be, we give students confident direction. this also creates a sense of longing for that from which they've been separated. For, certainly they will have to come to grips with the effects of the Fall upon their learning, and this gives us an even greater platform for reminding them of how good it is to see their need for Jesus.

9

OH SO BROKEN

Grid Question 6: Are we marked by mournfulness and repentance over sin and a broken world?

Several years ago, I came home completely distraught after a full day of teaching. By God's grace, this has only happened a handful of times in my teaching career. On this day I was cut to the core, having extended both mercy and grace to an entire class of students in an unprecedented way, only for them to throw it back in my face. Despite my best efforts to meet them where they were, they saw my vulnerability – and pounced!

I'm used to discouragement; unfortunately, it's par for the course in the teaching world. I'm used to seeing students perform below their best. I wasn't used to extending extreme generosity to them and seeing it devalued, unappreciated, and twisted as a weapon against me. As has happened many times in my home, I told my wife what had happened that day. She didn't need to hear me say how grieved I was; she could see it on my face. Not to cause me greater pain, but to re-center me, Katie responded, "What did you expect? They're sinners."

Obviously, we shouldn't approach each day expecting to see all the ways sinfulness shows up in the lives of our students and coworkers. Yet, it's critical that we both keep our heads in the clouds (recognizing and clinging to ideals) and our feet firmly planted on the ground (understanding the reality of a world marred by sin). While all forms of sin are violations against God's intent, we recognize that we can't have meaningful conversations about Christianity without speaking transparently about sin. As a result, any attempt toward being more gospel-centered in our schools requires honesty about the realities of sin in our schools. It requires that we have clear answers to the question, What's wrong with the world?

ORTHODOXY

I can't comprehend how modern "health and wealth" pastors can orchestrate entire worship services without mentioning sin. It's not merely *difficult* to talk about our standing before God, our need for Him, the beauty of the gospel of grace, or how Jesus speaks to the human condition without a forthright conversation about our sin; it's *entirely impossible.* I realize that they don't want to turn people away from church. They seek a comfortable experience which is more likely to fill seats than the Kingdom. They want people to leave the service feeling better about themselves. Though, we will necessarily miss the gospel if we avoid the dire predicament caused by sin.

In *Orthodoxy*, G.K. Chesterton says that sin is the one aspect of Christian doctrine that doesn't need to be proven. We don't have to look very far to realize that something's not quite right; things are not the way they're supposed to be. This is the root of any complaint we hear about political structures, natural disasters, or human suffering. We get upset because we realize these "bad" things shouldn't happen. All people (either religious or not) recognize there's a certain "ought," and are quick to point things out when others don't meet that standard.

Answering the Question

Nearly every mythic culture has a story which seeks to explain where the bad things in the world came from. Their narratives try to explain this because we all realize that something is very wrong with the world, and we long to make sense of it.

After considering how things should be, the next, logical step is to look around, observe that the world fails to resemble original intent and ask "Then, what happened? What went wrong?" These questions assume that we and our world have moved in a direction away from the original structure, and they seek to explain why that's the case. Answers to these questions require more than casual explanations; they also need to provide categories for defining "bad," "evil," or "wrong."

Some people try to dismiss these questions, because their belief-systems make it very difficult to believe in evil in an ultimate sense. The Naturalist can't believe in evil, neither can the Relativist. They can only talk in terms of dysfunction, preference, or discomfort. Because of this, they can't look at anything specifically and say, "yes, this is absolutely wrong" – at least, if want to be consistent with their worldviews.

They might relegate these events to some kind of natural disorder (like a chemical imbalance) or say something like, "wrong, who said anything is wrong?" or "I don't like it, but this is just the way it is." These two systems don't allow for real wrong, because they're either based on the assumption that there is nothing beyond what's physical (naturalism) or that there can't be absolute standards (relativism).

Filmmaker Woody Allen gave an interview with *Der Spiegel* magazine in 2005 and reflected this view which (if lived out) changes how we do education all-together. Essentially, he suggests that bad things happen; that's just the way the world works. So, we shouldn't feel as though horrific events like the Holocaust or the attack on the World Trade Center are overly unique. While we may be appalled at what Allen says, he's taking a worldview that doesn't allow for a personal God to its logical conclusion.

I can respect his attempt at consistency, but no one can fully live this out – not when tragedy hits home. I'd love to walk with Mr. Allen through the halls of St. Jude's Children's Research Hospital and see if his perspective holds up amidst the bald children we'd see. The fundamental problem with denying the existence of evil is that it can't be lived out. Deep down, we all know that something's wrong – a very dull, aching, wrong which can't be avoided.

We should be very concerned, because much of what we see in the modern educational system is the heritage of naturalistic and relativistic educational theorists which don't have a conviction of an absolute wrong. Education has an ethical dimension; so, questions of good and bad will come up routinely. Yet we wouldn't get very far in our schools if we couldn't label thoughts, actions, or events as evil and have a standard by which we do so. Students look to their teachers to provide categories and to help shape the way they engage their worlds. How can this be done without providing labels of good and evil? In *The Republic*, Plato insists that the purpose of education is to define and promote justice in the hearts and minds of the students. This is the purpose of their studies in history, logic, mathematics, and poetry.

Others may answer the question in a more dualistic way. They might say there are two forces at work: one good and another evil. Within these (typically spiritual) systems, bad things happen because the "bad power" caused it, and the good one couldn't stop it. The same is true of the good things which come our way. Additionally, both powers have been acting in this way for all eternity in a cosmic battle.

This problematically requires both of these powers to be equal to and independent of each other, wherein it becomes quite difficult to call one good and the other bad. Doesn't it just come down to us preferring the "power" that stands for things we happen to prefer, like honesty and justice? Within this perspective, though, it's impossible to say one is better than the other.

This view also assumes that neither the good power, nor the bad power need each other. However, Lewis points out that evil needs good. In *Mere Christianity*, he says it's "spoiled goodness." What he means is that you can define Truth without needing to use any variation of "falsehood" in your definition, but you cannot define what a lie is without some variation of the word "truth." All evil needs goodness to exist; it needs something to corrupt.

Other worldviews see only one force encompassing both good and evil; for example, Hindus look to Brahman, who is both Creator and Destroyer. In this scenario, the question ends up relatively the same: Why call one action good and the other evil, if they both precede from the same "god?"

In the end, any answer to the question needs to be "liveable." A person ought to be able to say that something is wrong, believe it's really wrong, and have a system that's not contradicted by this view.

A Biblical Answer

Christianity offers a far clearer answer to the question of the Fall category by insisting on a clear distinction between good and evil. Something bad actually happened. It's unique among many belief systems to have confidence that God created a good world that went bad. To say it another way, God's originally perfect creation is no longer what it was.

It's essential to make this claim, for if the "wrong" we see today mirrors the way it's always been, God's original desire was for sin to be knit into the fabric of what He made. If this was His intent, He must approve of it. And, if He approves of it, it can't be outside His nature. If God's nature allows for sin, we can no longer say it's bad and can't complain about its effects we see. This returns us to the same problem of the belief systems which suggest that God is both (or neither) good and evil.

Yet, the Christian answer says, "No! Things are not supposed to be this way." God created a perfect world and what we see now is a messed-up version of that. The Christian answer allows belief in an original intent and a God who is distinct from the evil that upsets us and Him. It allows us to have very real anger over the ravages of the Fall, because we can justly proclaim that God has no delight in these things.

At the moment we say God created a good world which has been distorted, we must address what brought about this change. Naturally, people want to know where evil came from. If God created a good world that went bad, where did that "badness" come from?

First, if God didn't create it, somehow this pre-existent evil crept into His world, and God couldn't keep that evil out. This certainly questions His power and pre-existence before everything else. Or, it also returns us back to the idea of there being two powers at work which can't defeat each other.

Secondly, if God created this evil, we're back to the problem of questioning God's goodness, because anything God creates will reflect His nature.[80] No wonder the problem of evil often makes us feel stuck!

I'm immensely thankful for Augustine's brilliance here, because his take allows us to be troubled by evil, acknowledge God's control, yet not blame Him for evil's existence. While I have no desire to get bogged down in a deeply philosophical discussion of the problem of evil, teachers need to have confidence in the essential tenets of the Christian worldview and be able to provide clarity for our students.

Augustine says that evil is not a real thing – as in a real substance you could capture in a bottle. Rather, it's a perversion of real things, like decay. For example, I can't draw a picture of decay; I can only draw a picture of something in the process of decay. Decay is not a real thing, it's what happens to real things.

God created all real things, but He did not create evil. He only created things which reflect Him, and all things which reflect Him are good. Satan is real, and God created him as a good being, not an evil one. All things that exist can only exist because of God; they owe their existence to God.

Though, by making real things, God made that which is necessarily less than Him. God can't make something equal to Him, because anything that God makes has a beginning point and would automatically be less than Him. Anything less than Him is finite, which isn't a bad word; Adam was finite. So are angels. So are we.

By definition, all finite things can change. Only something that is infinite can stay the same forever – infinitely. Yet, all finite things have the potential of experiencing some kind of change. God alone is immutable, and this is very much tied to the fact that He is infinite in his qualities as the Westminster Shorter Catechism reminds us.[81]

When it comes to people, God made "things" with the freedom to choose. I don't know why God gave Adam and Eve the freedoms He did, considering that the ultimate outcome of their rebellion would require Him to enter into the world and give His life for them and their descendants. We know that God is free, and freely makes choices. So, maybe God gave us this freedom as another way we could image Him. With that freedom, though, there came a potential that Adam could make the wrong decision. God didn't make sinful beings, but He did make people who had the potential of change from their original state of perfection.

By creating anything that could choose, God created people who could change from their original state. And, if that original state was one of perfection, a change from that is less than perfect – or evil. As Paul Harvey would say, "And now … the rest of the story."

Genesis 3's description of the Fall describes two people who took the one thing God gave to remind them that they were not God[82] and did with it what they weren't supposed to. There were obviously numerous ways they could have sinned. Adam could have refused to name the animals. However, it wasn't the beauty of the fruit or the mystery of sin that enticed them; it was Eve's desire to be like God. (3:5) Every sin since has been a form of wanting our way rather than God's – in essence, to be God.

As a result, every aspect of their beings was affected by this disobedience. Romans 5 tells us that Adam's rebellion in the Garden of Eden brought sin and death to all men. We understand that the effects of this sin went far beyond a breakdown of a relationship between God and man, resulting in death. The effects of the Fall were cosmic. Sin affects the entire cosmos; there is not a single portion of the created order unaffected by the Fall. When we speak of the effects of the Fall, we use words like distortion, fragmentation, and disintegration. The Fall did not destroy the created order, but it broke it; things became other than the way that they were supposed to be. But just because everyone and everything is affected by sin, sin isn't normal. It's actually abnormal, because it isn't supposed to be that way.

In *Engaging God's World,* Cornelius Plantinga further explains the effects of the Fall by defining evil as "a spoiling of Shalom" – or any time things are not the way they were originally supposed to be. As a result, sin is evil for which someone is responsible. Seeing evil this way provides greater need for a clearer view of the creational category. When Adam's relationship with God became fragmented, so did all his other relationships. The distortion of this vertical relationship between God and man radiated to his horizontal relationships as well. Obviously, such a distortion of the universals automatically led to a distortion of man's perspective toward everything else.

All creation fell and (as Paul tells us in Romans 8) still yearns for restoration from the bondage of decay. Because Adam acted as a representative of all creation as well as all people, God cursed even the ground, causing it to produce all sorts of frustrations. (Genesis 3:9-13)

Just as our relationships break down as a result of the Fall, the ways we reflect God's image are distorted as well. Not only do those capabilities break down (e.g., our rational faculties are now distorted) how these capabilities relate to each other breaks down. We compartmentalize our abilities (e.g., we try to live only as rational beings – as though we can separate rationality from spirituality). Our perspective of the world is skewed; we fail to see the unity that exists in the created order. For, we cannot isolate any one part of the ways we are supposed to image God and ignore the rest. This is another reason why we must be so careful in our schools to emphasize students' hearts and bodies as well as their minds.

God created a unified whole under His Lordship, while sin fragments everything into distinct pieces. Not only do we see the fragmentation of our relationships, we see break down in our thinking, bodies, and emotions. We should expect this outcome, given that our primary relationship has broken down and has filtered into everything else.

This should cause deep repentance and bring us to our knees, recognizing that we are not immune from the Fall; we are guilty, as Romans 3:10 tells us, "There is no one righteous." Just because everyone else is broken by the Fall, we can't minimize our guilt. We should be confronted by the reality of our standing before a Holy God. Typically, when people encountered the presence of God (e.g., Isaiah, Ezekiel, and the Apostle Paul), they were terrified, because they understood that their sin was in full view.

In the Sermon on the Mount, Jesus goes to unexpected places to help his hearers realize the infinite ways in which they have failed to keep God's law. God's law doesn't show us the things we need to become good; it shows us how much we need Jesus because we can't be good.

In Education

If we believe in the Fall and that alienation with God is our fundamental problem, we should expect this to change many aspects of education. Too often, we point to less significant issues as the primary problems education must address. As a result, schools continue to struggle to fix the same problems, because they often tackle symptoms rather than the real sickness.

Think of the many ways we have used schools to address racism in our country – treating racism like the problem rather than the symptom it is. Certainly, inequality and ignorance drive racism, but by focusing here, we undervalue what really needs to be addressed. We've mandated curricular changes to raise awareness, hoping that more knowledge about class-struggle and race relations will de-bigot students. We started bussing students between districts to remedy the significant inequalities in our schools and break down racial walls.

I remember reading theorists who assumed that having students in the same schools would reduce the inequalities and destroy some of the cultural ignorance driving racism. Not only did this not fix the problem, but it also led to further separation in many cases, as those who could afford to do so started private schools, many of them, "Christian." Believing in the Fall means we don't just go back to Adam's sin which started this mess. We willingly admit the sinful practices and assumptions at the root of starting some of our own schools.

We sin against God by either failing to meet God's standard of goodness or acting directly against it. Throughout His ministry Jesus draws attention to the many ways people had not done what they were supposed to. This is at the heart of much of what Jesus says in the Sermon on the Mount. It's humbling to admit that we spend more time focusing on the "evil doers" who break God's law, when Jesus focuses on the countless ways we have not kept God's law.

Because God has revealed himself so clearly in His Word, in our consciences, and through what He has made (Romans 1:20), we are without excuse for failing to do what we ought. The problem is significant – far greater than we can or are willing to admit. The

Bible goes so far as to say we are "dead" because of it. Dead people can't do anything; they can't fix their problem; we can't comprehend the gospel. This is where a biblical understanding of sin leaves us. This is why we ask: Are we marked by mournfulness and repentance over sin and a broken world?

ORTHOPRAXY

1. Create classroom environments which don't shy away from the realities of the sinfulness of the world in which our students live.

In *Back to the Blackboard,* Jay Adams asks, "How does a teacher cope with problems which grow out of sinful patterns rather than out of ignorance? How does the fact of sin in the student's life affect teaching methodology?"[83] Far too often, most of our problems and frustrations which stem from the effects of the Fall hijack our efforts because we don't ask the right questions. I don't have every answer, but I'm also quite sure that we won't make progress without considering questions like Jay Adams'.

Students come into each of our classrooms every day, bearing the scars of the Fall in very unseen, heartbreaking ways. Of course, they wear masks. We all desire to hide, and this shame goes all the way back to the Garden of Eden. I know for certain that I've had students incapable of focusing in my class because they got ready for school in a home where their parents were screaming at each other. There's been far worse stuff too in my school and in yours. The painful reality is that many of our students live in worlds that look far more like the Kingdom of Man than the Kingdom of God. And they bring it all with them into the schoolhouse.

We all know these things will necessarily affect the students' ability to learn or do well on any assessments we give them. Maybe it's not parental conflict, but they could be concerned over sick grandparents or even the exhaustion students have from the tireless rat-race which enslaves them and their families. If a student were to request to take a test at another time because she simply had a really hard night or morning, is your first response to be flexible, or do you tell the student that "rules are rules" or "deadlines are deadlines" because that's the way it works in the *real world?*

Of course, we need to push students toward ideals. However, when they blow it, they need to know that we are for them – because we also blow it. If they make a mistake, do we allow for hope? Or do we function as though the effects of the Fall are relevant everywhere except for our classroom?

A former student of mine once got a negative grade on a two-page paper he submitted to a former colleague of mine. The rubric for the paper led to so many point deductions resulting in a final grade below zero, and the teacher returned the paper with this negative number. Obviously, it was a poorly written paper. However, this sort of correction can only wound a student; it didn't remind the student that the teacher hoped for his growth. It crushed the student under his error. Rarely have I confronted peers about classroom policies, but I did on that one, and the teacher replied that students need to understand that there are consequences to actions. I don't disagree that this is part of what we want students to learn, but I'm doubtful that this teacher's approach was the way to accomplish it. People who believe that sin is real and love the gospel for that very reason are also the greatest lovers of mercy. You can't love mercy and give a student a negative grade on a paper.

On my first significant paper in college, I didn't get a grade from the professor. On each of the five pages, there was a big X covering the entire page. No other markings. At the bottom of the last page, there was only one word written: "No." I made really good grades in high school and went to a well-regarded Christian college. Looking back on that paper, I often laugh. It was probably a pretty bad essay. But I'll always remember the "grade," too. Giving someone a hard time is one of my love-languages, so this didn't crush me. However, I'm still amazed that the teacher was more interested in my knowing how gravely wrong I was than in trying to help me.

When students clearly don't get it, or they blow it, or they are overcome by circumstances they can't control, our response needs to reflect the recognition that we are not surprised that they aren't perfect. We should have high expectations of our students, and we should have high expectations about the infinite ways that sin is working on them. Also, our classroom policies need to allow for the recognition that sin will rear its ugly face. Don't be surprised.

Practically Speaking

- Put policies in place that allow for students to be broken people. Are mistakes allowed in your class without penalty, or do your policies look more like "zero tolerance?"
- For example, does your late work policy allow for the fact that students will make mistakes and their world isn't the way it's supposed to be?
- Do your policies reflect that you love to show mercy?
- Your classroom must be a safe place when a student blows it. And, not just because of your response when they do, but because you also protect them from their peers by how you shepherd their responses, too.

2. Willingly admit your own struggles and errors and be the first to confess when you're wrong.

I don't remember any of my teachers apologizing in class apart from dismissing typos on quizzes and tests. Had any of my teachers ever repented or asked forgiveness, I would have remembered; that tends to stick with a kid. I don't think any of them thought they were perfect or that they were too good to publicly repent, but my teachers missed this great avenue for modeling gospel-living.

I specifically remember one of my teachers absolutely losing her cool with our class, saying inappropriate things – to the point where it became so plainly obvious that she got embarrassed about what she said and walked out into the hall. We could see the shame. The following day she started class as though it never happened. What an opportunity lost! For both her and for us.

There are other times when teachers' errors are less obvious or public. The students are unaware, but the teacher isn't. When this happens and a teacher brings it up vulnerably for a class, it grabs students' attention in profound ways. Not only does it show students that the teacher is for them, but also that teachers struggle as much as they do. The recognition is liberating for them.

When children don't have Christian adults in their lives modeling what it looks like to repent, confess, or to ask forgiveness, it deeply misshapes their spiritual growth. It furthers the illusion that Christian maturity isn't marked by struggle. When students come to realize that the adults in their lives are marred by sin, they can also see that being near to Jesus is a daily need.

There may be nothing greater to model for them. For, as Jesus says – He came for the sick. If students are going to see vibrant faith in our lives, they need to see the *reason* why we need Jesus. Vibrant faith and denial of sin cannot coexist. If the formative teachers in their life won't model this for them, how do we expect them to learn it?

Practically Speaking:

- Considering that the Fall is real and that we all know we could do things better, or actually do things wrong, we should be talking about these shortcomings *regularly.* Dare I say, weekly.
- It's good to pause occasionally, and make sure students really hear you when you say you didn't do something well, or actually did something wrong.

- When you draw their attention to it, don't minimize it with sayings like, "no one is perfect" because we don't want them to minimize their errors either.

3. A true recognition of the Fall necessitates a culture of communal, professional growth and evaluation.

Any accreditation process will address a school's professional growth and evaluation model, because it has come to be an expected descriptor of school health. A teacher who isn't looking for opportunities for growth will become stagnant and will eventually fall behind, as advances and innovations change the educational landscape. Just to keep up with technology, learning styles, and new curricula, teachers must grow.

Our schools are learning environments first and foremost. And one of the most effective ways to foster a culture of learning is by having teachers who model that same passion. Many of our mission statements and school values express aspirations of students cultivating a passion for learning. Passion is efficacious, and so is a lack of passion. Therefore, students will necessarily reflect what they see in the lives of their teachers.

These are broadly pedagogical reasons why schools should insist on intentional, on-going, professional growth. But the theological reason is even more compelling. We all know that sin has significant effects on our souls, minds, and bodies, but we should connect the dots and realize that sin also has vocational effects. Sin causes us to be worse at our jobs than we would be without sin. It affects our judgment, our intentions, and our effort.

Because we know that sin's ramifications are vast, Christian schools should be at the forefront of harboring cultures of growth. Every single teacher needs to get better, because every single teacher is a sinner. It's that simple.

Of course, there are practical ways for faculty to grow, and a healthy school needs to stay current to educational trends and relentlessly pursue best practices. But we often need to pause and preach the gospel to ourselves, remembering that we truly do need to grow because we truly are sinners who need Jesus.

I love Jon Eckert's "4 R's"[84] in his book *The Novice Advantage*. He says that the best teachers **reflect** on their practice habitually, take calculated **risks** to teach in a new way, **revise** it when it seems to be working, and **reject** it when it's not. Not only is this a healthy, pedagogical best practice for students to witness, it's also theologically appropriate, because we should have an honest opinion of how flawed we are.

A school which believes in the cosmic effects of sin will embrace a culture of growth, transparency, willingness to change, and courage to accept correction. This is one of the same reasons why Christians need the Church and the fellowship of believers. Left to myself, I'll get stuck in my ways and stay blind to many of my sins. When we're authentically in relationship with other believers, we experience Christ more fully. Similarly, a gospel-driven school community is deeply committed to seeing its staff grow.

Practically Speaking:

- Take a hardline stand as a school to go even deeper into professional development opportunities, and do so for theological reasons, not just pedagogical ones.
- Openly tell your students and families both your theological and professional reasons for this decision.
- Create rhythms where senior/master teachers take the lead in conversations about what they're learning, not because they're the leaders, but because they should have the clearest understanding of their need to grow.
- Give junior teachers ample opportunity to teach senior teachers, not only because they may be more in tune with current trends, but to model a recognition that we truly need each other.

4. View student assessments as measurements of teacher effectiveness as much as student learning.

This sounds like general best practices for teaching and assessment. Why is it part of the orthopraxy section in the chapter on the Fall?

Educational theorist, Madeline Hunter, once said, "To say that you taught when students haven't learned is to say you have sold when no one has bought."[85] One of my friends once shared this with me and I bristled, thinking that there were many times when I taught a good lesson, but the students just didn't study hard enough.

Unfortunately, I was way too many years into my teaching career before I realized that my job wasn't primarily to "teach," but to help students learn. I imagine that many teachers have thought the same way. However, if a student isn't learning, what's the point of teaching?

Well, I taught some really good things and worked really hard at it.

How do you know whether they learned these good things?

That's what I'll find out on their tests.

How did they do?

Not too well.

Why do you think that?

Either they didn't study well, or I made the test too hard

The first thing that comes to our minds when students don't do well on a test should be something like, "Maybe I didn't teach this as well as I thought I did." It may be true that you taught the material well and there could be other reasons why the students didn't do well. But for teachers who believe the gospel (who truly believe that they are more affected by sin than they realize), our first posture should be open to the possibility that we maybe didn't do as good of a job as we thought. Our findings could be varied, but teachers who realize they need Jesus look at their assessments from a posture of humility and their own brokenness and make conclusions in that light.

Practically Speaking:

- Whenever you notice any trend where students didn't do as well as you thought they would have, err on the side of reteaching the material or giving students grace.
- Whenever we didn't teach something as well as we know we should have, rather than ignoring it, seize the opportunity to tell the students why you're reteaching it: you didn't do it as well as you thought, and you care about their learning. It's far better to slow down and do that than to plow forward.
- Prior to giving back graded assessments, pray that the Holy Spirit will make you receptive to questions, complaints, or even accusations from students rather than have a posture of defensiveness.
- If/When a student or parent offers critique, work hard to consider that they may be right and that we don't see things the way they do; it may mean that you're right. But starting with the approach of humble reflection will put you in the right posture to help.

5. Routinely create space in lesson plans to ask questions which target students' hearts and take them behind or underneath what's really going on.

Without question, your curriculum will deal with clear examples of a broken world – both in what's studied and within the environment of your classroom. Don't make the mistake of merely addressing these as concepts to teach, but use them as opportunities to talk about sin and the effects of the Fall. When studying clear examples of sinfulness/brokenness (like the Holocaust, or U.S. slavery), ask questions like, "what would cause a person to do such a thing?" "Why was he unkind?" "What must really be going on inside this person?" "What would a person have to value to think this?" Ask these questions as topics arise or include them to supplement their reading assignments. Journaling assignments also help to surface some of these issues.

With Older students, these sorts of questions wonderfully push students into Bloom's higher order thinking skills. With younger, concrete learners, it's also important to get them to understand what's underneath behaviors and see that they are also guilty of the same behaviors. Considering how concretely they think, it's also a wonderful opportunity for them to establish a foundation and habit for what we do when we recognize our own selfishness and greed – we repent and run to Jesus.

When reading stories, cause students to consider what's driving the characters – what's going on inside, what are their idols? Whenever possible, follow-up these questions with those which require them to think introspectively; make it personal for them. "When have you been unkind?" Ask students where they see these tendencies in their worlds and what's behind them. Don't let students default to simple answers when you talk about bad things (the usual suspects like murder or theft). Even when they talk about common culprits, force students to look underneath these issues as opportunities to discussions that will hit closer to home. What about personal selfishness, greed, and failure to consider others? Ask what other heart-issues are similar to these same problems. Ask them where they see these things in their own lives and even what it says about them if they have these thoughts.

This should be so intentional that it shows up in both lesson objectives and course essential questions, revealing an intentional and planned desire for students to see what's behind what they're studying.

Practically Speaking:

- It's always a powerful lesson for students to recognize that the evidences of the Fall they will learn about in school are not too distant from many of things within their own hearts.

- *Examples of Essential Questions*: Can students learn to see the impact of human selfishness on global events? Can students demonstrate that they further understand their own sin because of what is read in class? Can students distinguish between symptoms and core problems in society and connect them to the human condition?
- *Examples of Lesson Objective*: Students will consider how C.S. Lewis uses Edmond's rebellion to ask where we put our own desires before others'. Students will learn to see how the greed and impatience of Veruca Salt and Violet Beauregarde drives their foolish choices and ruins their ability to enjoy the Chocolate factory. Students will learn to see the hopelessness of the world that F. Scott Fitzgerald portrays and apply it to both Fitzgerald's conclusion and our own tendency to glamourize greed.

6. Be on the lookout for areas in your school which encourage fragmentation and confusion rather than wholeness.

I mentioned earlier that evil is a spoiling of shalom and that sin is evil for which someone is responsible. The school that functions mindfully of a healthy understanding of the Fall doesn't merely address the myriad places sin rears its ugly head in our schools. We also need to look for areas where shalom has been distorted.

We have all sorts of pressures which drive most of our decisions. But a school which is mindful of how education works best will also explore where we're doing what's less than our best. Because we're acutely aware of the conspicuous effects of sin, it's healthy to assume that everything in our school isn't the way it should be. It's our task, then, to search out those areas and address them. There will be many.

When speaking about our schools externally, it's normal to highlight our strongest aspects. While it's a typical marketing strategy, our attempt to celebrate successes should never inhibit our ability to face the reality of the many places where we haven't hit the mark. Unfortunately, I see far too many schools scared to acknowledge the extent of their brokenness. Because we believe the Fall is real, Christian schools should be the first to do routine, habitual analyses of our philosophy and practice.

If you do this exploration without fear or territorial protection, you'll uncover all sorts of areas which need to be addressed. Moving away from fragmentation and brokenness toward wholeness and shalom might mean you'll turn many things upside down – offering some things that other schools don't and not offering what most every other school does. Will you be brave enough to tackle the challenge?

Practically Speaking:

- Where does your school cause unnecessary anxiety and stress?
- Where does your school make learning more about meeting a temporary or vocational need rather than an all-of-life exploration?
- Where does your school further worldliness rather than godliness?

Why it's Christian

Everyone knows something's wrong, and none of us are happy about it. We're grieved by the world. Tired. Restless. Angry at times. We know it's not supposed to be this way.

Talking about these hurts, broken dreams, what seems to be chaotic or unfair, loneliness and so much more is of no threat to Christianity. In fact, this is where Christianity makes the most sense, because these all confront us with the painful truth: we're needy. That's not the only truth, though; there's an answer to that need.

Not only *can* Christians talk about sin, but we must. Our schools should never become places that try to function as though the effects of the Fall only have root outside the boundaries of our school grounds and communities. It's actually unchristian to function this way; it's part of why we've graduated so many Older Brothers. Christianity thrives in repentance, but this means we'll have to embrace who we really are.

ORTHOPATHY

In our journeys toward being more gospel-driven, we have no choice but to own our sin honestly. Unwillingness to do so stifles our opportunities to be visibly and authentically "Christian." But if we long to be true to our missions, we need to be deeply concerned by the many ways sin affects and resides in our hearts.

In *Desiring the Kingdom,* James K.A. Smith asks, "What if you are defined not by what you know but by what you desire? What if the center and seat of the human person is found not by the heady regions of the intellect, but in the gut-level regions of the heart?" This is very similar to Martin Luther's famous statement, "Whatever your heart clings to and confides in, that is your real god."

We help students by forcing them to dig deeper – to not let them off with the easy answer or the quick consequence. We help them by interacting with their hearts, and one of the greatest ways to do that is by modeling what it looks like in our own lives by transparently allowing them to see our own failures.

We also show students their need when we intentionally look for opportunities to help them understand heart-issues through spontaneous day-to-day interactions. It's far easier to focus on observable behavior and ignore the condition of the heart. It's more natural to be bothered by external actions of students than to dig into what's really going on inside the student. Yet, the Bible reminds us that the heart is what's driving what we see. The heart reveals who the student really is. Consider these passages:

- Luke 6:45: "The good person out of the good treasure of the heart produces good, and the evil person out of evil treasure produces evil; for it is out of the abundance of the heart that the mouth speaks."
- Proverbs 4:23: "Above all else, guard your heart, for everything you do flows from it."
- Matthew 15:18-20: "But what comes out of the mouth proceeds from the heart, and this defiles a person. For out of the heart come evil thoughts, murder, adultery, sexual immorality, theft, false witness, slander. These are what defile a person. But to eat with unwashed hands does not defile anyone.

Tragically, students who are rarely corrected about external behaviors inwardly violate the Greatest Commandment. We overlook how our loves are out of whack, because we spend most of our effort on behavior modification. However, if we do the harder work of pursuing students' hearts, we *will* see behavior change. When only focusing on their behaviors, we likely inhibit true growth as we push them toward either self-righteousness or rebellion and resentment. In both cases, it creates hard-hearted students, not those who readily accept and find joy in the freedom of the gospel.

This might require asking a student to talk to you after class about why she continues to do the same annoying things, rather than administering a swift consequence. You seek to understand what she's hoping to get from her behavior. She may be craving attention. Why?

She may be frustrated/angry because of what's going on at home. Why?

She may be bored. Why?

She may be lonely and not understand how to make friends. Why?

I'm not saying we should excuse what students do in our attempts to reach their hearts. Students need to understand the reality of consequences. However, if we only deal with behavior and don't pursue the hard and interrupting time to address the heart, our students conclude that we are *more* concerned about what they do than who they are. Of course, we all know that God's economy switches those priorities.

Those concerned about God's economy stay on the lookout for self-righteousness and pride, because Jesus was too. We often overlook these behaviors, because they're not immediately disruptive. Listen to what students say; look for condescension or self-righteousness. Don't ignore it when you see it. Actually – speak more to it than you do to disruptive behavior. You may find that when one student is corrected for bad behavior, others take it as a cause to further weaponize their own self-righteousness. How odd would it be if the greatest amount of the time you spent in class was dedicated to the responses of those who "didn't do anything wrong!" That would be a shocker.

Make a point to look for opportunities to address failures to meet God's standard – not simply times where it has been broken. When seen, don't ignore it. Address it – not as a weapon, but to prompt opportunities to talk about further reasons for needing Jesus. Bend the conversations toward introspective questions: what does this say about us, our loves, and our idols?

Many younger students typically struggle with impulsivity and navigating the pace of change in their lives while still being accountable to their parents' and teachers' authority. Cut them more slack on the impulsivity. It's often not willful, even though it's a result of the Fall. Rather than correcting students for their impulsivity as your natural go-to, emphasize opportunities to talk to students about idols – why they push against boundaries, what they're hoping to get out of it, or what they really want. In transitional years, it's important that students understand that we realize they are still learning and going through changes as we trying to help them properly shape their angst and awkward development.

Older students begin to formulate their own beliefs – both pushing against boundaries and questioning ideas and structures they previously accepted. Look for opportunities to talk about what's behind their questioning/tension/struggle. Be quicker to talk to them about their idols than their questions, angst, or apathy. It's easy to focus on what we see externally, but we should address why they push against these things, what they're hoping to get out of it, and what they really want. In these maturing years, it's important that students understand that we realize the changes they go through and that we hope to help them properly shape their angst and tension.

Let's not be schools who minimize sin by trite statements like "well, nobody is perfect." We shouldn't explain away sin to make excuses for failures. It's a lost opportunity to talk about Jesus! Let's not champion the successes of our students, alumni, and programs to the point where we ignore what's right in front of our faces – that we are surrounded by brokenness. We're all affected by it. Let's not be schools who leave students thinking that, somehow, they are supposed to be the only ones in the world who are not affected by the Fall.

When we model true honesty about and grieve over sin, we have a far richer ecosystem for a thriving gospel, because our commitments to talking about sin move us ever closer to embracing our need for Jesus.

10

REPAIRING THE RUINS: RUNNING FULL SPEED TOWARD HOPE AND RESTORATION

Grid Question 7: Are we actively proclaiming and seeking repair and restoration according to Jesus's plan?

"You awake us to delight in your praise; for you have made us for yourself, and our hearts are restless until they rest in you." St. Augustine[86]

I have a mild annoyance with a handful of church songs which don't seem to end properly. No matter how many times I've sung them and enjoyed singing them, they feel incomplete as though they're missing something in the last chord. I've never understood why the songwriter doesn't stick a resolving *something* on the end and just "fix" the song. I often think, "I get it. You're being artsy and creative. But your song still isn't right."

One of my friends who teaches high school band says that J.S. Bach's influence is so significant that even modern, popular songs still hinge on the structure of his compositions. We can hear the theme of Bach's Brandenburg Concerto #2 in the Beatles' "Penny Lane," but countless modern songs operate with his "rules." Bach wonderfully employed major and minor chords to establish primary themes, dissonance against these themes, and concluding resolution. Sounds like Creation, Fall, and Redemption, doesn't it?

Bach's "Air on G" moves me every time, in part because he contrasts a soaring tension above and against his initial theme. It almost hurts, because the beauty bleeds out a longing for the other. But the song doesn't leave me there; Bach brings about resolution at the end. It feels complete. It feels richly whole because of that resolved tension.

Similarly, I often think about the movies which most influenced me in my formative years. They tend to be on the heavy side and even dark at times. Yet I didn't gravitate to them because of the dissonance, conflict, or pain. It was the hope and resolution their conclusions provide.

Even though much of the movie is difficult to watch, I can't ignore "Shawshank Redemption" (1994). There's such injustice throughout the film, such pain, and horribly vile portraits of corrupt people. Toward the end, it appears that it's finally time to give up hope. Yet, joy comes crashing in as we're left with a picture of rest, friendship, joy and hope.[87] As Lewis says in his autobiography, *Surprised by Joy*, the truest of joys typically catch us most off guard.

A movie doesn't need to end in complete resolution for me to walk away feeling satisfied. I'm quite content with the slightest glimpse of it. "Magnolia" (1999) requires sitting through three hours of warped characters and great sadness to merely offer a splinter of hope at the end. "Slumdog Millionaire" (2008) doesn't provide the answers, but there's sufficient hope and resolution contrasted against profound despair. In other movies like "Braveheart" (1995) or "Gladiator," (2000) the heroes die unjustly, which I still hate every time. But, there's enough foreshadowed restoration to make the ending work. Even on a lighter side, "Sleepless in Seattle" (1993) merely *suggests* that the two main characters will live happily ever after. And it's enough.

Of course, some movies have "bad" endings and are still very good films, and we'll continue to sing the songs which don't end right. Yet I tend to believe that the reason we crave resolution is not that we've been trained by the story arc of typical Disney movies, but because we are *hard-wired* to long for restoration and redemption. It is the culmination of the grand story of Scripture and the story by which we judge all other stories. We gravitate to this story because of the important question, How is everything going to be fixed?

ORTHODOXY

"The good news is that God has addressed human corruption from outside the system, and it is on this gracious initiative that Christian hope centers." - Cornelius Plantinga[88]

My pastor for over three decades helped me learn to see that one of the most powerful biblical words is the Apostle Paul's use of the word "but." Billy Spink often drew our attention to this word, not because of the word itself – but because of its surrounding context. In several letters to first century churches, Paul takes great effort to explain the effects of sin. They're serious; we can't escape them; we can't fix ourselves; we're all guilty and deserving of God's righteous anger. *But.*

Reading the opening chapters of *Romans,* we see how dire the situation is.

"But..." (3:21)

That word signifies a shift. There's hope, and like Lloyd Christmas, we conclude, "So, you're saying there's a chance."[89] This tiny word offers a glimmer of hope. Just a little word. Yet it tells us that something can be changed. The "but" and the fix it suggests depend upon the action of God. It's most hopeful because of the context into which it collides.

To be specific, redemption is a monetary term which essentially means, "to buy free." Like going to a pawn shop to buy back something you pawned, redemption is paying something back into its right place. Christ's death on the cross provided a payment which accomplished two things. First, it satisfied the justice of God, by taking the punishment for sin. Secondly, because Christ lived a perfect life as Prophet, Priest, and King, His righteousness is given to us so we can be justified in order to do good works – to be a part of God's Redemptive plan. His death puts us and everything else back where we belong.

How someone answers the question of redemption (**How is it fixed?**) often most clearly reveals her worldview because these answers express what's truly ultimate for her and where she puts her trust and hope.

The Naturalist looks to physical fixes, to his own abilities, the government, technology, or education. The Naturalist puts his hope in finite sources like these because his worldview doesn't allow for anything outside the universe; he can only recognize something inside the system. Since he doesn't believe in any kind of original intent, he has a very difficult time articulating what the ultimate goal of any fix actually is.

Similarly, the non-Christian religious person also looks to human fixes. He believes his "god" provides a plan to follow, and it's up to people to follow it. While this person believes in something transcendent, his hope is placed in something natural because his "fix" is contingent upon a person's action. While many religions claim that their god is ultimate, they inconsistently look to what people can accomplish within the system.

If it's ultimately up to people and our efforts, we should have seen a "fix" by now. Considering that people have labored throughout history to better themselves, why don't we see radical repair to life's most significant issues? Of course, we've increased our capacity for communication, comfort, health, and can have hot food handed to us through a drive through window, but we haven't eliminated poverty, environmental catastrophes, cancer, or war. The problem becomes even more significant when we add loneliness, anxiety, and depression to the mix. Not only have we not solved these psychological ailments, but some might also say we're worse off.

We also see the same through religious practices. Despite our efforts to follow God's plan and better ourselves, we've produced hypocrites, conflict between religions, and disagreements within religions themselves. None of these religions seem to stand apart as bettering the human condition. The religions of the world haven't fixed it. Promised utopias have never materialized. The panaceas have vanished, leaving us disillusioned. But we're still left longing for a fix. Somewhere. Somehow.

What we Need

Imagine taking your car to a mechanic because it doesn't feel or sound quite right. You're no expert and can't diagnose the problem. Obviously, you want it fixed, and there are a few things you'd hope to result from the trip to the shop.

First, in order to fix the car, the mechanic needs to have a pretty good idea about the original condition of the car – and not just any car. This car. The mechanic needs to have access to manuals or diagnostic tools which tell him the condition of the car when it rolled off the assembly line. A repaired car runs like it's supposed to, and the mechanic must have clear knowledge of that "ought" in order to return the car back to correct operation.

Second, we expect that the mechanic not only knows what the car is supposed to be like, but also has the availability and knowhow to do the work. We'd be discouraged to hear, "yeah, I know what's wrong with your car, but I can't fix it" or "I'm booked for the next month."

Third, we expect the fix to last. Were a mechanic to properly diagnose the car and have the ability to fix it but not ensure that the repair would last more than a day or so, we'd look elsewhere. The same is true of a surgeon's diagnosis about a knee replacement. We want to know that the fix will last.

In the same way, we look around and see the brokenness of the world and our own roles in it and long for things to be better. We know there must be a fix. A fix which looks like the original. A fix which actually *can* be achieved. A fix which will last.

We could also consider our New Year's resolutions. Often, these hopes link to our personal images of "the good life" – scenarios where we're more disciplined, more in tune with God's Word, a few pounds lighter, and better friends, parents, husbands, or wives. I've never met a person whose New Year's resolutions are intentionally destructive; they're always for the better. This "better" often resembles our longings for what we wish we were; it's a response against the ways we personally experience the brokenness of the world.

Seemingly, the German word *sehnsucht* encapsulates this idea more fully than anything we have in the English language, for it denotes a deep frustration caused by yearnings for the unfinished or unmet ideals of life. In *The Weight of Glory,* C.S. Lewis suggests that this longing mirrors our desire to "get back in" or return to that from which we've been separated.

In one way or another, each of us experiences deep longing. This is one of the reasons why Martin Luther King's words resonate with us. Americans continue to celebrate his birthday because we still need to hear his voice. And, we should pay attention because Dr. King's words are often saturated with biblical images. They harken us both to God's original intent for humanity and to a vision of the New Jerusalem. Dr. King's "I Have a Dream" speech still makes me tear up (and I hope it always will) because I wish my "Lifetime Resolution" could mirror the image he creates. Simply put, we all long to be fixed.

As with the broken car example, we realize that the repair project needs to fit certain criteria. Whoever or whatever will set things straight must know what the original was like, can return things to their right place, and has the capacity to ensure that the repair will last. This "Somebody" must have an eternal perspective and be bigger than us, because we've seen the inadequacy of our fixes. This fits with what Socrates says, "Nothing less than ourselves can satisfy us." That's precisely why we need the promised Messiah.

Redemption is Cosmic

Immediately on the heels of the Fall, God set in place a plan to fix the problem of the world. He gave hope to Adam and Eve – foretelling the One coming to crush Satan's head. (Genesis 3:15) Through the covenants of Scripture, we see God's unfolding plan to repair the ruins of sinful man and sin's effects upon the rest of the world. The Snake Crusher didn't come just to restore the broken relationship between God and Man. He came to restore all our relationships. He came to provide righteousness in order to make "all things new." (Revelation 21:5)

When we think about this fix the way the Bible describes it, we don't merely see a fix for our souls. Romans 8:23 promises "redemption of our bodies," and Colossians 1:20 tells us that Christ intends to reconcile "all things" to Himself. At times, Christians can be a bit myopic, focusing on our souls whereas the Bible is clear: Jesus intends to restore everything to its right place. In Total Truth, Nancy Pearcey beautifully reminds us, "Redemption is as comprehensive as Creation and Fall. God does not save our souls while leaving our minds to function on their own. He redeems the whole person. Conversion is meant to give new direction to our thoughts, emotions, wills and habits." Certainly, Redemption should excite us.

As believers in Christ, we realize that we can't fix things in an ultimate sense, but Donovan Graham explains in *Teaching*

Redemptively that Christians are called to be a part of God's redemptive plan for culture through healing, reconciliation, renewal, deliverance, justice, and peace. In the same way God put Adam in the Garden of Eden to tend the Garden and to extend the beauty and order of the garden to the rest of the world, Christians are tasked with extending the redemptive order to the rest of culture as well. Albert Wolters says in *Creation Regained,*

> "The practical implications of redemption are legion. Marriage should not be avoided by Christians, but sanctified. Emotions should not be repressed, but purified. Sexuality is not simply to be shunned, but redeemed. Politics should not be declared off-limits, but reformed. Art out not be pronounced worldly, but claimed for Christ. Business must no longer be relegated to the secular world, but must be made to conform again to God honoring standards. Every sector of human life yields such examples."[90]

While the language has been more historically common among Dutch Reformed schools, it has recently become common for many other schools to use the biblical framework of Creation, Fall, Redemption, and Consummation. This framework shows up in many of the guiding principles of a truly biblical education, for it captures the entire tapestry of Scripture. In this context, the gospel flourishes, for the framework recognizes God's original design. However, it was thwarted by sin's perversions which have wedged their way into every nook and cranny of our experiences.

But...

The only One who could fix everything came to bring hope. By overcoming sin and death, Jesus accomplished what we could not, and He promises to make "all sad things come untrue" as Tolkien says.

While we live in a world where we're acutely aware of the reality that things are not as they're supposed to be, it would be tragic to focus entirely on the Fall and ignore Creation, Redemption, and Consummation. It's so easy to become discouraged by the effects of sin in the world to such an extent we lose hope or abandon our conviction that it never was supposed to be this way and one day *won't* be.

One of the most influential psychologists of the twentieth century, Viktor Frankl, said that living in the tension between the "is" and the "ought" might be one of the clearest markers of mental and emotional health.[91] This side of Heaven, we are destined to live in the mess. Gospel-driven, Christian education specifically seeks to enable students to navigate this struggle. We want students to have strong foundations which enable them to recognize God's design, appropriately lament, respond to what's wrong, and have passionate hope in the victorious Jesus.

The rhythm of this sort of life, though, is rather dissonant. It's not tidy or neat, for we must willingly enter the messiness of the world with a clear picture of biblical norms while dealing with our own idols. In doing so, a lot of people might see needing Jesus as desirable and beautiful.

The longer I'm in Christian schooling, I'm convinced we could be at the tip of the spear for engaging our broader communities with the power of the gospel. In order to do so, we have to embrace the unique giftings and differences of the vastness of God's kingdom, rather than forcing conformity on our students. Celebrating our differences brings healthy tension. Even more so, a community which handles differences well is most equipped to navigate the "is" and the "ought." We'd also be most fit for imaging Dr. King's words to the onlooking world.

Being at the tip of the spear, though, is undoubtedly uncomfortable at times. The tip is where division happens. It's where pain occurs. Dr. King and others like him were at the business edge for accelerating the systemic change our society continues to need, and they obviously suffered division and great pain. Being committed to the gospel *will* shake things up because it naturally wars against the idols we hold most dearly.

The prophet Isaiah wrote to the Jews in captivity, "Forget the former things, nor consider the things of old. See, I am doing a new thing; now it springs up. Do you not see it? I am making a way in the wilderness and streams in the wasteland." (43:18-19) Thinking and teaching redemptively requires that we recognize the wasteland of the world around us and run toward the streams God makes.

We work daily to equip students with a foundation which enables them to make sense of the world by not only recognizing the wilderness around them, but by running to what God's doing. That's what our schools should be about – enabling our students to run headlong into the wilderness in search of God's streams, knowing that He is their vanguard. Sometimes we don't think about it, but parents and teachers alike are sharpening these little arrows in our school quivers because one day they will be shot out.

Teachers have the task of helping students recognize their role in culture. Students cannot reject it – thus giving the world over to the enemy. Nor, can we allow students to accept the world as it is. We must continue to speak toward the world in its intent, according to creational norms. Looking to these norms, we must then point students to see the perversions resulting from the Fall. Yet, we must reclaim culture as agents of God's redemptive plan. Redemption is re-creation.

I can't help but pause in reflection on that word: recreation. Each of us looks forward to recreation, whether reading a book on the beach or hammock, taking a leisurely walk with a loved one, or playing your favorite yard game. We may not all look forward to vacations (they can tire us out more than our normal routine), but we all look forward to recreation. We look forward to being rejuvenated. To be restored and returned to the way we're supposed to be. Re-creation.

Cornelius Plantinga says that believing in Jesus means believing in his program. In Jesus's first public statement in Luke 4, He says that He came to proclaim good news to the poor, to proclaim liberty to the captives, to give sight to the blind to give liberty to the oppressed, and proclaim the year of the Lord's favor. That seems to be a profound mission, and if that's what Jesus is about, we must be about the same things. This is certainly what Erasmus means when he says, "If Aristotle, who was a pagan and a philosopher too, painted such a picture among men who were not holy and learned in the Scriptures, how much more is it fit for one who moves in the place of Christ."

In his essay, *Of Education* John Milton writes the end of education is "to repair the ruins of our first parents by regaining to know God aright, and out of that knowledge to love him, to imitate him, to be like him," so we may "perform justly, skillfully, and magnanimously all the offices both private and public, of peace and war."[92] Do we teach as though what we are about is a process of repair?

This question should be considered throughout the totality of the Christian school ecosystem. If we truly think about our schools as pointing students toward a restorative view of all things, we need to question all aspects of our school, so that our curriculum and program can be a part of "repairing the ruins." What would it do to our classrooms and our schools if we operated from the standpoint of these truths being pro-life? That's why we ask the question, <u>Are we actively proclaiming and seeking repair and restoration according to Jesus's plan?</u>

ORTHOPRAXY

1. Our schools should physically reflect commitments to restoration, repair, and rescue.

Maybe my favorite part of *Shawshank Redemption* is a scene where the main character, Andy Dufresne, gets himself in trouble for playing part of Mozart's "Marriage of Figaro" over the prison's loud speaker without permission. The music catches the prisoners by surprise, but they all freeze, captivated by the beauty of the two women singing. Red, another prisoner and the narrator in the movie (and in Stephen King's book), voices over the powerful images,

> "I have no idea to this day what those two Italian ladies were singing about. Truth is, I don't want to know. Some things are best left unsaid. I'd like to think they were singing about something so beautiful, it can't be expressed in words, and makes your heart ache because of it. I tell you those voices soared higher and farther than anybody in a gray place dares to dream. It was like some beautiful bird flapped into our drab little cage and made those walls dissolve away, and for the briefest of moments, every last man in Shawshank felt free."[93]

Amid such a dark place as the Shawshank prison, something beautiful brought life. It made hopeless prisoners feel free. Isn't that what rescue is about! Andy Dufresne gave prisoners a glimpse of what it would be like to be rescued by bringing something beautiful into a place of misery. Of course, it's just a movie. But human history is riddled with stories of broken people being softened and won-over by beauty. By grace.

If beauty can liberate prisoners in a hopeless place, we need to think intentionally about the spaces that surround our students. John 1 tells us that the Word has come into the darkness to bring light and life. Certainly, this speaks in spiritual terms. But it's also a very physical proclamation. Jesus physically raised people from the dead. He brought sight to the blind. He cared about the restoration of the physical world.

My wife is an interior designer. Whenever we visit churches, she takes in the aesthetics of the visuals around her, often considering how she would redesign the spaces. She can't turn it off. There have been times that these spaces have diminished her ability to worship. The lack of beauty has created dissonance for her. She isn't the only person who's wired that way. On the other end of the spectrum, most of us have experiences when the beauty around us has driven us toward worship and wonder. There's a profound connection to what our senses take in and what happens to our hearts.

As image bearers, students are relational beings; they are creative beings. They're physical, emotional, tactile and kinesthetic. When we expose them to things which are true, beautiful, and good we give them glimpses of restoration. Exposing students to beautiful things should be part of our restoration projects.

I once visited a school where every inch of the campus reflected an intentional effort to protect the "brand." Teachers could display only a few items which fit within approved schemes – and only in designated bulletin-board type locations. With "safe," and tidy colors, it looked like what you'd expect in a country club or top shelf retirement facility. True, the school reduced the "clutter," and nobody was embarrassed by certain teachers' tackiness or lack of style. While things looked very "nice," the environment didn't inspire wonder. It was orderly, but vibrancy was stifled. In fact, when the school finally painted an accent wall the students buzzed with excitement! This sliver of beauty and interest enlivened students like they were prisoners at Shawshank.

Walk around your classroom and those of your peers. Does the "feel" of your classrooms engender hope and beauty? What about creativity and wonder? How are the sounds, textures, and images driving your class vibe? Is it minimalistic and boring? Is it over-stimulating? Is there order and structure? Too much? Too little? Is there intentionality? If you don't have an eye for design, bring a friend into your room who does. It's that important.

Play good music. Often.

Not only should our classrooms expose students to beauty, but we should also take the appearance of our campuses seriously. If students stay indoors most of the day, we need to get them outside, not just for the physical benefits of fresh air, but also as part of the rescue project. They need to be exposed to good things – not just good ideas, because they are multi-faceted beings. Remember, Adam and Eve were created in a Garden; and we need to think of our Christian spaces as imaging Eden.

I've become friends with a man who teaches high school in Georgia. As students come into his class, he has music playing. Most of the time, it's relaxing music. Sometimes, it's "pump up" music. When the bell rings to start his class, he requires students to sit in silence for five minutes. He encourages them to close their eyes and pause. No, he's not teaching them to meditate. His students have come into his class from somewhere else; their minds can only handle so many different frames of thinking at once, so he requires them to pause. They're not allowed to do homework. They're not allowed to do anything except unwind; he believes it's important to give them that space before he begins the lesson for the day. And he's convinced that, since doing this, his students are more productive.

Most of our schools talk about educating the whole student, but maybe these students have more of their "whole" persons engaged. We need to consider how our senses move us toward wonder, awe, and joy, or hopelessness, darkness, and sadness. Our physical spaces should be "pro-life."

Practically Speaking:

- Commit to finding something beautiful, inspiring, or wonderful to expose students to (at least) every week.
- Find areas of your school that distract from order, structure, and beauty. Involve students in figuring out how to make it better. Even a little bit – that's a glimpse of restoration.

- When students find something beautiful, give them space to talk about it, and remind them that it is an echo of a longing each of us have for when all sad things will be made untrue.

2. Emphasize where your curriculum moves students toward redemption and provides pictures of hope, restoration, and repair.

An underlying assumption of a well-developed philosophy of Christian education must proclaim that truth in its varied forms is fundamentally good for humans. It brings us closer to the Source of that truth. It restores us; it repairs the ruins of the Fall.

In Shakespeare's *Hamlet*, Polonius interrupts young Hamlet and asks him what he's reading, and the prince responds, "Words, Words, Words." Clearly, he's not that interested in or moved by what he is reading. It's just "words" to him.

How often have students left our classrooms learning mere words or facts? Even if we don't sound as warbled as Charlie Brown's teacher, it may be that the content of our classrooms is just as confusing or uninteresting. Granted, there are days when students will struggle to pay attention or keep focused, but there are also days when we're clearly not captivating them – because of something we're doing, or not. There have been lessons where I could tell that the students weren't connecting, and I just pressed forward, because I needed to get through the lesson.

Sin fragments things by disconnecting them from the One who made them. Redemptive teaching looks to restore connections, and connections create meaning. They give us hope that learning will last.

In his *Poetics*, Aristotle says that poetry is far truer than history. How could that be? Poetry is imaginative, and it plays with words, metaphors and similes. History is about facts. But Aristotle suggests that poetry sticks with us, because it's uniquely human. It goes beyond what happened and goes after the soul – the guts of a person. That's why Plato suggested that art should be censored, because it is what most pierces the soul.

Though living thousands of years ago, Aristotle understood what's most likely to stick with a person. And, as an educator, he understood that true learning is fundamentally about lasting change; it should affect the learner. Not that we shouldn't teach physics, or math facts, or geography, but when we do, we must always think about connections. Relationships. Motivations. The "so what" that will stick with a student.

In *Building Better Schools*, Jon Eckert says that we take our "students' learning for granted, mistaking what we teach for what students learn."[94] We're not simply teaching things. We all *know* that, but sometimes, it's easy to focus on all the things we need to push through – what we need to teach – that we sometimes forget why we teach.

When we make curricular decisions, we must consider how the material is good for students – beyond "it's something they need to know." How is studying the animal kingdom good for them? How is a Reading good for them? How is Art good for them? How is creative writing good for them? There are very godly answers to these questions, and they need to be our driving motivations.

As we ask these questions, we need to think about "good" in terms of hope, restoration, and repair. How can Physical Education bring about restoration? How can studying Western Civilizations nurture hope and repair? How can Art History nurture reconciliation?

As we ask these questions, we need to work into our curriculum different lessons, images, ideas, projects, and essential questions which specifically focus on getting students excited when they see things being restored back to the way they're supposed to be. Aim your curriculum at helping students become fans and quick recognizers of restoration. In the same way that a restaurant menu can make your mouth water before the food even arrives, the Christian school curriculum should grow our students' hunger for redemption.

Find stories and examples of restoration, repair, and hope and sprinkle them throughout your curriculum. Get your students so used to seeing, hearing, touching, and thinking about these examples that they realize that something's wrong when they aren't given examples of it. Something is wrong, and that's why we need redemption. Your curriculum should be "pro-life."

Practically Speaking

- Math classes can incorporate situations where Math fixes problems.
- Science class can tell stories about how scientists used the methods God has given us to solve difficult questions. There are so many things here that can amaze students by what science can repair.
- History is rife with examples of restorations, revolutions, reformations. Make sure to draw special attention to these when you come across them.
- In reading/literature it's nearly impossible to find plots that don't have some kind of rescue, redemption, or restoration.
- Remember to help students connect these fixes to the recognition of how they return things back to the way they were supposed to be.

3. And do the same with your assessments …

I shouldn't need to distinguish between curriculum and assessments, because assessments are married to instruction and curriculum. However, I want to make sure we're thinking intentionally about each.

Imagine that David (one of your students) fails a test on chapter 10, and not by a few points. David *really* bombed it, getting more questions wrong than he got right. To add to the scenario, the average on the test was 89%. Clearly, your test wasn't unreasonable; in fact, you probably could have made it more challenging. However, David was the significant outlier.

I'll confess what my response were in my early years as a teacher. I moved on without thinking twice. Chapter 11, here we come.

Worse confession: I remember saying to students in these same early years, "if you got a poor grade on a test and don't say anything to me, I'll assume you're content with your grade. Unless you ask for help, I'm going to move on." And, that's what I'd do. I wouldn't intervene. I didn't initiate any kind of rescue. I let kids drown.

Thankfully, the Redeemer intervened on our behalf and hasn't let us drown. He entered into our failure 2,000 years ago to pursue us and rescue us. That should tell us something.

Let's consider David again. If he failed Chapter 10, why would I ever take him to Chapter 11 without addressing what he doesn't know? Doesn't moving on without pressing into David's need almost guarantee his learning gap will grow? Even more critically, why would I allow him to get further behind in a subject where the chapters and units build on each other (like Math or World Languages)? Tragically, I've done this when I should have made it a priority to use David's Chapter 10 performance to reveal what he knows so I can chart a plan to help him fill in those gaps. I should have had a rescue plan in mind, informed by what I learned about him from his Chapter 10 test. We don't just assess students because we're required to give grades; we should think of them as guides to help us chart what our rescue plan looks like.

Considering that Christianity hinges on the idea of redemption, my classroom practices should also model restoration and repair – more so than what we'd see in a secular classroom. The instruction should be geared toward restoration – making them whole – not just cramming knowledge into their heads. Similarly, my assessments should be part of a process of repair and restoration. In fact, our assessments might be one of the best tools in our toolboxes for this repair plan. Don't miss the opportunity to use them appropriately.

If this is true, most of my assessments should be formative. I should think about all the assignments and measures I give along the way to repair and restore students. Our assessment procedures shouldn't beat students down. They should bring them closer and closer to the ultimate goals we have for them. And we should create language and class cultures around teaching students to learn to see assessments as part of this hopeful restoration.

Do I see my assessments as part of a rescue plan? If I do, it likely affects the sort of assessments I give and the frequency with which I give them. Of course, this presupposes that I have a clear idea of the end in mind and have charted out the various paths I'm going to take students down to arrive at our end goal. It requires a healthy dose of backwards design. Our assessments are artifacts which reflect our underlying objectives, values and beliefs. They should promote our students' dignity, allow for brokenness, and pursue God's redemptive plan. Our assessments should be "pro-life."

Practically Speaking:

- Either offer opportunities to repair learning deficiencies from former assessments or introduce reviews on following assessments to incentivize them learning the things they didn't do as well last time.
- Give quicker feedback on formative assessments to enable students to better fill in gaps before summative assessments. This should be a top priority – not because administrators require it, but because we see feedback as necessary parts of the restoration process.
- While I had to figure out ways to speed up grading processes, I saw much higher grades on summative assessments when I allowed students to retake formative assessments. Now I know some might balk at letting students retake things, but isn't the goal to see students succeed on summative assessments?

- Consider putting a plan in place to allow students to delay taking major assessments until they are ready to take them.
- Have a plan in place for when students demonstrate that they really don't know the information you're teaching. It's better to involve outside resources sooner than later.

4. And with your approaches to classroom management and discipline.

Several years ago, I listened to an administrator from a Christian school in Connecticut describe his school's approach toward student discipline. He said that, if a student submitted to their discipline process, there was nothing a student could do (barring clear threats to student safety) to result in an automatic expulsion. Questions came up about drinking on campus, student pregnancy, or students "coming out." The administrator reiterated that, as long as the student adhered to their process, the school wouldn't expel him or her.

I was all ears.

This school had three expectations within their discipline model which trickled down into basic classroom management guidelines. Were students to overstep boundaries:

- There would be a form of discipline, consequences, or punishment to serve as a tangible reminder that students had done something they shouldn't have.
- There was some measure of accountability going forward.
- There was a plan for restoration to the community.

Clearly with major offenses, the consequences, accountability measures, and plan for restoration would be weightier. However, the school was willing to walk alongside students for any reason with the goal of restoring whatever had been broken.

Someone else asked if this administrator had been burned in the process. He said, "only twice." He admitted that the process was often messy. He admitted that there were times that students didn't follow through on the process and they ended up having to leave the school. But, in listening to him describe their model, I was moved by their willingness to formalize a process which seeks restoration as an ultimate goal.

In a similar way, we need to think about our structures with "restoration" as an end worth pursuing. It's helpful to know that even negative consequences can be restorative.[95] At times, the goal of our management or discipline policies and structures is "order" or "quiet." While these have a place in school, we need to realize that students *will* overstep our guidelines, and our models need to be designed not merely so the student won't do it again, but that the consequences and accountabilities bring about wholeness. When we aim at wholeness, we might also engage more subtle or quietly divisive attitudes which aren't disruptive on the surface.

I once observed an elementary school teacher and marveled at her focus on wholeness and restoration. A student was repeatedly disruptive in class to the point where the teacher calmly told the student to wait in the hall until she would talk to him. As the student walked toward the door, another student said "he's always like that" as others *hmphed* or rolled their eyes. The teacher asked the assistant teacher to go outside in the hall with the student. Then, the lead teacher addressed the rest of the class about their condescension and self-righteousness and how their attitudes were more of a threat to the class than what this student was doing.

She walked out into the hall, spoke to the student before bringing him back in. The student came in and apologized to the class for being a distraction, and one of the other boys said, "We weren't good friends to you, and that's even *badder*. I'm sorry." He did this even though the teacher never told the students they had to apologize. I'm quite sure that this is the only time I've ever cried while observing a classroom. Not only was the distraction addressed, the teacher viewed restoration on a far deeper level. She didn't just deal with the most glaring symptoms; she looked at the brokenness before her and brought about the sort of restoration students need to see in their classrooms.

Every year, I re-listen to Paul Tripp's series, "Your Christian School: A Culture of Grace?" I do this because I need to be reminded that we're supposed to be believe the gospel, and that schools that believe the gospel function differently than other schools do. Tripp suggests that, if there were a classroom management program that guaranteed results, we would no longer need Jesus. He also says that our primary difficulties in school result from "expecting rules to accomplish what only grace can."

Thinking redemptively about our discipline and management plans means we need to be more willing to have policies in place which allow for treating students and situations differently. We need to be more for the child and the supremacy of Jesus than our precious policy matrix. Of course, that may mean that we're not "fair" or that things get messy. But, the gospel hinges around a Savior who entered into our mess and showed radical grace, rather than what was clearly deserved.

Practically Speaking:

- Always insist that students see consequences as necessary aspects of restoration.
- When disruption happens, the first question needs to be "how do we bring about reconciliation?" not "how do we punish this, so it doesn't happen again?"
- Be ready to defend your practices with students and families – that you are more interested in hearts that see hope and forgiveness than in ensuring that everyone is treated the same.
- Make both asking for and giving forgiveness as important in your classroom as other classroom values.

5. Seek the welfare of the city.

I have previously referenced the prophet Jeremiah's charge for the Israelites to seek the welfare of the city where they had been taken in exile. Rather than secluding themselves from Babylon's pagan influences, Jeremiah told them to build houses, plant gardens, have flourishing families, and pray for the welfare of the city. (29:5-7)

Christian education is also inherently outward facing. We have failed students if our alumni retreat from the world around them – forming safe, tidy, Christian atmospheres, showing little evidence of engaging God's world. Our schools should prepare students to see the Church's ministry of redemption and reconciliation in a broken world. The truth, beauty, and goodness they learn should require something of them: they should reflect it into every area of their lives. While many non-Christians know Christians by the things they're opposed to, our alumni should be known as better neighbors, entrepreneurs, citizens, artists, plumbers, police officers, activists, parents, and friends – all because we believe in and long for the redemption of all things.

Nearly every school, whether Christian or not, now includes words like "service" and "leadership" in their mission statements. Apart from a Christian understanding of redemption, these concepts make little sense. Yes, we should long to see our students become servants and leaders, but certainly not to keep up with other schools or to pad students' resumes. It should flow out of our beliefs that Christianity celebrates transformation and restoration. It champions hope.

Often, people serve out of a desire to help. But, if we're not careful, it creates hierarchical thinking – "from a position of being one of the 'haves,' I'm helping you who is one of the 'have nots." The greater helps the lesser, and might even look down on the one who is served. But if we properly teach students to be fans of repair, they'll naturally jump at opportunities to see restoration firsthand. When we marry opportunities to serve with school-wide commitments to restoration, students get to see and feel redemption. It gives them a foretaste of Jesus's return and aligns them with what Jesus came to do. It's not about me helping you; it's about seeing what Jesus is doing. It's about running toward the fixes (even when they're messy) because we're fans of Jesus entering into our mess to usher in His fix.

Stay away from the temptation to make service opportunities only "extra-curricular" or "add-ons" in your school. We want students to be servants, because they understand how Jesus came to serve, they are enamored by Jesus's plan for restoration, and because they see their roles in the Church's mission to engage the world. Yes, we might need to start with programs to create traction toward others-minded service and restorative engagement becoming part of the school culture. But we look for a way of life, not "events" because the goal isn't service itself. Rather, it's a byproduct of a passionate commitment to redemption within the school and flowing into the communities our schools touch.

Practically Speaking:

- There should be some place in your school curriculum that focuses on learning more about your city: its history, its people, and the current events.
- Find places in your school to talk about the good things happening in your city and push your community toward being quick to celebrate when you see good things happening.
- Address some of the obstacles, evils, and challenges in your city; pray for them; charge students with the task of figuring out how your school can bring about change.
- Do not retreat from the city. Even though many of our schools have moved into the suburbs, we still need to find avenues for engaging and being healthy contributors to our cities.

6. Thrive in the messiness of redemptive endeavors.

It's vitally important that we never forget that only God can *really* fix things. At best, we might be blessed to be instruments of change, of repair. We cannot view ourselves as functional saviors; that's never what we were called to be. Yes, we must be huge fans of restoration and reconciliation, but those things can only be brought about, ultimately, by God.

Christian schools can often be more committed to success and repair than we are to the God who brings it about. Again, our task is not to seek and promote a "victorious Christian life" or "victorious Christian students." Throughout the Bible, we see that restoration is God's work, and (at times), He allows His people to be instruments of bringing it about. But it's still His work. Consider Psalm 40:1-3, "I waited patiently for the Lord; he inclined to me and heard my cry. He drew me up from the pit of destruction, out of the miry bog, and set my feet upon a rock, making my steps secure. He put a new song in my mouth…"

God is the one who rescues the Psalmist; it's the Psalmist's work to wait and to witness what God is doing. In Exodus 3, God calls Moses to be the front man of His plan to rescue the Israelites out of the hand of the Egyptians. In a way, Moses (and all Israel) was rescued from a pit of destruction. He had lost everything and lived as a shepherd in the wilderness. That was his own miry bog. But God lifted him up, set Moses on a rock, and "put a new song in his mouth" when Moses and the Israelites would worship God on that very same mountain.[96] God was also very insistent that everyone understood that it was not Moses' abilities or Pharaoh's kindness that caused the Israelites to go free; it was entirely God's power. Yet, God used His people to participate in what He was doing. This is no less true throughout the rest of the Bible.

Believing this, "waiting patiently for the Lord" means that we look to see what God is doing, and recognize that He may be using us to accomplish His purposes. Yet, as we know from the Exodus story, Moses' part in God's rescue plan wasn't absent from a lot of mess and heartache. Complaining. Unfaithfulness. Idolatry. Rebellion. Yet, God's plan was not set on hold during these times; they were part of His plan.

Being in the business of repair and restoration doesn't mean we look for tidiness, success, simplicity, or victory. It means we seek what Jesus is doing and recognize that growth is often found in the midst of hurt. Heathcliff Huxtable once said on *The Cosby Show,* "I'm not interested in Justice; I just want quiet" to his arguing kids. We laugh, because it comically captures where many of us have been as parents and/or teachers. It's extremely easy to want quiet, calm, obedience, compliance, etc., when the deeper problems are ignored, only to surface in more dangerous ways later. We do this, because it's easier to focus on symptoms than problems.

It's foolish to think that projects of repair will only see prosperity. Actually, real growth is most likely to happen in the midst of adversity. The best coaches often talk about fears of easy success. They know that team growth requires conflict and challenge. Similarly, if you want to get in physical shape, you'll have to tear some muscle fibers along the way. The growth doesn't happen despite the pain; it happens *because* of it.

For our schools to have pronounced commitments to redemption, we can't run away from the messiness which necessarily results from broken teachers and staff pursuing broken students in broken schools surrounded by a broken world. Rather than running away from it, maybe we should run toward it. Of course, this is counter-cultural, but it's also life-giving to the school and its members.

You'll know it's' working when a student begins to see the goodness and mercy of God and remarks to a teacher, "Wait. You're proud of me, even though I'm nothing like the students who do everything right?" You don't expect me to be like them?" We want students to be the people God created them to be, but what we push them toward needs to allow them to be the messy, untidy, oddly unique persons they are.

The restitution at the end of the parable of the two sons is not that the Prodigal Son starts behaving like his older brother. The restoration is that he came home and celebrated with his father. The relationship is what's primary. In the same way, the images of repair, redemption, fix, reconciliation, restoration, and success must not be such that our students feel pushed toward becoming Older Brothers. Older Brothers don't think they need Jesus, even though they so deeply do. Consequently, redemption in our schools must look like growth while not minimizing the goodness of needing Jesus.

Practically Speaking

- Work to be known for praising growth, more than "performance." They don't have to be mutually exclusive, but if you had to err on one side, it ought to be the former.
- Whenever you see student behavior less than "ideal," rather than trying to fix it and force conformity, enter into it with the student. Students need to know that their teachers are there with them, regardless of who they are and what they do.
- When students or events create tension in your classroom and school, rather than first addressing the symptoms (the noise, conflict, energy, frustration), be willing to tolerate that if it means you're addressing student hearts.
- Always remember that Jesus didn't come for the healthy, but the sick. So, the goal isn't to nurture a veneer of healthy people, but to cultivate a school where sick people are allowed to be sick, because that's when they'll know how good it is to be met by the Healer.

Why it's Christian

Everyone longs for a fix. Yet, Christians realize that trying harder, doing more, and being better won't bring about the sort of fix we really need. We also embrace that we're not the ones making the fix happen. We look to Jesus, and have confident hope in His fix, because He has already done what's necessary to ensure it will all come true. The Bible often talks about this restoration with such certainty, that it uses what reads in English as past tense. It will happen. We are both recipients of that fix and His people called to be parts of His plan.

Christians recognize that Jesus's fix is a restoration of all things. We don't look to be transported to an other-worldly existence. Rather, we look to a New Jerusalem, which is very much like this world – because God cares about it so much that He wants to see all of it repaired.

This being the case, Christians should be people of confident and joyful hope, because we rest in the only One who can bear the weight of our hopes. We can truly care about the world around us, because it clearly matters to God in an eternal sense. So, caring about the world and longing for redemption are uniquely Christian, because only Christianity seeks to see a fix that's restorative, not an escape.

ORTHOPATHY

Love is at the epicenter of anything we can call Christian, because Christianity is rooted in God's love for us and requires us to respond in love of God and others. The primary reason Christians should root for restoration is because we love what God is about and we love seeing repair, because we are beneficiaries of the very same rescue mission.

If we want students to long for redemption and to learn to see their place in God's redemptive plan, they need to be people of hope. If they're going to be people of hope, they need to see it in us. Maybe it's good to remember that teaching is inherently one of the most optimistic professions there is. Unfortunately, a lot of teachers become ground down by the systems in which they work, but the very notion of teaching assumes that something good is going to come out of our efforts. We're supposed to be optimists; yet, so often teachers become complainers. I've done my fair share of it. But we need to hold each other accountable – accountable to being people of hope.

Students need to see us being hopeful about what they're learning in class on any given day, about how they will do on a test, and how the Lord will use what they're learning in their lives. That doesn't mean that we need to be Pollyanna all the time. Hopeful people can grieve over sadness and loss, but we can't give up.

When Middle Earth is near its darkest point in *The Lord of the Rings*, Gandalf stands before Denethor, the Steward of Gondor – the last bastion of hope against the rising tide of Mordor. Hopeless and territorial, Denethor accuses Gandalf of meddling in his kingdom, to which Gandalf replies,

> "All worthy things that are in peril as the world now stands, these are my care. And for my part, I shall not wholly fail of my task, though Gondor should perish, if anything passes through this night that can still grow fair or bear fruit and flower again in days to come. For I also am a steward."

Like Gandalf, we should be stewards of anything that can bear fruit. Our students will bear fruit of one kind or another, and they have been entrusted into our care. Our hopeful care must be geared toward them "growing fair" and flowering. To flourish. Full, flourishing wholeness. *Shalom*. And in that shalom, we see how good it is to live and flower in need of Jesus.

11

ENOUGH PHILOSOPHIZING ALREADY!

Applying the Grid in Increasingly Specific Ways

Though in opposition to a "worldview in a box" curriculum, I still recognize the need for tangible examples of using the framework I've detailed in the previous chapters. For those who got through the seven questions and ask, "How do I *use* these questions," this next chapter is for you.

There's no limit to the level of specificity I could provide. How does the Grid apply to a certain lesson? How do we use it in a specific context or situation? What does it look like when we apply it to actual programs and processes? Even though my hope for my follow-up book *Gospel Above Grades* is to address school life in even more tangible ways, there's no way to properly address each specific question and need. That's why I've tried to provide follow up ideas in each chapter to go along with the Grid questions.

If you've ever had to teach a new curriculum or methodology, you know that it takes significant time before you feel like you've got a good handle on it. Even when working with a specific curriculum for many years, the best teachers grow along with their curricula.

In the same way, you'll likely stumble through these questions as you work through them within your own context. However, I fully believe that you'll get better at them. I've seen it in my own practice, and I've seen it in others' too.

Having taught this framework for more than a decade now, I've gotten used to the sorts of questions teachers ask as they process through the categories and ideas. I've also watched people wonder not only how they could use these questions in their schools but even how they could go about building a program to have these questions (or something like them) be used to build a professional development curriculum or program.

This chapter is intended to provide some direction. Were a teacher to think specifically about her discipline or were a school to build a worldview development program, what would that look like? While this won't answer all your questions, maybe it will make it easier to get an idea of what it could look like in your school. If you do get to the point where you have specific questions, it would be a great honor to be an ongoing resource to you. That desire was what drove me to start teaching this framework to other schools and that same desire is the very reason I wrote this book.

And, if I can help you apply any of these questions in a more specific way, please let me know. There are few things I enjoy more than exploring these sorts of questions with schools and teachers. Email me: noahsamuelbrink@gmail.com.

We all have room for improvement in the philosophical and theoretical dimensions of our schools, but I've also seen schools bog down when theory is separated from practical, actionable plans. For the purposes of providing a context of practical use, let's walk through an example of grid-theory applied to an aspect of the school I've rarely seen discussed.

I'm going to target the World Languages department – not because I understand it particularly well, but because these Grid questions are sufficiently applicable. I'd far rather see a World

Languages department ask and struggle with questions like these than one which never gets beyond assigning Bible verse translations.

To those of you who teach in another department, stay with me. Even though I'm zeroing in on a specific department, my methodology should demonstrate ways to employ some of these larger questions, regardless of your context. The same can even be true of age groups; there are certain things you can do with students differently from what you can do at other stages. There will be unique opportunities of each.

The easiest disciplines for "doing biblical integration" are in the Humanities.[97] Of all the humanities, literature absolutely seeps with conversations which take us back to the gospel, because it deals with the human condition – with images of oughtness, brokenness, hope, redemption, heroes, and beauty which brings people to worship. For this reason, I've observed that many schools' "worldview champions" tend to be literature teachers.

There are also ample resources which speak toward a Christian approach to the sciences, and I've seen lots of schools utilize these to equip students to respond to the pervasiveness of naturalism in scientific study. So, many schools have begun conversations about what it looks like to teach biology, chemistry, astronomy, and physics from a Christian perspective. So, I don't see the same vacuum here I see in the World Languages department.

[I can't avoid a brief sidenote here: Many of my former students returned years later to say they felt unprepared to deal with the naturalistic insistence of their college professors. At first, I was a bit surprised to hear this, our school used secular textbooks and supplemented them with books addressing naturalistic evolution. I *know* our students were exposed to evolution; they weren't sheltered away from it. But they expressed that they didn't know how to *think* about evolution.

Christian science teachers have the unique task of emphasizing God's hand in creation while providing caution against naturalistic, theistic philosophies which remove God from his lovingly creative work. I've seen many Christian science teachers who work very hard to provide these perspectives. Maybe there's even more work to do.

Books which target errors in evolution or seek to provide a defense against it certainly have their place, but they prompt students to default into opposition-mode the moment evolutionary buzzwords are mentioned. That's not training thinkers; it's training opposers. Unfortunately, this resembles how we often teach students to deal with secular ideas, literature, art, and film. I'm not sure how it's Christian to only point out non-believers' errors. Thinking means far more than merely pointing out what's wrong.

I'm far more interested to see what happens when students read books like *The Language of God* by Francis Collins, who believes both the primary tenets of evolution and the gospel of Jesus. A book like this would challenge students to think about evolution, because it forces them out of their traditional categories, where they hear "evolution" and think "OK, I got it … it's atheistic … it's wrong." If we want to train students to think, we must allow them to see *where opposing views are right* – not just where they're wrong. In *Mere Christianity*, Lewis says it's actually impossible for other religions to be totally wrong from top to bottom. Because this is true, we can't allow students to develop bad habits in response to non-Christian things. What will they do when confronted with ideas which make sense, when all they've heard is how wrong these other views are?

Of course, this takes much more work; it's not easy. It's not tidy. Encouraging students to reflect on ideas contrary to God's character and nature may mean they are not repulsed by what they see. It might mean that some of them entertain thoughts that are different from ours. That's where we need to guide them and walk through their exploration with them, rather than crafting them to think and be exactly like us.]

Back on task …

Many schools seek to increase their ability to teach subjects from a Christian perspective, but I haven't found many asking where the gospel shows up in specific departmental objectives or how their departments' curriculum shapes both hearts and bodies. When it comes to the World Languages departments, I find the conversations barely existent, and I haven't found many resources to help.

We may teach world languages because state boards or university admissions offices require it, but (like many other programs in our schools) not necessarily because our commitment to a gospel-worldview is pushing us in these directions. We include them because of external pressures – all the while insisting that we do "everything" from a biblical worldview (as I clear my throat and raise my eyebrows).

Recently, my concern grew even more when an administrator explained to me that her school teaches world languages so students can fulfill the Great Commission and evangelize the nations. Certainly, this is a better answer than meeting state and university standards, right?

Right?

Even though global missions is a biblical mandate, when it comes to teaching world languages, this answer is neither sound theologically nor pedagogically. There has to be a better way. While I don't have nearly every answer, I want to use the Grid questions to raise ideas which World Languages departments can consider in pursuit of the gospel. Lord willing, this brief exercise can demonstrate how these seven questions should function in the life of a school that tries to use gospel-guided principles to shape its school's programs.

I also hope this chapter will reinforce the fluidity of the questions. There's a lot of overlap in what we find when we habitually ask these questions. By the time we've gotten through all seven questions, you'll see repeating themes.

Every department won't answer each question in entirely unique ways. Some departments will go deeper with certain questions than others will. And some questions will be answered essentially the same way by every single academic department. These questions are designed to ensure that we're mindful of fundamental ideas.

Grid Question 1: Are we declaring and pursuing God as ultimate over everything else?

I would rejoice to hear that a high school curriculum springboarded student's calling to evangelize the nations. Yet, saying that the primary reason for teaching world languages is for global evangelism is educationally narrow; it's also man centered. This contrasts against the first question of the Grid which seeks the supremacy of God above everything else. Yes, we should be concerned about others, but not to the detriment of forgetting the ultimate goal for our studies – to know and love God more.

God requires the Church to go to the nations. But every student won't go into vocational, international missions, and they're not disobedient for choosing not to do so. My younger brother is a missionary. My older brother is a dentist, and his vocation serves the Kingdom just as powerfully as my younger brother's.

Because most students won't use what they learned for evangelistic purposes, the limited justification we gave them for their studies seems to minimize lasting meaning in it. This is the problem with giving students "lesser" answers to the routine question: "Why do we have to know this?" While many of our answers are true (Yes, they *could* use it for evangelism. Yes, it will influence the ACT or SAT, etc.), students see right through flawed answers, because they recognize how temporary it is to learn information merely for limited purposes. This doesn't change their hearts; it simply fulfills pragmatic desires and likely fuels their propensity toward self-centeredness.

When asking how our departments or specific classrooms proclaim God's supremacy, it forces us to structure what we're doing so God's supremacy becomes the primary objective. And this can very much guide our motives for teaching World Languages.

In *The Four Loves,* C.S. Lewis writes about the death of his close friend Charles Williams, and his reflection shows that it wasn't only the relationship with Williams that he lost. He also lost those things which Williams brought out of J.R.R. Tolkien. Lewis says,

> "By myself, I am not large enough to call the whole man into activity; I want other lights than my own to show his facets. Now that Charles is dead, I shall never again see [Tolkien's] reaction to a specific Charles joke. Far from having more of [Tolkien], having him "to myself" now that Charles is away, I have less of [Tolkien]."[98]

This wonderfully details what relationships are designed to bring about; the difference of experience causes us to see things that, otherwise, we wouldn't see. They broaden our lines of sight. They bring out new emotions. They connect in ways we naturally wouldn't.

When we desire for our entire school program to proclaim God above all else, we consider how our individual departments help in this endeavor. Knowing more about other languages helps us to know more about God, because it shows us something He has revealed about Himself which we would not see without that exposure. This should actually be at the heart of our justification for adding any new program, but the world languages teachers have a special claim to it.

I'm jealous of my brother's family. They are full-time missionaries, currently living in their second European country. My middle school-aged niece and nephew are now tackling their fourth languages, and I'm confident they have the advantage of developing a broader and fuller view of God than my children will likely ever have. I've seen a little bit of this when I've had international friends describe how their languages translate biblical passages. Hearing these differences has caused me to notice things about the Bible in ways I wouldn't have, left to my own experiences.

When we learn about other cultures, we see the different ways God has revealed Himself. We see the largeness of the Church and different ways people worship God. This even goes back to the Garden of Eden, for God could have created someone just like Adam to be his helper. But God created a woman who was anatomically and psychologically different; these differences would be for each other's benefit, as these distinctions would enable each to perceive fresh things about the world and the One who made it.

Viewing diversity as a tool to know more about God provides a renewed motivation for learning about the varied cultures of the world and their languages. We have to realize how a limited view of the world will necessarily lend to a small view of God. The more of the world we know, the more we can know of God, who is bigger than it all. Seeing how different people groups experience and worship God should bring about wonder and amazement. A World Language department (and the subjects and individual classes that make up that department) should be built around celebrating diversity for the purpose of knowing more of God. It should be cognizant of fostering students' awareness of the "bigness" of God who is above and Creator of the people groups of the world.

Seeing this diversity can also return students to the uniqueness of the Triune Godhead. God LOVES diversity, because He is diverse at His core. In the Trinity, we see three Persons, yet one God. Thinking in a trinitarian way, a World Language department ought to get excited about its advantages to talk about one, diverse Church.

The Bible also teaches about God's heart for the nations, and this is the context within which the Great Commission makes the most sense. So, if God has a heart for the nations, we must also – both out of concern for other people groups and to be passionate about what God is passionate about.[99]

I'm a fan of schools that have adopted the title, "World Languages Department." In a way, it's less centered on us. As Americans, it's easy to think that anything else is "foreign." Foreign to us, maybe, but not to people in those countries. The more we think of these languages as foreign, the more likely we be to keep them at a distance. However, when we talk about them as "world languages," it provides a broader and more welcoming perspective. These languages give us a glimpse of the wealth of languages spoken around the world.

There are many languages, because the world is a big place, and God is bigger still. These languages, collectively and individually, help us to have a fuller perspective of who this God is, and this should excite us to see how these departments have a unique task in helping students to be enlivened by the world.

Questions which flow out of Grid Question 1:

- In what ways do other cultures understand God differently than we do? What does that tell us about Him?
- What do students learn about God specifically from studying another language and the people who speak it?
- Loving God looks differently in different cultures. What can we gain from that?
- What does it reveal about God that He created the world and its different customs, languages, and desires?
- How do we take what we're learning about God into other disciplines?

Grid Question 2: Are we modeling and encouraging dependence upon God's Truth wherever it's seen?

Much of the goal of this second question is wound around embracing our own limitations when it comes to truth, while still having great confidence in the truth God has revealed. So, world languages should always be taught to remind students how finite they are but also inspire them to wonder – because of the ways a global perspective broadens their appreciation of truth.

Deep study of other cultures (any study of language will inherently be a study of culture, because the two are married) should nurture an appreciation for truth, beauty, and goodness in a way which recognizes that we don't have a monopoly on any of these. The labor required to better understand world cultures and their languages should yield a broader view of truth and recognition of human limitations. It's always good for us to have things in our lives to serve as reminders of how finite we are; for this is very much at the heart of what it looks like to proclaim the gospel to ourselves.

Many Americans have the tendency to think the world revolves around our own country, and we desperately need to repent of it. It's easy to think the rest of the world would work better if it functioned more like the U.S. But, when we work to understand more of the world (cultural beliefs, values, institutions, and artifacts) we have new contexts which speak into what we always assumed to be true. Rightfully seen, these cultures (and the languages which they reveal) enable us to see truth more fully – truths we wouldn't be able to grasp within limited, nationalistic perspectives.

Any time we can use a subject to reinforce students' limitations it creates space for conversation about the gospel. Because of the difficulty of language acquisition and the limitations of our national perspectives, the World Languages department can create plenty of gospel-directed fodder for discussion. It should also nurture awe, as students are directed toward seeing their own dependence within the vastness of ways God has revealed Himself among the nations.

There's also great power in words. Words matter so much to God that He chose to reveal Himself through words – even as *the* Word. (John 1:1) My own vocabulary has been broadened by very rudimentary attempts to learn aspects of other languages. It has cultivated a more vivid landscape of word meanings.

I've seen this in attempts to understand the Greek and Hebrew words our English translations of the Bible have tried to capture. For example, throughout the New Testament, multiple words for love are used, yet English speakers have one. So, we inherently miss some of the original intent of biblical passages.

Our languages have limitations. In disciplining ourselves to study the nuances of syntax differences and the oddities of idioms, it gives us a broader appreciation for the power of words and their meaning, for the immense wonder and diversity the world has to offer, and for the greatness of this God who still reveals Himself to these people in ways they can understand.

I've also had people tell me that certain books, like *Les Misérables,* are best read in their original language. Apart from my scoffs in the general direction of people who make such statements, it makes complete sense. There's no way an English translation can fully capture the meaning or the beauty of the words and phrases Victor Hugo used to write his masterpiece. Similarly, teaching world languages helps students see truth and beauty in the fullest intent of the authors. This discipline could even teach us something about how we handle God's Word.

Thinking along these lines could ignite a wonderful conversation about seeing the world as God intended it to be seen, which forces consideration of the Creational norms and the perversions of the Fall. This would help students see the connections and overlaps between these different categories of the Grid.

Questions which flow out of Grid Question 2:

- What are some of the other languages' words we don't have good translations for? How does this reflect our own limitations and broaden our perspective on words, meanings, emotions, and the fullness of God's world?

- What can we learn about word meanings and God's intent for how we learn language and Truth?
- What are some concepts we could understand more fully from learning the languages of other cultures?
- How can studying world languages cause students to see how much more there is to learn out there? When they see this, do you launch into talking about the God who is above it and our dependence upon Him?
- How do students feel when they fumble through the learning of a language? What does this teach them about themselves? Can this be used to remind them of how needy they are? Can it be used to nurture their dependence?

Grid Question 3: Are we honoring the full nature of all members of the school community?

In Matthew 22, Jesus makes a quite shocking statement when asked what the Greatest Commandment is. Any Jewish scholar would have known that the *shema* (Found in Deut. 6:4: "You shall love the Lord your God…") was the Greatest Commandment. But Jesus grabbed everyone's attention by attaching another commandment alongside it. He says there's one "like unto it." It would have perked up some ears to hear that loving my neighbor as myself is like unto the greatest of all commandments. Yet, that's what Jesus says; we are supposed to deeply love others.

In his book, *Fool's* Talk, Os Guinness reminds us that Jesus never talked to different people the same way, and we shouldn't either. For, we recognize the dignity of the individual. We're called to love individuals and to recognize their dignity. Yet we cannot love people properly if we don't know anything about them. Christian education seeks to provide a knowledge base so students can better love God and others well. It's not knowledge for knowledge's sake, it's knowledge so we can love rightly. It's about shaping our loves.

Going a step further, how can we truly know, understand, or value people if we don't know their language? Certainly, we can have fondness toward people who speak other languages. I've experienced deep bonds with international friends who I couldn't understand, but I know full-well that these relationships would be much richer if I could speak their language. The language barrier always gets in the way. Yet, removing obstacles and leaping over them is central to the heart of what is required to adequately love someone.

It's immensely embarrassing that Americans have put so little value on language acquisition; it seems like we are the only industrialized, educated country with so little emphasis on language acquisition. Nearly all my international friends know multiple languages. They've made great effort to speak my language, and I've made so little to speak theirs. This says something about the dignity we ascribe to other cultures.

Within our own school contexts, we have families from very different cultures; the conversations surrounding diversity and racial reconciliation are very present and necessary in our schools. World Languages departments can be instrumental training grounds for students learning what it looks like to celebrate our differences, not just tolerate them. For, students need these differences so they can see their own needs and have a fuller appreciation of God's nature. This can be a great laboratory for building a culture which doesn't shy away from the dialogues of race and class, because students will increase their awareness of what it looks like to live in God's world on His terms.

We also have to recognize that students have different giftings; they aren't all good at math, science, literature, or P.E. But some of them are wired so learning a new language comes very easily to them. These classes provide a platform for such students to excel in areas which can be celebrated. Too often, we focus on excellence in Math, Science, and English above others, in part, because these are the subjects which are most recognized on standardized testing. But, doesn't this show how much we have relegated learning to certain areas alone?

Questions which flow out of Grid Question 3:

- How do we recognize individual students' abilities to excel in the world languages? Do we put this gift on the same par as other disciplines?
- How can we intentionally use our World Languages department to recognize the dignity of all persons? Can these conversations be used to encourage students to become more sympathetic to differences within the members of the school community? If our students are willing to learn more about cultures overseas, why aren't they more willing to learn about "different" ones here?
- What cultures elevate certain dimensions of what it means to be image bearers and prophet, priest, and king better than others? How can this increase our ability to dignify people within our own cultural context?
- How do other cultures show value for persons? What can we learn from this?

Grid Question 4: Are we cultivating a culture of grace-prompted obedience?

In Chapter 7, we addressed the reality of God's desire for His laws to paint a picture of how life works best. While they do condemn us, that's not the purpose of God's laws. They aren't intended to restrict but enhance the fullness of life.

Similarly, we can never allow students to think the reason they have to learn a different language is because of weak answers such as college requirements. This creates a stigma which often surrounds World Languages departments – it's not useful for the students. It's just something they have to do. This is a common accusation I hear from students; they don't see the benefit of learning a language they won't use. It becomes like a "do and don't." More rules.

Just like every other department of the school, world languages teachers must be diligent in their efforts to smash student assumptions that the discipline of learning a language isn't good for them. It *is* good for them, not just because of what it gets them, but because it can teach them more about God, themselves, and how they ought to live in a world – especially one which is increasingly flattening.

We all tend to have internal assumptions of what "the good life" looks like. But, when we start to learn about other cultures, our perspectives of *eudaimonia* should be challenged. Some cultures value relationships above all else, to the extent that punctuality isn't a priority for them. Modesty looks quite different in different cultures. Some would say that hard work and efficiency are of greater value than communal bonds. As a result, identities get wrapped up in what cultures value. Do cultures decide what's right and wrong, or is there something above culture?

As we learn the languages of other cultures, we also learn to see their value. If we care to learn it in such a way that we are willing to be shaped by what we see in other cultures, it provides a clearer perspective of what true right and wrong look like. Every time I return from visiting other countries, it always takes a few days to get back into the way of doing life in the United States. I also realize certain things I'm reluctant to go back to. An enlarged global perspective gives us a greater ability to sift through the clutter around us and enhances our maturity to distinguish between those which are essential to godliness and those which are merely cultural nuances.

Another aspect of Christian ethics we must always be mindful of, regardless of what we're teaching, is the importance of gratitude. Obedience doesn't make us good; only Jesus does. Obedience doesn't change our standing before the Father, because Jesus already accomplished that for us. So, the motive for obedience is gratitude for the greatness of God and what He has done for us.

How, then, can studying world languages further gratitude? Just as learning about other cultures can offer a critique against our own culture, it should prompt thankfulness for what we do have. Our gratitude can also be enlarged as we learn to see various ways that God has revealed Himself to the nations. We should be overjoyed to see what God is doing and how He is worshiped and celebrated.

Questions which flow out of Grid Question 4:

- What do we consider to be right/wrong that another culture would find disagreeable? Why? Could this show us anything about what real goodness looks like? What should we do when we see that some values are entirely cultural, not globally moral?
- Are there ways that other cultures apply God's commandments differently to their lives? Could it cause us to do a better job of living godly lives?
- How can World Languages lessons enhance student joy and thankfulness?

Grid Question 5: Are we pursuing, celebrating, and resting in God's original intent?

Even though we could trace many language differences to the sinfulness of the Tower of Babel, it would be unreasonable to think no cultural differences (and maybe even dialects and languages) would arise over time, even if sin had never entered the world. And, as those differences developed, sinless people would find great joy in learning about cultural distinctives; they would cherish the opportunity to expand their view of the wonderful way that God was revealing himself to and working through these cultures.

Because of our sin, we get frustrated by differences, but that's not God's original intent for difference. God created diversity as a gift and vital part of the shalom of the Garden, not a hindrance to it. The helper which God created for Adam, though like him in ways that other animals weren't, was still very different from him. And, it was for his good to have the perspective of a female who's emotional "wiring" would be very different than his own.

By going through the previous four questions, I've already tipped my hand when it comes to what I think about the "oughtness" of language learning. Living rightly in the world requires having a big view of God, an appreciation for what He's doing, a desire to understand and know more of the world (because it's His), and a deep love for others. These would have been true in the Garden of Eden; they're true today; they will be true in the New Earth. Thinking creationally about world languages requires that we consider how the department objectives can revisit each of these truths.

Questions which flow out of Grid Question 5:

- How does studying world languages nurture wonder, curiosity, and exploration in ways that other departments can't?
- How does studying world languages help students broaden and deepen love for the world?
- How does World Languages enable students to understand that human flourishing looks like a celebration of difference and distinction?
- How does World Languages nurture global stewardship – to tend, take care of and have dominion over what God has made?

Grid Question 6: Are we marked by mournfulness and repentance over sin and a broken world?

Not only can studying World Languages reveal our own limitations, it can also point out our sin. First, it can push against our unwillingness to invest the care to learn other languages. It does say something about our culture that we are not overly bothered by how handicapped we are in our abilities to communicate with others.

Without fail, I've witnessed my multi-lingual friends' capacity to treat non-English speakers with dignity in ways I cannot. I have a ceiling on what I can do because of my language barriers. But I have seen these friends be able to connect, speak to needs, and make the "alien and stranger" feel valued. It's not because of sin that I can't do what they can; but it is sinful if I'm unwilling to take steps to do it.

Secondly, studying languages and the cultures which connect with them can reveal some of the communal sins we have accepted as normal. When Katie and I got married, she moved to the South and had to learn about the cultural nuances which, for her, almost made it seem like living in a new country. I failed to prepare her, because I didn't properly think to address many of the things which would have helped her understand life in Tennessee, because I took them for granted – as normal. For example, she didn't know that moms smock their daughter's church dresses, and she didn't expect to feel like an outsider for not having been in a sorority in college. She received a few "well, bless your heart" statements (for those of you who aren't from the South, that's not as good as it sounds).

One of the advantages of having a Midwestern wife is her ability to point out things I passively accepted. Not that there's anything wrong with smocking or sororities; they aren't exactly normal to someone who's not operating from a Southern perspective. But there *have* been some things she pointed out which need to be repented of. My immersion in my own culture dulled my radar to notice it. Sometimes, we must be dragged away from our own norms to see what needs to be seen.

I also remember listening to a pastor friend talk about the ways he has been routinely convicted by his international friends. In one instance, he talked about American missionaries' tendency to expect the conveniences of an American lifestyle while "suffering" on the mission field. He hadn't ever really thought anything about it, but when a seminary friend who was from a developing country pointed it out as something that's easily noticed by the locals, it grabbed his attention.

James K.A. Smith says our internal and even unspoken views of the "good life" often reveals our deepest idols. The "American Dream" is typically more about personal peace and prosperity. But this dream is commonly seen as selfish to other cultures who cannot imagine lives of isolation from others. Even though there's currently a lot of debate about building walls, much of the American dream requires hedges and walls to protect what's often vital to shelter our idols. As much as it hurts, it's good for others to address these idols. We need it.

Third, studying World Languages can reveal our ignorance about the rest of the world and people in it. I remember visiting another country as a chaperone for a school trip. After being in the country for a week, one of our students remarked in a self-deprecating way how he had always assumed people in that country didn't wear shoes. The other teacher and I picked our jaws up off the ground.

It wasn't malicious, and we all got a good laugh out of it – not because we shared his misconception, but because the student was laughing at himself and his own ignorance. It was still a tangible example of why students need to get a true exposure to the rest of the world. It tore down his flawed perception. By the end of the trip, the student didn't want to leave his host family's home, and I know he has visited this country multiple times since and has had his international friends come to visit him. His heart was changed, and that change required a shattering of his illusions and idols.

Questions which flow out of Grid Question 6:

- What are some of my culture's sins, and how do other cultures sharpen my ability to see that? How can our studies sharpen this? Where does it show up in our curriculum?

- What have we accepted as normal within our own school that we should repent of? What do we do when we see it? Do we ignore it or pause and reflect? How are you modeling a movement toward repentance and creating space for it?
- How can we be intentional about shattering flawed assumptions about the rest of the world and the people in it? In recognition of our failures, what should repentance look like.
- What idols can World Languages point toward that other disciplines can't? Go there.

Grid Question 7: Are we actively proclaiming and seeking repair and restoration according to Jesus's plan?

This is the grammar of the gospel at work. Learning about world languages helps us to see how very needy we are. The World Languages department isn't any more equipped to talk about redemption than other departments, yet these classrooms have an acute ability to heighten students' awareness of their limitations, their idols, and their errors. But we should never draw attention toward these without using this as a platform to talk about Jesus and His plan to restore all things.

Though the Bible gives us several images of Heaven, I have very little idea what to expect in the New Heaven and New Earth (the New Jerusalem of Revelations 21). I've heard several people say we should expect to see something very much like our world, except without the effects of sin.

I don't know what to think about language, though. Revelations 7 suggests there will be people from every nation and every language (v. 9), and that they will praise God together in one voice. (v.10) Could that mean these people will praise God in their own languages? Will we retain our language differences in Heaven? I have no idea.

However, I do know God's kingdom is represented by people from many nationalities who speak a multitude of languages, and this great diversity is celebrated in Scripture. So, I tend to think learning additional languages is a form of preparation for citizenship in the kingdom of God.

World Languages teachers can whet the appetite for God's redeemed kingdom in ways other departments can't; they can create a longing for the world and for its diversity. My wife and I have been watching Netflix's "Somebody Feed Phil." It's not just a show about food, even though its focus on food is wonderful. Every episode causes me to love the world more, because it gives me a broader view of the beauty that's out there. Phil Rosenthal is not a Christian, and I doubt the show's writers are believers either. But they cause me to long for a diverse New Jerusalem. How much more can a Christian teacher of world cultures do that!

I once heard a preacher say that Pentecost (Acts 2:1-12) is a restoration of the confusion of the Tower of Babel. (Genesis 11:1-9) At Babel, language divided people. They could not work together, and it drove people apart. On the day of Pentecost, we see one Church with many languages spoken. Rather than this frustrating the Church, it galvanized the believers, and 3,000 people come to saving faith. (2:41) The Bible is clear that God is about fixing broken things, and a World Languages classroom can be a microcosm of Acts 2 where these differences come together to create awe and wonder.

Questions which flow out of Grid Question 7:

- How does World Languages repair the ruins of the Fall (think about Bable)? What specifically is repaired and restored?
- How does World Languages enable students to be kingdom minded?
- In what ways does World Languages restore an appreciation for people, uniqueness, diversity?

If you teach a different discipline, you can replace "World Languages" with your own department in some of the questions I've asked. Other things I've outlined won't be immediately applicable to all departments, but I hope that this has provided an example of what can result from applying these questions. And this is only the tip of the iceberg. It's a first pass; there are an infinite number of places you can go, and I'd love to hear how you've applied them in your school.

While the Grid questions have shaped my own ability to consider the gospel's effect in the life of the school, I don't think this is the only framework which works. It's what I gravitate to whenever I work with schools, but I realize that it may not be the best structure for every school. However, I do believe it has the necessary components schools need to consider.

There are essential questions every school needs to ask. For instance, if there is no category in a school's program which addresses the school's approach to truth and knowledge, I would have significant concerns. I prefer having some categories where the questions would fit, rather than having a list of twenty-something questions core to the school's ethos. In the same way we learn in the classroom, it's easier to remember and conceptualize the questions when they're grouped together into an organizing scheme.

Simply, we all need to have a framework of questions we ask ourselves to be more aligned with the grammar of the gospel, and we need to willingly accept what answers we uncover. There are many reasons to be hopeful about where you can go with this. Along the way, you'll likely step on some landmines; you'll probably realize that some of it didn't go over nearly like you hoped. You might blow it. Those are all reasons why Jesus came, and we deeply need Him, too. Even for this.

ACKNOWLEDGMENTS

To my wife, Katie, who during the process of writing this book never even seemed to consider that this would be hard for me. Your blanket confidence in me cannot be explained or repaid. Thank you for loving me and walking with me yesterday, today, and for years to come.

To the "Brinklings," Elsie, David and Millie. You have believed in me and cheered me on without the slightest hesitation. Being able to be your dad has taught me even more how much I need Jesus and given me a fuller perspective of the need for what's at the very heart of this book.

To my dad, Mark, who has spent more than four decades as a teacher and who can articulate Christian education better than anyone I know. Dad, it's not just that you speak so well about the gospel and education, but you have lived it. Your faithfulness, wisdom, and grace have modeled for me what I would hope to become as an educator, husband, and father, and friend.

To my mom, Sandi, for putting up with dad's and my philosophizing. Nurturing me these many years also meant nurturing this book inside of me.

To Josh and Lissa, Daniel and Katy, Jim and Julianna, and Steve and Tiffany for your prayers and for constant encouragement. And to my wonderful in-laws, Dave and Mary Gieser, for your remarkable, undying, and joyful support.

To Lisa Morse Ginz who predicted twenty-five years ago that I would someday be a writer. I doubted you but said that I'd give you credit for calling it first. "Words are for those with promises to keep." - W.H. Auden

ENDNOTES

1 Gene Frost, *Learning from the Best: Growing Greatness in the Christian School (*Grand Rapids: Christian Schools International, 2007).

2 I recommend James Sire's *The Universe Next Door* and R.C. Sproul's *Lifeviews* as a first pass because both are accessible for lay readers.

Chapter 1

3 Mentioned several times in his video/audio series "Your Christian School: A Culture of Grace?" 2006.

4 One of the most compelling studies is Christian Smith's book, *Soul Searching* (2009), in which he concludes that the dominant worldview of today's "Christian" youngsters is "Moralistic Therapeutic Deism."

5 Jay E. Adams, *Back to the Blackboard* (Simpsonville, SC: Timeless Texts, 1998), 14.

6 Richard Niebuhr, *Christ and Culture* (1951).

7 "Multiple Choice: How Parents Sort Education Options in a Changing Market." ACSI. 2017

8 Michael S. Horton, *Christless Christianity* (Grand Rapids, MI: Baker Books, 2008), 15.

9 Stanley Hauerwas, *Hannah's Child: A Theological Memoir* (2012), 10.

10 *The Abolition of Man* by C.S. Lewis Ó copyright 1943, 1946, 1978 CS Lewis Pte. Ltd. Extract reprinted with permission.

11 I reference my involvement in this course at greater length in the Introduction.

Chapter 2

12 For the very reason that most teachers would give different definitions, my school in Memphis decided to fix that and created a required a course to ensure that all our faculty were on the same page. The course I taught

to help create a common vocabulary for our faculty is much of what has driven the writing of this book.

13 James Sire, *The Universe Next Door* (Downer's Grove, IL: InterVarsity Press, 1997), 16.

14 Charles Colson, *How Then Shall we Live?* (Carol Stream, IL: Tyndale House, 1999), 14.

15 Albert M. Wolters, *Creation Regained: Biblical Basis for Reformational Worldview* (Grand Rapids, MI: William B. Eerdmans Publishing Co, 2005), 2.

16 Francis A. Schaeffer, *How Should we Then Live?* In *The Collected Works of Francis A. Schaeffer, Vol 5.* (Wheaton, IL: Crossway Books, 1993), 83.

17 Armand Nicholi, *The Question of God: CS Lewis and Sigmund Freud Debate God, Love, Sex, and the Meaning of Life* (New York: The Free Press, 2002), 10.

18 R.C. Sproul, *Lifeviews* (Grand Rapids, MI: Baker Book House, 1986), 25.

19 C.S. Lewis, *Miracles* (New York City: The Macmillan Company, 1971), 8. *Miracles* by C.S. Lewis Ó copyright 1947, 1943, 1944, 1952 CS Lewis Pte Ltd. Extract reprinted with permission.

20 For a far more in-depth look at the history of Worldview, I recommend David Naugle's book, *Worldview: A History of a Concept.*

21 My dad was a freshman at Wheaton when Schaeffer was the key-note speaker for a week-long lecture series. It was the notes and transcript from these addresses which were refashioned as Schaeffer's first book, *The God who is There.*

22 Kuyper's statement from *Lectures on Calvinism (1898)* is one of the primary reasons why I wanted to name my son after him is, "There is not one square inch of the entire creation about which Jesus Christ does not cry out, 'This is mine. This belongs to me!'"

23 Dorothy L. Sayers, *Creed or Chaos?* (Manchester, NH: Sophia Institute Press, 1995), 31-32.

Chapter 3

24 Frank E. Gaebelein, *The Pattern of God's Truth* (*Colorado* Springs, CO: Association of Christian Schools International, 1968), 18.

25 Cornelius Plantinga, *Engaging God's World* (Grand Rapids, MI: Wm. B. Eerdmans Publishing Co., 2002), 74.

26 This quote was first shared with me by my twelfth grade English teacher, Joyce Herring. The fact that I'm still holding onto this quote years

later shows the power of a teacher whose place in my life will always be remembered.

27 Sally Lloyd-Jones, *The Jesus Storybook Bible* (Grand Rapids, MI: Zondervan, 2007), 14-17.

28 While I struggle with several of her conclusions, I appreciate Kristin Kobes Du Mez' point in *Jesus and John Wayne* (2020) that far too many Evangelical leaders have focused more on political power and financial prosperity than on what Jesus would have ever wanted for His Church.

29 James K.A. Smith, *Desiring the Kingdom* (Grand Rapids, MI: Baker Publishing Group, 2009), 17-18.

30 C.S. Lewis, *Mere Christianity* (New York City: HarperCollins Publishing, Inc., 2001), 32. *Mere Christianity* by C.S. Lewis Ó copyright 1942, 1943, 1944, 1952 CS Lewis Pte Ltd. Extract reprinted with permission.

31 Barbara Duguid, *Extravagant Grace.* (Phillipsburg, NJ: Presbyterian and Reformed Publishing, 2013), 30.

32 *The Pattern of God's Truth,* 17.

33 *Piety and Philosophy,* 86.

34 *Educating for Life,* 25.

35 *Desiring the Kingdom,* 32-33.

36 While more practical than the "orthodoxy" sections, I recognize that I'm still asking rather broad questions, but hope that these questions will lead schools toward building practical momentum. My follow up book *Gospel Above Grades* seeks to take these questions to even greater practical applications.

37 Even as I type this, it makes me think of Jesus' ironic words in Mark 2:17 about coming for the sick, rather than the healthy.

Chapter 4

38 While I take theological issue with the song, "Something Good," it's still a wonderful song.

39 Francis A. Schaeffer, *The Complete Works of Francis A. Schaeffer. Vol. 1* (Wheaton, IL: Crossway Books, 1993), 287-288.

40 From "The Principle or Foundation" (1882). You'll find this quote in various, out-of-order arrangements all over the internet, but the full article and paragraph is absolutely wonderful as Hopkins wrote it.

41 *Liturgy of the Ordinary*, 23.

42 By Jay McTighe and Grant Wiggins (1998)

Chapter 5

43 Romans 11:36

44 Not only did my students try this, but I also witnessed it when Christians would hear about my discussion group with atheists and bring these arguments thinking they were going to defeat the skeptic. On one occasion, a Christian showed up to the group trying canned arguments on one of my secular friends (a self-professed relativist) who said, "there's no absolute truth." The newcomer responded with what is so often portrayed as an automatic check mate … "well, isn't that statement an absolute truth?" The Christian grinned, thinking he had exposed a chink in the non-believer's argument. My secular friend responded wonderfully, "Good for you! You exposed my inconsistency. Did you ever consider what it means that I'm a relativist; I don't have to be consistent."

45 *Mere Christianity* by C.S. Lewis Ó copyright 1942, 1943, 1944, 1952 CS Lewis Pte Ltd. Extract reprinted with permission. P. 40.

46 G.K. Chesterton, *The Ballad of the White Horse* (San Francisco: Ignatius Press, 2001), 60.

47 *Summa Contra Gentiles* Book 1, Chapter 7

48 Rosaria Butterfield, *Openness Unhindered* (Pittsburg, PA: Crown and Covenant Publications, 2015), 15.

49 It's actually the name of one of Peterson's books … a book about the unexpected places we find Jesus at work.

50 I realize that there are people who question God in the Bible and are rebuked for that. For example, Jeremiah complains to God, as does Job, and God puts them in their place. However, my point here is that there is ample reason to say that there is biblical justification for Christians' struggle to understand.

51 I highly recommend Matthew Lee Anderson's book *The End of our Exploring* to shape what it looks like to be a person who lives a life of questioning well.

52 Chesterton discusses this idea in Chapter 6 or Orthodoxy, in saying that we all need mystery in our lives if we are going to stay sane. Sane people are always more concerned with truth than with consistency, because they are ok with paradox.

Chapter 6

53 I'm not trying to insult those who taught in the 1950's or who are products of the 1950's. I'm merely thinking of the *Leave it to Beaver*

idea of a teacher who wrapped students on the knuckles, and whose professional separation from the students couldn't be more understated.

54 *Mere Christianity* by C.S. Lewis Ó copyright 1942, 1943, 1944, 1952 CS Lewis Pte Ltd. Extract reprinted with permission.

55 G.K. Chesterton, *Collected Works,* Vol. 1 (San Francisco, CA: Ignatius Press, 1986), 222.

56 C.S. Lewis, *The Weight of Glory* (New York City: Touchstone Books, 1996), 39. *The Weight of Glory* by C.S. Lewis Ó copyright 1949 CS Lewis Pte Ltd. Extract reprinted with permission.

57 Mason, Charlotte. *Toward a Philosophy of Education.* Book 1, Chapter 5.

58 The address is accessible online, and it also appears in a collection of writings entitled *This is Water.*

59 From the introduction to Dorothy Sayers, *Mind of the Maker* (San Francisco, CA: Harper Collins, 1987), xvii.

60 It's impossible for me to adequately reflect how highly I recommend for school leaders to read *Shop Class as Soul Craft* (2009) by Matthew Crawford.

61 I could recommend many, but I'll start by suggesting: Deci, E., & Flaste, R. (1995). *Why we do what we do: Understanding self-motivation.* New York: Penguin Group. Pink, D. *Drive.* The Surprising Truth about what Motivates us. New York: Riverhead Books, 2009. Tomlinson., C., & Moon, T. (2013). *Assessment and student success in a differentiated classroom.* Alexandria, VA: Association for Supervision and Curriculum Development.

62 Jonathan Eckert, *The Novice Advantage.* (Thousand Oaks, CA: Corwin, 201697.

63 I'm not suggesting that God was at all threatened by mankind or that the Fall was ever outside His control. Yet, if God were like us, He certainly wouldn't have made people who would one day want to kill Him. He would control the situation so it would never happen. Yet, God did grant that freedom, and the great mystery is that never once have any of our choices ever been outside His control.

Chapter 7

64 Unpacked in Aristotle's *Nicomachean Ethics*

65 Question 14

66 *Engaging God's World,* 74-75.

67 I appreciate Jon Eckert's (2016) emphasis on the word "uphold" when it comes to our classroom boundaries - rather than using words like "enforce" or "punish" when it comes to consequences. P. 98-99.

68 *Educating for Life*, 272.

69 *Educating for* Life, 268.

Chapter 8

70 I find this word to be fascinating, even though I've been prone to overuse and miss what's clearly right there in the word. We all look forward to recreation because we all long to be restored to creation - to the way things were supposed to be. It's amazing to think that our rest and play - what rejuvenates us - is part of a restoration project.

71 *Engaging God's World*, 23.

72 Nancy Pearcey, *Total Truth* (Wheaton, IL: Crossway Books, 2005), 88.

73 Donovan Graham, *Teaching Redemptively* (Colorado Springs, CO: Purposeful Design, 2003), 28.

74 I borrowed this from Paul VanderZwaag – one of the best teachers I've ever witnessed.

75 Sir Ken Robinson, *You, Your Child, and School* (New York: Penguin, 2018), 18.

76 This statement comes from the 1965 musical "Man of La Mancha" by Dale Wasserman. Though these words are never specifically said in the book, *Don Quixote*, this idea is very much at the heart of what Miguel de Cervates is making.

77 *Collected Works*, 263-264.

78 It also makes me rethink the very nature of what we're after in the business of educating children. We do not want them to grow out of those things which cause them to have the very sort of faith Jesus desires to see in us.

79 *Educating for Life*, 18

80 These two problems put together are very close to the primary argument for David Hume's (1711-1776) against the existence of God, and his point has been oft used by many skeptics ever sense. He says that God can't be both omnipotent and good if evil exists. For, if He is good, then he wouldn't allow evil or suffering to exist. And, if He had infinite power, He certainly could prevent it. The fact that evil does exist, then brings one of these two into question.

81 Question #4.

82 Chesterton suggests that the Tree of the Knowledge of Good and Evil, in part, was sacramental because it stood as a physical reminder of the grace of God. In God's goodness, he put the tree in the middle of the garden – so they would have seen it every day. And, in seeing it, they would have been reminded that they didn't have infinite dominion. The tree stood there to remind them that they are finite … that they weren't God. And, that was good for them.

83 *Educating for Life,* 16

84 *The Novice Advantage,* 46-47.

85 Timothy P. Wiens and Katherine L. Wiens, ed. *Building Better Schools.* (Stony Brook, NY: Paideia Press, 2012), 161.

Chapter 10

86 *Confessions* (ca. A.D. 400). Book 1, Chapter 1.

87 Even though the movie is so powerful, it's not the sort of movie that's easy to recommend because of the language and darkness. So, I'm careful to talk about this move (and others like it) with students, because I don't want to stumble into a student watching it and then saying it was recommended by Mr. Brink.

88 *Engaging God's World,* 68.

89 I bet you never would have imagined to see a quotation from *Dumb and Dumber* (1994) in a book about Christian education.

90 Albert M. Wolters, *Creation Regained.* (Grand Rapids, MI: Eerdmans Publishing Co., 2005), 71.

91 A significant theme of *Man's Search for Meaning* (1946).

92 "Of Education." A brief essay written in 1644 to Master Samuel Hartlib

93 (1994) Castle Rock Entertainment, written and directed by Frank Darabont

94 *Building Better* Schools, 161.

95 *The Novice Advantage,* 99.

96 Exodus 3:12, "He said, "But I will be with you, and this shall be the sign for you, that I have sent you: when you have brought the people out of Egypt, you shall serve God on this mountain."

Chapter 11

97 I think the easiest age group for doing integration is at the elementary grades, because teachers see all the pieces better, and you can more

easily find areas and overlap between what students are focusing in on in individual lessons and find alignment to something you might be learning in Bible lessons or other gospel-emphases you might have.

[98] C.S. Lewis, *The Four Loves.* (New York: Harcourt Books, Inc., 1988), 62. *The Four Loves* by C.S. Lewis Ó copyright 1960 CS Lewis Pte Ltd. Extract reprinted with permission.

[99] This idea central to the heart of John Piper's perspective of God-centered missions as expressed in his book, *Let the Nations Be Glad: The Supremacy of God in Missions* (2010).

Made in the USA
Columbia, SC
13 November 2024

46417710R00186